UNLOCKING
the
TAROT

About the Author

Lisa Papez is an author, tarot educator, tarot deck creator, and YouTube content creator whose work has always been founded on her passion for self-worth and personal empowerment: the common threads that connect everything she does. For over twenty-five years, Lisa has been working with the tarot for herself and others. She is intensely passionate about making tarot accessible for everyone as she believes it is one of the most powerful tools available for accessing greater self-awareness and leveraging personal growth. Because learning such a comprehensive system can be overwhelming, Lisa's work is focused on providing innovative methods that both new and existing tarot enthusiasts can use to deepen their relationship with this empowering tool. Visit her at SupportiveTarot.com.

To Write to the Author

If you wish to contact the author or would like more information about this ·book, please write to the author in care of Llewellyn Worldwide Ltd. and we will forward your request. Both the author and the publisher appreciate hearing from you and learning of your enjoyment of this book and how it has helped you. Llewellyn Worldwide Ltd. cannot guarantee that every letter written to the author can be answered, but all will be forwarded. Please write to:

Lisa Papez
℅ Llewellyn Worldwide
2143 Wooddale Drive
Woodbury, MN 55125-2989

Please enclose a self-addressed stamped envelope for reply,
or $1.00 to cover costs. If outside the U.S.A., enclose
an international postal reply coupon.

Many of Llewellyn's authors have websites with additional information and resources. For more information, please visit our website at http://www.llewellyn.com.

UNLOCKING
the
TAROT

Create Your Own Keys

LISA PAPEZ

LLEWELLYN
WOODBURY, MINNESOTA

FIRST EDITION
First Printing, 2024

Book design by Christine Ha
Cover and chapter opener art by Brittany Keller
Cover design by Verlynda Pinckney
Interior art
    Card spread diagrams by the Llewellyn Art Department
    Tarot Original 1909 Deck © 2021 with art created by Pamela Colman Smith and Arthur
        Edward Waite. Used with permission of LoScarabeo.
    Tarot of Marseille. C. Burdel Schaffhouse, 1751. Used with permission of LoScarabeo. (*The
        Lovers* appears on page 45)

Llewellyn Publications is a registered trademark of Llewellyn Worldwide Ltd.

Library of Congress Cataloging-in-Publication Data (Pending)
ISBN: 978-0-7387-7665-1

Llewellyn Worldwide Ltd. does not participate in, endorse, or have any authority or responsibility concerning private business transactions between our authors and the public.
    All mail addressed to the author is forwarded but the publisher cannot, unless specifically instructed by the author, give out an address or phone number.
    Any internet references contained in this work are current at publication time, but the publisher cannot guarantee that a specific location will continue to be maintained. Please refer to the publisher's website for links to authors' websites and other sources.

Llewellyn Publications
A Division of Llewellyn Worldwide Ltd.
2143 Wooddale Drive
Woodbury, MN 55125-2989
www.llewellyn.com

Printed in the United States of America

Other Works by Lisa Papez
The Self-Worth Path: A Guided Journey to an Empowered Life

Forthcoming Works by Lisa Papez
Unicorn's Journey Tarot
Sassy Dragons Tarot
Unicorn's Journey Oracle

To all the friends who became my family.

Contents

Foreword

If we are very lucky, people come into our lives during troubled times and, like a lifeline, help us stay afloat until we find solid ground. The Supportive Tarot YouTube channel found its way onto my feed in 2019, amid a troubled time for me. Through her work, the host, Lisa Papez, unknowingly provided comfort and connection to a lowly soul. On a personal level, her work touched me, and I will always be grateful for that. As an acquiring editor always looking for new voices in tarot, Lisa's friendly manner and her sparkly, optimistic-but-practical personality won my heart. Her smart and curious brain won my respect. Her ability to be absolutely delighted by decks or images or ideas made me want to hang out with her. I watched the videos with a smile as this vibrant voice for reasonable, healthy connections with tarot grew in experience and confidence. While the host is still one of the most supportive people in the tarot world, her channel now operates under her name. Some of you may already know Lisa Papez from her wonderful videos. For some, this may be your first connection with her. If so, do check out her other work. She's good people and very good energy to be around.

Meeting Lisa in person at a tarot conference in 2022 was an absolute delight. Sitting in the sun, eating sandwiches, and talking tarot like old friends ... what could be better? We discussed her many project ideas, landing on this one to start. Let me tell you about this brilliant book, why you are going to love it, and how it will help you.

Very often, the best teaching methods come from adapting ways we've taught ourselves something. It's a great process because we have the benefit of knowing what worked, what didn't, and what could be improved.

In addition, finessing the material through classes and presentations allows a high level of adaptation and refinement in creating a method that is suitable for a broad audience. This is precisely what Lisa has done with *Unlocking the Tarot*.

Lisa developed a process that works not only because it arose from her experience but also because it mimics how tarot works. Back in the day, we used to call the major arcana cards "keys." They are considered keys because they open doors to the mysteries of life, to various interpretations, and to a multitude of potentials. Unfortunately, in the 1990s, using keywords became unpopular as readers shifted from predicting the future to exploring psychological applications, personal growth, and spiritual practices. The argument was that each card meant so much that it was folly to assign a single word to any card. The intentions were good: to help tarot evolve and shed the charlatan reputation that surrounded tarot, particularly the images of Miss Cleo and the Psychic Friends Network.

The trouble with the wholesale forsaking of things is that sometimes babies get thrown out with the bathwater. Perhaps in the old days keywords lent a shallow or fortune teller feel to interpretations. Like many old practices, keywords didn't need to be thrown away; they needed to be revised for modern readers and to reflect the evolution of human consciousness. Properly used, a keyword does not limit one's understanding. On the contrary, the very act of developing a keyword requires, first, comprehension, discernment, and awareness of the scope of a card. Second, one must then be able to identify, in that ocean of meaning, the essence of the card. This is varsity-level knowledge and is what you will find in most excellent readers. Once you've discovered your keywords, every time you flip that card, it is like turning a key that opens a door to all that is possible.

Here is the thing about smart keyword usage: using someone else's keys won't work. The reason they are effective is because they come from your well of wisdom and from your understanding of and relationship with the card. Lisa isn't coy; she shares her keywords and explains why they work for her. She also shares an overview of interpretations for each card and guides you as you create your set of keys. Creating keys is useful even if you never use them. The very act of developing them will embed the card meanings into your brain and psyche. It is so easy to say a card means thirty things; it is another thing altogether to name the quintessence of a card. Brevity and precision are the signs of a true master. From *tarot with training wheels* to master card slinger—this is definitely a journey worth taking. There are few people I'd trust to guide me on that journey. Lisa Papez is one of them.

Using keywords and more importantly developing a set of keywords is an often neglected but incredibly effective practice. I'm so grateful to Lisa for sharing this work with all of us and for her supportive, friendly, and wise presence. Just imagine all the excellent tarot readings that will happen in the future because of this wonderful book. You are in good hands. Relax and enjoy the ride!

—*Barbara Moore*

Introduction

I threw my first tarot guidebook in the trash.

Please don't take this the wrong way. It was an excellent guidebook. Every card was beautifully described and explained. It was a powerful and beautiful tool. I read it cover to cover precisely once, and it was an absolute pleasure from start to finish.

You might be wondering, if the book was so good, why would I dispose of it in such a permanent way?

The answer is simple: I wanted to learn to trust and build a relationship with the tarot. I knew that if I had kept that guidebook close at hand, I would refer to it every time I read the cards. I would never know if it was me interpreting the tarot cards or if I was letting the book do that job for me.

Yet, here I sit, writing a book that I—admittedly—hope will serve as the sort of resource you can come back to time and time again: a book that will support you in learning the tarot and remain relevant long afterward. Well then, what gives?

I'm a massive fan of tarot guidebooks. They are marvelous tools and often facilitate a greater understanding of the tarot. Every tarot deck's accompanying guidebook offers a peek into that deck creator's view of the cards. The ability to expose ourselves to a variety of perspectives on the tarot is a gift I benefit from every time I acquaint myself with a new tarot deck.

Over the years, I have looked back on the moment I discarded that guidebook with both annoyance and gratitude. The annoyance I feel stems from the fact that I missed out on years of reflections on that original guidebook.

1

The gratitude I feel stems from the ways the absence of that guidebook positively impacted my tarot journey.

Years after building my solid relationship with that particular deck, I longed to revisit the beautiful stories and parables in that once-read guidebook. Thankfully, it was still readily available, and I was able to repurchase it. Anyone who tends to acquire tarot decks the way I do will know that it can be challenging to reacquire decks or their guidebooks once a fair amount of time has passed. I was lucky that the deck was still in print, and I was able to repurchase a set with an intact guidebook. It still sits safely on my bookshelf beside my other beloved tarot guidebooks.

I don't regret my original decision to discard the guidebook. If I had it to do all over again, I would do the same thing. Well, except perhaps—to be safe—I would ask a friend to hold on to the guidebook for me rather than throwing it away.

Allow me to explain.

The tarot deck I used then differed from the one you might imagine. Instead of the usual card titles like the Fool, Death, and the World, it had keywords or phrases such as *innocence, transformation,* and *completion.*

Because expansive keywords were right on the cards, I wanted to get to know the deck without relying on the guidebook. I knew that if I kept the guidebook too close, I would rely on it instead of myself. I was always a rule follower, but I wanted to do things differently with the tarot.

I was right.

Once the book was out of reach, I found myself interpreting the cards using what was in front of me on the table: the artwork on each card and its associated keyword. It was incredibly freeing. Reading tarot began to feel more like a conversation I was having with the cards instead of merely a tool and its instruction manual.

Over time, I learned to trust what first popped into my mind when reading those keywords and reflecting on the artwork. My interpretations became meaningful and accurate, hitting home with the friends and family who would let me practice on them.

And I practiced … a lot. I took my tarot cards with me everywhere, always carrying a deck in my purse. I offered to give readings to anyone I thought might be open to the experience. I gave tarot readings to friends, family, acquaintances, people I chatted with at restaurants and bars, coworkers, and even perfect strangers. Looking back, I am pleased with my boldness. I'm rather shy, especially about approaching people I don't know, but my desire to practice reading tarot helped me overcome my shyness.

Tarot became an integral part of my life. I began turning to my cards whenever I was feeling lost, sad, angry, or confused. I turned to my cards when I needed another perspective or some helpful advice for navigating a sticky situation. I pulled cards to make the big decisions in my life, and I pulled cards to recognize my successes. But most of all, I pulled cards for querents—people who came to me with questions they wanted answered by the tarot.

Eventually, I decided I wanted to read tarot professionally. I began offering to read tarot for strangers in online forums and groups in exchange for honest feedback about their experience. That feedback was invaluable and gave me the confidence to take the next step: selling tarot readings on eBay.

I know it sounds odd, but that really was a thing in the early 2000s, and it was a great way for me to get practice reading for paying clients. I would get the question and a few basic details about the client when the order came in. Then I would pull cards and lay them out in a spread—usually a Celtic cross—and write up a full report explaining the reading and email it back. I still remember some of the first pieces of feedback I got from those eBay readings. People I'd never met told me how accurate their reading was. At first, I found it hard to believe that long-distance tarot could be so effective, but the proof was in the pudding. I had happy clients who kept coming back for more.

Those early eBay experiences gave me the confidence to read professionally in a variety of settings. Reading for others in person wasn't the least bit intimidating after my experience providing tarot readings long-distance. It was easier to have that in-person connection with someone sitting across from me at a local festival, a public park, or a bar. When I became a yoga teacher, I hosted tarot and tea events at yoga studios in my area. When I opened my own yoga studio, I brought those tarot and tea events with me. I still remember what it was like to sit for hours on end, giving fifteen-minute Celtic cross tarot readings for walk-in clients. It was exhilarating!

One of my favorite parts about those long days reading for walk-in clients was reading for the skeptics. There was always at least one person who walked in already pretty convinced that tarot couldn't possibly "work." I related to them. I had felt the exact same way when I experienced my first tarot reading. I wondered if any of them would ever pick up a tarot deck of their own and learn to read themselves.

It was around 2015 that I discovered YouTube when I went looking for a tutorial for how to apply eyeshadow. One thing led to the next and I found myself watching YouTube for fun. It was only natural for me to wonder if anyone was out there making videos about tarot. That's when I discovered what some of us affectionately call "TarotTube." There was a whole group of people making videos about their love of tarot! I lurked for a long time, then I began commenting, and eventually, I started a tarot YouTube channel of my own. I called it Supportive Tarot, because of how strongly I felt about tarot being a tool that supports and empowers us.

Making tarot content on YouTube changed my life in ways I couldn't have imagined. I could finally talk as much as I wanted about a subject that I had been passionate about for years, and I began making friends with others who were just as enthusiastic as I was about the cards. Making content on YouTube also made me more comfortable with the idea of offering tarot services via video on Etsy and eventually my own website, which I named—you guessed it—Supportive Tarot. There, I continued to offer professional tarot services, and eventually, I added tarot courses, one of which became the inspiration for this book.

Creating content on YouTube isn't always easy. The internet is forever, as they say, and being online in such a public way taught me about what mattered—and what didn't. I learned that some people will understand you and some won't but that it was important to remain true to myself regardless. I changed my channel name from Supportive Tarot to my real name, Lisa Papez, when I realized it was time to stop hiding. In that moment, I claimed all of me in the most public of ways. Taking that action was a rite of passage, and what made it easier was the ways that tarot has become more—dare I say—mainstream in recent years.

Tarot used to mostly be perceived as something dark, mysterious, and scary. These days, it's much more accepted. And yet, it remains a practice that is full of magic and mystery.

But how does tarot *work*?

I've spent more time than I care to admit trying to answer that question, looking for some sort of logical or scientific basis for its successful operation. How can stacks of paper give such insightful, accurate answers to questions, big and small, about the human condition? How can I discover the secrets of perfect strangers by laying cards on a table? But after all these years, I have yet to find an adequate explanation that would satisfy every skeptic—so I stopped trying to find one.

Now, when asked—and I am asked often—"How does tarot work?" my answer is this:

I don't know *how* it works. I only know *that* it works.

It's the things we don't fully understand about tarot that makes it so special.

It's been more than twenty-five years since I first learned how to read the tarot with that deck that had a keyword on every card. To this day, when I pull the Wheel of Fortune from any deck, I can easily recall the imagery from that first deck and its associated word. Those original keywords became an integral part of my tarot vocabulary and are still with me to this day.

The only thing that could have been better was if I had assigned my own personally meaningful keyword to each card. That is the experience I hope to offer you in this book: an experience of building your own personal set of keywords for the cards so that any tarot deck you pick up will feel like it was tailor-made especially for you.

Supplies

In addition to this book, there are a few things you are going to need as you work your way through the pages ahead.

A Tarot Deck

You will need a tarot deck but not just any deck; you'll need an affordable and easily replaced deck.

Why? Because I'm going to ask you to mark up the deck you use with this book. Yes, I will ask you to write your chosen word on each card as you go through this process with me. You may even want two copies of the same deck: one you can mark up and one that you can keep pristine.

I have been teaching this method for a while now, and I've seen people try to avoid writing on their decks—using washi tape or other methods. While that is an option, I don't recommend it. Even the thinnest washi tape will make your deck thick and difficult to shuffle. I want your marked-up deck to be usable. Trust me on this; pick up a deck you are okay with writing on.

Make sure whatever deck you choose is based on the Rider-Waite-Smith tarot system and has scenic images on all seventy-eight cards.

Most importantly, pick a deck you like both physically and aesthetically. A deck you want to look at and enjoy handling and shuffling makes all the difference when you're trying to learn, and it will make it much easier for you to choose the best keywords for you.

A Fine-Point Permanent Marker or Pen

You're going to need a writing implement that you can use to write your chosen keywords on your cards. I suggest a permanent marker or pen because it will typically hold up the best over time, and you want those words to stick around! Don't worry if you make a mistake. Remember, the deck isn't precious. The messiness is part of the process. Embrace it!

A Journal

It's helpful to have a place to make a note of your exploration of each card and possible keywords that might work for you as you go through this process. This can be a paper journal or a notes app on your phone, tablet, or laptop. I also heartily encourage you to write all over this book. Whatever helps you explore possibilities as you go through this book? Do that.

Learning the tarot is hard, but it doesn't have to be. Let's get started.

Chapter 1
Setting the Record Straight

"Do you want me to read your cards?" The tarot reader asked while we sipped tea in the living room of one of the coven elders hosting this social.

"Sure," I replied nervously.

We sat opposite each other on the floor. After carefully unwrapping her deck of cards from a square of silk, she laid the fabric out between us, setting the stage, and began to shuffle.

I didn't know what to expect. I wasn't even sure if I believed the cards could have anything to say about me: past, present, or future. The woman sitting across from me, shuffling cards, knew nothing about me—though we would one day become friends. So, I wondered how she could possibly tell me anything true about my future with only a pack of cards.

I guess you could say I was curious but skeptical. It was only paper, after all, and I tended to approach everything—even my spirituality—with a logical approach. I usually worked best with tools whose purpose I could understand intellectually, but tarot cards seemed mysterious in a way I couldn't wrap my mind around.

The tarot reader laid out a Celtic cross tarot spread and began telling me things about my past she had no way of knowing, insights about my present that blew my mind, and predictions for my future—and it wasn't all positive. In fact, some of it was intensely challenging.

The predictions made that day provoked a viscerally negative response in me. She predicted that my then long-term relationship would dissolve after I met an older dark-haired woman whose personality she went on to describe in detail. I would find out later that she was correct.

I contemplated my experience that day for a long time afterward. I couldn't explain the experience I'd had. Awestruck, I assumed that tarot readers must have a special gift. No regular person could interpret tarot cards.

I couldn't have been more wrong.

Curiosity—more than any actual hope that I could competently read the cards—led me to wander into a metaphysical shop and purchase my first tarot card set.

I am so incredibly grateful that I had never heard that my first tarot deck was supposed to be a gift. I am not sure I would have ever bought that first deck if I had. And if not for that first tarot deck, I wouldn't be sitting here right now, writing this book.

Common Misconceptions

Let's talk about the assumption that your first tarot deck must be gifted and other common misconceptions about the tarot.

#1: Your first deck must be a gift.

Around the time tarot began to be used as a form of divination, it would have been common to receive your first deck as a gift. After all, tarot decks were not readily available and would most likely be luxury items that only the wealthy would own. I suspect that is where the idea that your first tarot deck must be a gift came from.

Even in the last few decades, tarot was hardly mainstream. Few people would have access to metaphysical stores, and you certainly wouldn't see tarot decks at your local Barnes & Noble, so it stands to reason that most new readers were given their first decks by a friend or family member who read cards. Today's tarot readers are so enthusiastic about our practice that we love introducing someone else to it. It's such an honor to have the opportunity to give someone their first deck!

What are the chances that someone would develop an interest in tarot and meet a tarot reader close enough to them that they might hope to one day be given a deck by that person?

What likely began as a practice borne of necessity morphed over time into a superstition that has stopped quite a few aspiring readers in their tracks.

About once a week, someone will wander into a tarot discussion group and ask, "Do I have to be given my first tarot deck as a gift?"

The answer to this question is no.

I purchased my first tarot deck. You can, too. The best deck you can choose to be your first is one you have picked out for yourself and are excited to learn how to use.

#2: You must be born with the gift to read tarot.

I used to think that only those born with special gifts were able to read tarot. The practice of working with tarot cards felt utterly unattainable to me—until I decided to try to learn anyway and found it was possible after all.

I learned you don't have to have some unique genetic trait to learn to use tarot. Tarot is a system; like any system, you can learn to use it by applying time and energy to studying and practicing.

With that said, some readers learn more quickly than others and take to it like a fish to water, but fish aren't the only creatures who swim.

Let's replace tarot with math.

There are plenty of people who naturally pick up and retain math easily. I wouldn't count myself among them. (See what I did there?)

Still, I passed all my math classes in high school and college. I even brought home a decent grade in one or two math classes. I am not somehow excluded from holding my own mathematically simply because it comes less easily to me than it does to others.

Like math, reading tarot cards is a skill anyone can learn by putting time and energy into the attempt.

#3: You must wrap your tarot deck in black silk. You must put your new tarot deck under your pillow while you sleep for 100 nights. You must never let anyone else touch your deck. You must store your cards with a clear quartz crystal. You must cleanse your deck between every reading. You must charge your cards under the light of the full moon. And, so on…

Your tarot cards are pieces of paper—cardstock, ideally. They may or may not be laminated or coated in something to offer them some protection, but they are pieces of paper.

Your tarot deck is as sacred as you want it to be or as you intend it to be. You can treat it as a holy object, but you don't have to.

You can reach into your messy backpack, pull out your deck of tarot cards, extract them from their rapidly disintegrating paper box, lay them on the sticky bar table you're sitting at, and get down to the business of reading tarot quite effectively.

I wouldn't necessarily *recommend* treating your cards so casually, at least if you want them to last. But I guarantee you there are readers for whom that casual approach works best. You might be one of them. There's nothing wrong with that.

A large number of the beliefs around how cards should be handled, stored, or used correlate directly to the idea that tarot cards hold energy. For those that subscribe to this belief, the idea is that tarot decks absorb energies you push into them through activities like charging them by the light of the full moon or with crystals or bonding with them by sleeping with them under your pillow. It also means that they can absorb energies through the readings you do with those cards or from those that touch, shuffle, or use them.

If you believe that your cards can absorb energy, you may very well find it helpful and appropriate to cleanse your cards regularly or between readings, or you may feel as though wrapping them in a special fabric or bag or storing them with a crystal keeps them protected from unwanted energies. If you believe that your cards are bonded specifically to you, the reader, you may not be comfortable lending your cards to others or letting your querents touch or shuffle the cards. Every reader's approach to these things is different. All approaches are valid.

I am in the camp of those who believe our cards can absorb energy, though I like to think I'm pretty laid back about it. I have a few decks that are particularly precious to me, and those I treat with special care and don't let others touch or shuffle them. Generally, I don't mind if people I know touch or use my cards, and I even prefer that in-person querents shuffle before I pull cards for them. I use simple energy-cleansing methods between readings and occasionally give my deck collection a soak in moonlight or cleanse them with crystals. I almost always use a reading cloth beneath my cards, and I keep nearly all my tarot decks in special handmade bags (mostly for convenience) because I'm spoiled enough to have a wife who makes them on demand. All of this makes sense for me based on how I view and interact with my tarot decks.

If you believe, as some others do, that your tarot decks are inert objects, tools, and not carriers of energy, then you may find that these prescribed practices are unnecessary and a waste of your time.

There's nothing wrong with treating your tarot cards as sacred. There's also nothing wrong with treating them like pieces of paper. Some of us dabble in a bit of woo with our cards. Some of us don't. The point is: you can do whatever you want with your tarot deck.

#4: Only witches or Pagans read tarot cards.

Okay, hear me out.

As a self-identified Pagan witch, I understand how easy it is to assume that tarot is a Pagan practice. Arguably, witches and Pagans played an enormous role in popularizing the tarot. Most witchy folk I know have at least dabbled with tarot.

In recent years, however, I've met a number of fantastic tarot readers who self-identify as atheists or follow an Abrahamic religion, such as Christianity or Judaism.

Tarot is not inherently spiritual. While some people work with tarot on a spiritual level, the cards themselves are simply tools. For example, some witches may use cast-iron cauldrons in their magical practice, but plenty of people only use cast-iron cauldrons over a fire to make delicious soups and stews.

Tarot may be relatively popular among witches and Pagans, but it is certainly not exclusive to us.

Anyone with a desire to work with tarot can.

#5: Tarot is for predicting the future.

The idea that tarot is strictly for predicting future outcomes is so limiting.

The tarot can open a world of possibilities to you, and only one of those possibilities includes uncovering your future. Several tarot practitioners I know use tarot—first and foremost—to discover deeper information or advice about current circumstances or situations. Others, including myself, turn to tarot for the same reason a sailor consults a compass: to navigate rough waters.

Sometimes that involves looking to our future, but often it is more about understanding the present and—almost as commonly—processing the past.

Some people don't believe it's even possible to forecast the future. I focused exclusively on the past and present when reading tarot for the first several years. There's nothing wrong with that approach.

Nowadays, it's more common for tarot readers to use the tarot as psychological or spiritual support than to predict the future, and that is a totally valid approach.

While I continue to use tarot to process the past and navigate the present, I also use it to predict the future. In fact, I would argue that most tarot users divine their futures in some form or another. We want to know what the day has in store for us, what we need to know about our career or school, or how our relationship will go.

I believe the future directly reflects our choices and actions rather than a fixed outcome we have no control over.

Reading the future with tarot cards is like watching the ripples in a pond from a tossed stone. The tarot helps me see the consequences of the behaviors, actions, and choices made in the present. Even the tiniest change can interrupt those ripples.

To understand what I mean:

1. Try—or imagine—throwing a pebble in a pond.
2. Watch the ripples spread out from where the stone makes contact with the water. You'll be able to predict where they will go.
3. Try this again, but as the ripples spread outward this time, throw another pebble and watch the pattern change to one that is more difficult to predict.
4. Imagine it begins to rain or a leaf falls.

You get the idea.

Reading the future is, well, tricky.

While it's true that most tarot readers—to one degree or another—are looking forward, most are also trying to empower themselves and their querents to make the best decisions in the present, decisions that serve their long-term greatest good.

If I felt that tarot predicted a fixed future, I'd have gotten bored with it long ago, to be honest. What use is a tool that tells me what will happen but doesn't empower me to figure out what I can do to craft the future I desire or prevent futures I don't want?

Like any tool that taps into human experience, there are many ways to work with the tarot, and all are equally valid. The only opinions that ultimately matter in your tarot practice are yours.

#6: Tarot cards originated in ancient Egypt (or some other ancient civilization).

While it is possible that the beliefs or practices of ancient civilizations, such as those in Egypt, had an influence on the evolution of divination, tarot cards were a European invention.

As far as we know today, tarot cards originated in Europe in the fourteenth century from unique playing card sets commissioned by the wealthy to play specialty card games. They continued to be used in parlor games by the affluent for hundreds of years until around the middle of the eighteenth century—when we first encountered references to tarot and divination. Tarot grew in popularity as a divination tool until it eventually spread outside of Europe and took on a life of its own.

In the late nineteenth century, the Hermetic Order of the Golden Dawn—an occult group interested in multiple forms of mysticism—was formed. At the turn of the twentieth century, Arthur Edward Waite and Pamela Colman Smith, both members of the order, created a tarot deck that would go on to be published by the Rider company in 1909: the Rider-Waite-Smith tarot—commonly referred to today as the RWS. Not long after, Aleister Crowley, also a member of the order, partnered with talented artist Lady Frieda Harris to create the Thoth tarot, published for the first time in 1944.

Both the Thoth and the RWS tarot decks are still popular today. While they are both founded on the principles and practices of the Golden Dawn, the RWS tarot has become the most popular system for today's tarot readers. It is the system that forms the foundation of most modern tarot decks.

#7: Tarot and oracle are the same thing.

I can't count the number of times I've heard the idea that tarot and oracle are the same. While we use both types of tools similarly, tarot and oracle decks are different.

An oracle deck can be any deck of cards, of any quantity, with or without any accompanying structure, used for divination.

A tarot deck follows a specific structure. The tarot's structure and key concepts distinguish it from other divination systems. Let's take a closer look at that structure.

- **Major Arcana**

  The major arcana is the trump suit in a tarot deck. It consists of twenty-two uniquely named cards, beginning with the Fool and ending in the World. These cards carry more weight in a reading as they represent significant experiences in life.

- **The Minor Arcana**

  The minor arcana contains four suits. Each suit corresponds to one of the four elements: fire, water, air, and earth. Each suit includes ten numbered cards, ace through ten, and four court cards (i.e., page, knight, queen, and king).

If a deck omits any of these components, I have difficulty viewing it as tarot. Some tarot deck creators have played with this structure by reordering the major arcana, renaming the suits, or changing the court structure slightly while leaving the system intact. These alterations can offer us a different perspective on the traditional system. However, when a deck creator omits parts of the system itself entirely, such as leaving out the court cards, the deck ceases to be a tarot deck.

#8: All tarot decks are the same.

All tarot decks are not the same, but it's complicated. Let me explain.

There are multiple tarot systems; the Rider-Waite-Smith tarot is the most common.

The Rider-Waite-Smith tarot system includes twenty-two major arcana cards numbered zero through twenty-one; sixteen court cards ranked page, knight, queen, and king; and forty numbered minor arcana cards. In the RWS structure, you can expect that each numbered minor arcana card will feature a scene of some sort, though some RWS-based decks may skip the scenes in the numbered minor arcana cards and show a number of pips, or suit symbols, much like playing cards. Most modern RWS-based tarot decks feature scenic minor arcana cards rather than pips.

The Thoth tarot system is similar to the RWS in that it also contains twenty-two major arcana cards, forty numbered minor arcana cards, and sixteen court cards. However, the rank of the court cards is different. Instead of page, knight, queen, king, the Thoth court is princess, prince, queen, knight, which can confuse new readers. Additionally, the Thoth tarot system leans much more heavily into astrological and esoteric references, and the numbered minor arcana cards depict suit objects in certain formations instead of scenes.

The older tarot systems, like Marseille, Sola Busca, Trionfi, and others, have other distinguishing characteristics. For example, Marseille tarot's minor arcana cards are always non-scenic and feature pips arranged consistently across the decks.

It's important to understand that there are different tarot systems. As a beginner, you'll find learning much easier if you start with one system and stick with it until you're comfortable. On that note, I recommend the RWS system, as it's the easiest to learn. The scenes on the cards are a massive help to those learning tarot, and it is the system I recommend you use along with this book.

Now you know.

Chapter 2

About Keywords

Tarot, for me, is like buried treasure. You can spend your entire life never knowing it exists, let alone having an opportunity to experience it. And yet, the wisdom it offers is right there—within reach. From the moment I had that first reading, I knew tarot was special, but I had no idea how to unlock its mysteries.

When I opened my first box of tarot cards, I found seventy-eight keys. Each of these cards and their associated keyword unlocked a unique part of the tarot.

A keyword is exactly what it sounds like it is. It's a word that acts like a key to unlock a broader meaning. This quality makes the single-keyword method of learning the tarot incredibly powerful.

Imagine standing at the seaside. Your toes dig into the sand. The wind whips around you and through your hair. The waves lap peacefully nearby. Choose a word to capture this feeling.

Some words that immediately come to mind for me are *freedom*, *peace*, *calm*, *home*, or *bliss*. I'll choose the word *bliss*.

Picture this exact scene on a card. Written on the bottom of that card is the single word you chose. Then, imagine pulling this card in answer to the question "What should I focus on today?" This card, with that single word, has the solution for you. What is it telling you?

My word was *bliss*. So, I might see that card draw as a reminder that, today, I should do something that helps me tap into bliss or that I should look for small moments of bliss during an otherwise hectic day.

What answer would you get from your word?

Keywords help you extract layered meanings from a simple, expansive word that can bring related feelings or thoughts to mind whenever you pull that card.

The tarot is a comprehensive system. Every card has astrological, esoteric, elemental, and color associations. It's a lot to take in. But at its core, tarot is a system for understanding and relating to life: whether past, present, or future.

A simple keyword can help you tap into the heart of tarot in a way that is meaningful for you. When each card means something to you personally, you'll find that working with the cards becomes easy and natural.

Once you're comfortable with the essential meaning of each card, the sky is the limit. With a good keyword as your foundation, you can spend the rest of your life adding more and more layers of information to this basic meaning. That single keyword will eventually sit at the heart of a virtual mind-map of other words, ideas, and concepts.

Let's face it: most of us don't just want to understand tarot; we want to use it! When I got my first deck, I was eager to put it through its paces immediately, and I was able to do that because my first deck had a keyword printed on every card. You can do that too if you write your own keyword on every card. With your own set of personalized keywords, you'll be able to hit the ground running and can start reading with your cards right away.

There is a sneaky side benefit to this method, too. By really thinking about what each tarot card means and trying to pick a word that best aligns with your understanding of that meaning, you're creating a personal, intimate connection with that card.

As you go through this process, you'll find that each word will become a memory trigger, taking you back to the experience of picking the word in the first place. In other words, you will train your mind to recall the more expansive meaning of the card simply by referencing that single keyword.

Pretty cool, huh?

But Wait, What about Reversals?

When you shuffle your cards, you might discover that some are upside-down when you flip them over. Some readers read the cards differently when that happens.

You can, for example, read a reversed card as the opposite of its usual meaning. You could view a reversed card as if the usual interpretation or energy is blocked or resistant. You could also view a reversed card as the more pessimistic version of its meaning, whereas when it is upright, you look to the more positive version. Or vice versa.

Some tarot readers believe that working with reversals brings more balance to the tarot, allowing for a secondary meaning for every card. Other tarot readers ignore reversed cards when they arise or shuffle their decks so that the cards remain pointed in the same direction when laid out for a reading. Neither is correct. Both methods are valid and valuable.

I believe that tarot is already inherently balanced between light and shadow. Some cards speak to lighter or brighter topics. Other cards illustrate challenging issues. Even the cards that appear the most negative contain a favorable interpretation, just as every seemingly positive card has a negative one. Light cannot exist in the absence of darkness. And darkness cannot exist in the absence of light. Life isn't binary and neither is tarot. I believe that physically reversing cards is usually unnecessary and can create extra complexity and confusion—especially for new readers.

However, I'm not a purist when it comes to this topic. While I *typically* don't read with reversals, I do occasionally shuffle them into my deck—usually when I want to quickly identify blocked or challenging energies or obstacles in a reading. Truthfully, I simply find it easier to examine the artwork on the cards if they are all pointed in the same direction. I also typically prefer having the flexibility to lean into the more positive or negative meaning of the card depending on what my intuition tells me in the moment or where the card appears in the spread.

Bottom line: If you don't feel like working with reversals, you don't have to. You can read each card in whatever way feels appropriate to the question, the situation, the tarot spread you're using, and the surrounding cards. When you take your time to feel your way through every card in a tarot reading, you learn to trust your own insight more. Strengthening your intuition helps to make you a better tarot reader over time.

Regardless of how you choose to approach reversals, I highly recommend beginning with a neutral keyword for every card whenever you can so that you have the freedom to take your reading in the direction that feels right in the moment.

What Is a Neutral Keyword?

A neutral keyword is a word that does not immediately feel positive or negative when you think of it.

The keyword *bliss*, from my earlier example, is a positive keyword. Or is it? Bliss is a happy experience. But could *bliss* also be used negatively?

What about being blissfully ignorant, for example?

Keep in mind that it doesn't matter what anyone else thinks about how neutral or not your keyword is. What matters is that you can use that keyword to interpret that tarot card in a variety of ways—positive or negative.

A simple way to test your keyword for neutrality is to use that card to answer both questions:

- What blessing will come my way today?
- What obstacle will I face today?

If you can use the keyword you've chosen to answer both questions, you're good to go!

Some cards feel inherently negative or positive. In those situations, you may find it challenging to find a truly neutral keyword for every card, which is absolutely okay. I only suggest that you do your best to aim for neutrality as much as possible.

It's now time to begin the process of choosing your seventy-eight keywords. But first, let's establish a few ground rules, shall we?

Rule #1: This book is not precious (assuming you own it!).

If the copy of this book you are reading is yours and only yours, please write in it, dog-ear the pages, highlight words, write in the margins, and deface it in whatever way will help you dig into this process! After all, this will be an exploration of words.

If you've borrowed this book, please have a notebook handy to scrawl all your thoughts and takeaways in.

Either way, writing things down helps fix them firmly in your mind. Besides, you'll be grateful to be able to look back on your notes later. I wish I had kept the notebooks I jotted in when I was first learning tarot.

Rule #2: You're the boss.

I'm not the boss. Your best friend whose grandmother taught them to read tarot is not the boss. Your favorite tarot YouTuber is not the boss. That other tarot book you read last month is not the boss.

You are the only person who gets to decide what word you will use for each card.

You're the boss.

Rule #3: Gender is irrelevant (unless it is helpful).

The Rider-Waite-Smith tarot images show people of various genders in various stereotypical gender roles. Today, we understand that gender is more nuanced than a strict binary of male/female and that people can be in all sorts of relationships and can fulfill all sorts of roles.

You may find that it is, occasionally, helpful to incorporate the gender or gender role of the people pictured on the cards into your reading; however, it's important to remember that anyone can be an emperor, empress, queen, king, page, or knight. The cards depict situations, energies, personalities, and the dynamics at play between people, and their meanings can be applied to anyone of any gender.

Regardless of how you choose to perceive the people pictured on individual cards, I do think it's important to avoid assuming the gender of your querent or the people important to them. As a queer woman married to another woman, it's awkward when a reader refers to my husband. The reading is still valid, of course, but the discomfort of that moment is totally avoidable. I really appreciate it when other readers avoid making assumptions about gender, and I like to do the same for my querents by following their lead. If my querent refers to her husband, then I refer to him as her husband. If it's not clear, I will use gender-neutral language like *partner* or *significant other*. Using the language used by your querent shows them you care.

Rule #4: There are no wrong answers.

There are no incorrect keywords. You might opt for a word that fails to work as well as you want it to over time. You can choose a word that you eventually don't like and want to replace. You can even choose a word that leads you astray. When that happens, you'll change it. Your understanding of each tarot card will evolve. That's part of the fun. So, remind yourself of rule 1, cross out whatever word isn't working for you, and write in a new one. It's all good.

Chapter 3
The Big 22:
The Major Arcana

L et me introduce you to the big twenty-two: the major arcana.

The definition of *arcana* is secrets or mysteries. And the major arcana are the major mysteries—the big stuff.

These cards carry more weight in a reading as they depict significant events in one's life. The major arcana is where you will find the cards most often associated with tarot, such as the Fool, the Wheel of Fortune, Death, and the World. Each card shows up to teach us about major events in our lives: past, present, or future.

The Fool's Journey

Each card in the major arcana appears in a particular order—an order that illuminates a journey: the Fool's journey, to be precise.

The Fool's journey refers to the storylike progression of the major arcana. It begins with an archetype for new beginnings, the Fool, and ends with an archetype for endings that lead to more new beginnings, the World. Unlike a linear story, the Fool's journey is circular. You begin at the Fool, make your way to the World, and then start again at the Fool.

Life, like the major arcana, is also cyclical. All the cards of the major arcana, in the form of the Fool's journey, combine to create a more extensive archetype for the cycle of life. Cool, right?

Familiarizing yourself with the Fool's journey is incredibly helpful in understanding tarot's major arcana.

Let's break it down with an example from mundane daily life:

Sarah recently graduated from college with a degree in clinical psychology and decided the time had come to apply for counseling jobs. Having never worked in the field before, she approached this new adventure with all the hope and naivete of a bright-eyed, bushy-tailed recent graduate (Fool).

Sarah spent years preparing for this. She studied well, got excellent grades, and learned how to apply her knowledge. She had all the tools she needed to succeed (Magician).

While reviewing the classifieds for opportunities, Sarah had a bad feeling about some and a good feeling about others. She listened to her intuition and added the good-vibe options to her list (High Priestess).

After thoroughly reviewing the options on her list, Sarah applied for the positions that seemed the most personally fulfilling (Empress).

Sarah's applications moved forward with several of her picks, and now she had to face the interview stage. She was intimidated by the prospect of meeting with lead psychologists at the clinics she wanted to work at. She knew their focus would be on protecting the well-being and interests of their existing staff and their patients. If she wanted to perform well at these interviews, she'd have to meet high standards (Emperor).

During the interview process, Sarah learned that she would not have a lot of freedom to work creatively. Her future boss would expect her to follow existing rules and operating guidelines. She knew she would need to approach any new position with a focus on learning from those with more experience— at least until she established herself (Hierophant).

Sarah interviewed well and received two different offers that she would have to choose between. One opportunity was for a position that focused on helping patients over the long term with personal growth. At that clinic, she would have the opportunity to build long-term relationships with her patients. The other offer came from a clinic that helped patients with more urgent but short-term needs. There, Sarah's focus would be helping at-risk patients reach a point of stability that would allow them to move on to other clinicians supporting their long-term mental health. Each option offered unique challenges, and each would build a different skill set. Sarah knew this choice would significantly impact the long-term trajectory of her career (Lovers).

Ultimately, Sarah decided the best choice for her was the urgent care clinic. Shortly after she began her work there, however, she realized she may be in way over her head. Worries, doubts, and everyone's needs seemed to pull at her from all directions. She knew that if she wanted to succeed, she had to remain focused on helping her patients get what they needed to ensure long-term wellness (Chariot).

Sarah's first challenging patient taught her so much. She learned the importance of recognizing her abilities, but also her limitations. To serve this vulnerable patient, she needed to bring gentleness to her approach while remaining confident in their sessions. Slowly, this patient began to trust her, a rewarding experience that gave Sarah newfound confidence in her abilities (Strength).

After several long weeks at work, Sarah was exhausted. Despite the social invitations she'd received, she knew it was best to stay home. She needed to recharge her batteries and, more importantly, needed to reflect and integrate all she'd been learning as a clinical counselor. This reflection was essential if Sarah wanted to be her best for herself and her patients (Hermit).

After two years at the clinic, Sarah was delighted to be told she was being promoted. She would continue to support her patients directly but would also help bring new clinicians onboard. The promotion came with a sizable salary increase and some much-deserved recognition. Sarah insisted that the additional workload would not interfere with her ability to manage her current caseload. She could adapt to her new duties and manage the shifts in her workflow (Wheel of Fortune).

Several months after the promotion, the lead psychologist called Sarah into his office to review her performance. Some of Sarah's patients hadn't been progressing as well as expected, so he made the decision to reduce Sarah's caseload so she could manage her responsibilities better. Sarah wasn't managing the workload as well as she'd hoped and the quality of care she was providing had dropped, so an adjustment had to be made (Justice).

Unfortunately, despite the reduced caseload, Sarah still struggled to give her best to her patients and the new clinicians. Overwhelmed, she decided to take a leave of absence to catch her breath. She planned to use the time away from work to learn what she could from her experiences and explore new perspectives to help her determine the next best steps for herself and everyone relying on her (Hanged Man).

While Sarah was on leave, her boss called to let her know that her role would be changing. He was removing the onboarding support from her responsibilities, and she would be focusing solely on the clinical work with her patients when she returned to work. Her boss assured her this was best for all involved, but Sarah was devastated. She recognized that it was probably best to let go of the additional responsibilities, but she had enjoyed onboarding new clinicians and felt like something had been taken from her (Death).

Eventually, Sarah recognized that trying to do it all wasn't working and that getting back to working with a moderate caseload of patients would be best for her. She returned to work, determined to avoid biting off more than she could chew in the future (Temperance).

Sarah was feeling fulfilled with her work again, and her patients were having good outcomes. All was going very well until the new administrator joined the team. David was charming and incredibly attractive and constantly flirted with her. Sarah knew she should keep her professional boundaries in place and focus on her patients, but when David asked her out on a date, she caved. She'd been single for ages and needed a night out on the town. She didn't think there could be much harm to bending the rules this once, but once turned into twice, and twice turned into dozens. Sarah told herself that as long as no one in the office found out, they could continue to see each other outside of office hours—except for that clandestine kiss they exchanged in the copy room (Devil).

It turned out that Sarah hadn't been as careful as she thought. Office gossip was rampant, and her affair with David was no longer a secret. During an uncomfortable meeting with the lead psychologist, David blamed the entire thing on Sarah, and they were both fired. Everything in Sarah's world has come crumbling down. What a mess (Tower).

Afterward, Sarah did some soul-searching. She knew how everything had gone wrong and knew what role she had played in what had taken place. She decided that giving up was not an option. Instead, she picked herself up and dusted herself off, determined to get back on track with her goals. It was time for a new beginning (Star).

Sarah perused the job ads again, but every single one raised red flags. This one sounded too corporate and materialistic. An egomaniac runs that one.

Perhaps these opportunities were disasters waiting to happen, or perhaps Sarah was leaping at shadows. To get to the truth, Sarah needed to determine whether each job really was a walking red flag or if she was viewing each ad through the lens of her past experiences (Moon).

Sarah finally found herself back at work. After reapplying, she had been hired at the long-term patient clinic she had previously considered. It turned out that it was the perfect fit for her. Helping her patients meet their personal growth goals was the most fulfilling work she'd ever done, and she finally felt like she was on the right track. The office culture at this clinic was great. Sarah could be herself with her coworkers, no longer felt she had anything to prove, and enjoyed her work with her patients. She'd finally landed her dream job and the future looked bright (Sun).

One day, Sarah received a call from her alma mater, the university she graduated from. They'd heard about the work she'd been doing and wanted her to come on board as a professor of clinical psychology. Accepting that offer would mean leaving behind the job Sarah had grown to love, but she knew she could do great things as a university professor. When she said yes, she knew her life would be changed forever (Judgement).

Sarah worked at the university for fifteen years before being offered tenure. When the offer came, she didn't even hesitate to accept. She knew the university believed in her, but more importantly, Sarah believed in herself. She knew this was where her career had been leading her all along, and it was perfect for her (World).

Sarah's story demonstrates the way in which the Fool's journey offers you a glimpse into the narrative qualities of the major arcana, showing how the Fool moves through every card and how this suit encompasses all the biggest moments we experience throughout our lives.

The Dreaded Three

There are three major arcana cards that have terrible reputations they don't necessarily deserve. Yes, I'm talking about the Devil card, the Tower card, and the most terrifying (thanks, Hollywood!) Death card. Let's have a chat about these.

The Devil

While the concept of the devil can undoubtedly make some people uncomfortable, the Devil card in tarot does not represent the literal embodiment of evil.

Instead, the Devil represents bad habits, temptation, selfishness, self-sabotage, and other unhelpful behaviors.

The Tower

The Tower card depicts a sizable physical structure destroyed by a lightning bolt. It can be scary because it shows people falling from the tall structure toward their likely doom.

This card certainly shows a lot of destruction, but it's important to remember that the Tower doesn't have to represent total disaster.

The Tower card does point out where things are falling apart. Often metaphorically, the Tower represents the breaking down of some existing system, structure, or element in our life to create space to rebuild or begin again.

Sure, it's not light and fluffy, but it's also not literal.

Death

Speaking of not taking things literally, let's talk about the Death card.

The Death card is arguably the scariest card for someone who has never worked with the tarot or had their cards read before. Thanks to its disproportionate (and misrepresented) coverage in modern media, we associate this card with dramatic predictions of someone's early and untimely demise.

This card is a metaphor for endings that we cannot change but must come to terms with.

I'll never say that the Death card never represents an actual physical death because I have seen this card come up to mean physical death—often when there is a blockage to grief or when grief significantly impacts my querent—but this is a rare exception, not the rule.

These scary cards are only frightening when we look at them literally. Tarot cards aren't literal. They're archetypal.

What Are Archetypes?

Archetypes are examples. They are ideas or concepts that can be used as a model to explain something: a type of person, an experience, or a feeling.

The mother, for example, can be an archetype for someone who is nurturing, caring, and supportive and tends to take people under their wing.

The tarot is made up entirely of archetypes. Whether it's the Death card modeling the concept of loss or the Fool modeling the idea of innocence, openness, or someone with an unguarded heart, every tarot card is a model for a person, experience, or feeling we will face. It's what makes tarot such an excellent and flexible tool—one that we can use for everything from processing the past to predicting the future.

Now, grab the major arcana cards from your deck, your permanent marker, and your journal, and let's get down to business.

As you read each card's entry, reflect on possible words that might work for you. You can use one of the keywords I share or choose an entirely different word that doesn't appear in this book!

Remember that the most important thing you can do is select a word that makes sense and will help you recall the card's meaning. Choose the card's keyword before you move on to the next card.

The first word that feels right is right for you—at least for now. You can change it later. For now, go with your gut. Try not to linger or second-guess yourself.

Trust me on this. It's going to work out. I promise.

The Major Arcana
The Fool: Risk

My keyword for this card is *risk*. The definition of *risk* is moving forward in the presence of danger.

Of all the cards in the tarot, the Fool is the card that inspires me the most.

There's openness, trust, and boldness to this image: a person whose gender is ambiguous walks straight ahead, not looking at their feet but trusting in the journey. They don't know—or they don't care—how arduous the trip will be. They know they want to move forward—do something, learn something, experience something.

The Fool has had experiences. They've had successes, and they've had failures. Look how light they travel! There's no way they have even an extra pair of shoes in there. I could never pack so lightly, literally or metaphorically.

In life, we always bring our experiences with us. We jokingly refer to having emotional baggage. The only experiences the Fool can fit in that tiny little pouch are those necessary for the present journey they are beginning and nothing more. They don't lug around their failures and their fears. They step forward with total faith that, somehow, everything will work out.

Sure, the Fool is about to step off the edge of a cliff, but they aren't concerned. They truly believe the universe has their back. There's no way they could come to any harm. Or could they?

In truth, the Fool could be walking forward into something spectacular or something devastating. Those who see how big the risks are see only a fool.

Those who find the Fool's openhearted enthusiasm for life inspirational—and who wish they could trust so easily—see a genius.

The Fool also brings a lot of new beginning energy to the tarot. After all, even the card's number is the absolute beginning: zero—the number that comes before one! This card points us in the direction of new beginnings.

The Fool reminds me of Zen Buddhism's beginner's mind concept, which describes the beauty and power in approaching any part of life as if you are a beginner, even when you aren't. This card invites you to consider the beauty and power of setting aside preconceived ideas or worries so that you can have an experience. It's incredible what you can accomplish when you assume you know nothing and open yourself up to everything.

Oh, and one more thing: the Fool is not alone. They have a companion. In the card you see here, our Fool's companion is a fluffy white dog, full of energy, bounding beside our Fool and yapping away. I like to think of the Fool's companion as their instinct: the part of them that will warn them of real danger or encourage them if the way is clear—if they pay attention, that is.

The unknown future of the Fool is what I find so thrilling. The Fool is not a planner; they are a doer and are open to whatever life throws at them, good or bad. The Fool is spontaneous, a free spirit.

As a blessing, the Fool invites you to take a glorious, openhearted leap of faith without worrying whether other people might think you foolish for doing so. The risk is worth the reward!

As an obstacle, the Fool can represent the fears that stop you from taking risks, opening your heart, trusting, or taking a step forward on a new path. Being blocked from trust and openness or letting past failures get in your head and in your way can undoubtedly present obstacles. The Fool as an obstacle can also be about being reckless and ignoring your instincts about red flags or pitfalls out of a stubborn desire to pretend everything is better than it is.

With the Fool card, there is always an element of danger. How you approach or interpret the card will depend on whether the threat you perceive is worth facing or better avoided. Based on this, *risk* works best for me as a keyword for the Fool.

Consider what word might work for you if *risk* doesn't fit the bill. Here are a few other words that you may want to consider:

Naivete/Innocence

Naivete, the quality of being naive, describes the result of someone lacking in life experience, or at least lacking in the type of life experiences that make one more cautious, making it an excellent keyword for the Fool.

The word *innocence*, like *naivete*, suggests someone relatively untested by life. It also suggests the idea of purity or a blank slate, which can be a helpful way to look at the Fool.

Beginning/Beginner

The words *beginning* and *beginner* work well to capture the starting energy of the Fool. If this quality of the Fool jumps out, either of these keywords will work well for you.

Trust/Faith

Trust and *faith* are interesting words for the Fool because they remind us of the interpretation of the Fool as a leap of faith.

The Magician: Potential

My keyword for this card is *potential*. The definition of *potential* is anything that can become actual. It is a word of possibility and creation, which I associate with the Magician.

I don't know about you, but I think of magic tricks when I think of the Magician. When I have seen magicians perform, I've found them to be tricky characters who made me think or see one thing when another thing was true. They are artists of illusion. It's no wonder that the Magician in the tarot is so often misunderstood.

Don't get me wrong—the Magician can certainly represent a trickster, someone who creates illusions, which is how older tarot decks depicted the Magician.

In the RWS tarot, however, the Magician is reborn with more depth than the performative Magicians of older tarots. The Magician stands at his table with three of the four elemental tools on display: a sword, cup, and pentacle. The fourth tool—a wand—is pointed at the sky in one hand while the other points down to the earth.

We could view the sky the Magician points to as the heavens, the universe, another plane, or even his own higher self. The Magician's other hand points to the earth, where plants grow in abundance at his feet. This positioning directly references the Hermetic saying "As above, so below."

The Magician is a creator, but what's incredibly mind-blowing is that what he is creating already exists; it just isn't visible yet. What a powerful idea!

It's why my favorite representations of the Magician card, in some way, illustrate the idea that everything you need—all the materials you require to produce anything in life—you already have within you. That pure potential allows the Magician to manifest their reality by transforming spirit into matter.

If the Fool is the blank slate, then the Magician is the chalk. When the Fool finally realizes what they are truly capable of, that is when they begin to embody the Magician (or, to stick with the metaphor, it's when they pick up the chalk and begin to draw).

The incredible thing about the Magician is that whether or not we see the potential, it's there. Ideally, the Magician helps us identify internal possibilities so that we can tap into them and build the future we want.

It's not all lilies and roses with the Magician, though. Someone who is aware of their capabilities but doesn't yet feel they have any rules to follow (don't worry, we'll get to that) can be a dangerous character—the sort of person who could be deceptive or manipulative.

What I find especially intriguing about the Magician is that we can look at this archetype in so many ways. How the Magician interacts with their potential can change the flavor of this card!

As a blessing, the Magician is a potent reminder of your inherent ability. You are not at the mercy of anyone. You have the ability to change what is and manifest what has not yet been realized. Everything you need or require is available, and nothing is out of reach. The Magician represents the essence of creation.

As an obstacle, the Magician can represent the ability to trick and deceive. Sometimes this energy shows up as worrying too much about impressing others or caring more about getting one's way than getting things done. The Magician, as an obstacle, can also represent the experience of underestimating one's own capabilities.

The word *potential* works well for this card because it marries the ideas of inner power and possibility—what better combination for manifesting whatever we want or need in life?

Consider what word might work for you if *potential* doesn't fit the bill. Here are a few other words that you may want to consider:

Manifestation

The definition of *manifestation* is to make something visible. This word does a fantastic job of representing the idea that whatever you want to do or create already exists in some form. The word *manifestation* also reminds you that you have the power of drawing toward yourself whatever it is that you want in your life.

Capability

Capability would be a terrific keyword if you want to focus on having the skills or abilities you need to accomplish your goals or manifest your desired future. *Capability* identifies that what you want is innate to you, which is a grounded way to look at the Magician.

Manipulation

To manipulate is to work with something skillfully. It could also imply someone who twists reality through clever words or actions, which makes *manipulate* an effective keyword for the Magician.

The High Priestess: Intuition

My keyword for this card is *intuition*. The definition of *intuition* is the knowledge that excludes conscious thought.

The High Priestess is an absolute mystery, and that is entirely the point.

Often depicted seated between two pillars, one black and one white, as in the tarot image you see here, the High Priestess seems calm and still.

It is the sea behind the enigmatic High Priestess that my eye always seeks out in this card. No matter how it's illustrated, I want to see that dark moonlit sea—what the High Priestess seems to guard and protect. The sea is a beautiful symbol for the subconscious, that deep well of knowledge available to us if we only tap into it or access it.

The High Priestess is the gateway to the unconscious. It's interesting how little of the sea you see in the image here. What is between you and that deep well of knowledge? Only you.

On her lap, the High Priestess holds a scroll that hints at the knowledge she holds but chooses to keep concealed. When the High Priestess speaks, it's not a shout but the softest whisper you will hear.

More importantly, the High Priestess will not seek you out. Instead, her secrets are ready when you are and wait for you. The High Priestess will answer only when you ask the right question.

In the Fool's journey, the High Priestess represents the point at which we begin to realize that we have innate knowledge that we can access whenever we choose. For some, this deep-down knowledge of the unconscious is a collection of ideas, memories, impressions, and experiences cataloged throughout our lives that we can call upon when needed to interpret the present. For others, this deep well of knowledge is more energetic or psychic.

Most of us can point to a time when we knew something we didn't have a reason to know. Perhaps it was a suspicion that someone wasn't being entirely honest with you, and you found out later they were lying to you. Maybe one day, you had a funny feeling and decided to go to work a few minutes earlier or later than usual, only to discover there had been an accident on the freeway. Perhaps you felt someone was good to have in your life, and it turned out they were. Or maybe you felt like someone was bad news, and they were.

The High Priestess represents the unknown, but the veil on the card is thin; if you look closely, you can see behind it. If you want to access your own inner wisdom—the secrets the High Priestess guards—you have to carefully dial it in, much like how you have to adjust an old-fashioned radio to get past the crackle to clarity.

Whenever this card comes up, I feel called to get out of my logical mind and into my gut. What does my gut tell me about the situation at hand? What messages from my inner knowing have I been ignoring? Are there red flags or green lights I'm overlooking because I'm too caught up in rationalizing or making pro/con lists? How can I lean into my inner knowing and turn down the volume on everyone else's opinions? These are the questions I ask myself when the High Priestess comes up in a reading.

As a blessing, your intuition offers knowledge, answers to your questions, and a clear way forward; you must tune in and listen.

As an obstacle, you aren't hearing your inner voice, you aren't listening to your inner voice, or you're ignoring the truth or feeling blocked from the information. There could be a lack of self-trust.

I love using *intuition* as my keyword for the High Priestess because it immediately brings to mind the connection between the High Priestess and my unconscious. It reminds me that I can't find the knowledge I seek outside of myself. The answer lies within, perhaps deep within, but within nonetheless.

Consider what word might work for you if *intuition* doesn't fit the bill. Here are a few other words that you may want to consider:

Secret/Mystery

A secret is a piece of information unknown to you that you want to learn more about. This word is good for you if you find the concept of intuition to be too slippery but want to retain the connection to the unknown. *Mystery* is similar to *secret* but adds more magic to the equation. A puzzle can feel more inviting than a secret, so using *mystery* as a keyword might feel more neutral.

Inner Voice/Higher Self

Inner voice and *higher self* are short key phrases you could use for this card. These can remind you that the knowledge you seek is within you if you tune into it.

Riddle/Puzzle

Riddle and *puzzle* represent needing to work to get the answer. I find these a little trickier for the High Priestess because, in my experience, gaining access to the information this card has for us is more effortless than these words imply, but one of these might work beautifully for you!

The Empress: Nurture

My keyword for this card is *nurture*. To care for something is to nurture it.

The Empress card is the ultimate archetype for the mother, with all the beauty and baggage that comes with it.

When I think of a mother as an archetype, I think of a divine mother—a power that is fierce and powerful, sensual and soft, nurturing and protective. Remember that the mother archetype has nothing to do with gender but represents the broadly applicable qualities of mothering.

The Empress is about more than caregiving, though. This archetype also represents sensuality and connection with the earth. If the Empress were a person standing on the beach, she would dig her toes into the sand, throw her arms wide to the wind, and be fully present in the experience. The Empress cares, but she is also fierce and protective.

The Empress, as depicted here, sits on what is, arguably, the most comfortable furniture you'll see throughout the entire deck but doesn't lay back lazily. She seems attentive and alert despite her relaxed posture. Her dress flows around her like water, the land around her is fertile, and the fields are ripe with wheat, ready to be harvested.

While a vast number of modern RWS-based tarot decks depict the Empress as pregnant, there is no noticeable baby bump in the RWS tarot image. It's easy to use pregnancy as a depiction of the maternal archetype, but I see it as an oversimplification of the meaning of this card. After all, I don't think someone needs to be pregnant to be a divine, nurturing presence in the universe.

To nurture something is to keep an eye on it, watch it, tend to it, and help it grow. We often think of this word in the context of nurturing others, but you can also nurture projects, jobs, or yourself—especially yourself.

The most important thing to remember about the Empress is that this card is not about creating something and walking away. It's about creating something, holding it by the hand, and stewarding it to its destination, safe and whole.

The Empress doesn't exist purely to care for others but also reminds us to unabashedly care for ourselves and enjoy life's sensual, earthly pleasures. This card isn't only about sustenance, but about nourishment.

As a blessing, the Empress helps you identify what, or who, needs your support and attention. This is the time to support and nourish your creations. This maternal energy helps you grow and expand in the direction of your dreams and offers support and a reminder to tend to yourself deeply.

As an obstacle, the Empress can indicate too much focus on the self or that your connection to the self is blocked. You may not feel you have the right to the good in your life or the right to feel whole and nourished. You may be self-sabotaging, or your way to creative growth may feel blocked.

The word *nurture* works well for me for the Empress because it brings to mind the deep care and attention required to help anything in life grow.

Consider what word might work for you if *nurture* doesn't fit the bill. Here are a few other words that you may want to consider:

Mother/Motherhood

My hesitance to use the word *mother* for this card concerns the complex, nuanced relationships that so many of us have with our mothers. Good or bad, healthy or toxic, these relationships can muddy our interpretation of the Empress. If, however, you can separate this word from your own mother and, instead, associate it with the maternal archetype, you might find this word works well for you. On the other hand, working with the Empress to explore a complicated relationship with your mother can provide additional nuance to how you read the card.

Divine Feminine/Goddess

The Empress is, indeed, a representation of the divine feminine. If you have a solid connection to the divine feminine or goddess archetype concept, then either *divine mother* or *goddess* could be an effective keyword for you to use!

Create/Creation/Birth

Creation used to be my favorite word for the Empress because this card is strongly linked with the idea of creation and birth, so *create*, *creation*, and *birth* all work well for this card.

The Emperor: Authority

My keyword for this card is *authority*. The definition of *authority* is, at its core, about having the power to rule others or direct their behavior.

If the Empress is commonly associated with the mother archetype, then it should be no surprise that the card's counterpart, the Emperor, represents the father archetype. As with the Empress, this is not about gender but about the qualities we typically associate with the idea of fatherhood.

Visually, the Emperor seems relaxed, sitting on his throne, but when you look closer, you'll see that, beneath his flowing red robes, he wears a full coat of metal armor. The Emperor is ready for battle and will not cede any territory. When protecting what is important to him, the Emperor becomes an immovable obstacle that makes no apologies for maintaining order. When actively pursuing opportunities, the Emperor becomes an unstoppable force that you dare not oppose.

When I think of the Emperor, I think about his domain because that ultimately defines this character as a ruler. Without something to oversee—and the accountability that comes with it—there is no ruler. The Emperor is ultimately accountable for everything and everyone within his domain. Sure, it seems like a great job to be commander of all the things, until you realize the weight of responsibility that rests on your shoulders when you're in charge.

A lot of tarot readers struggle with the Emperor. I wonder, sometimes, if that is because we struggle with authority—whether because we struggle with the ways it strips our autonomy or because we find it frightening to step into leadership roles ourselves. The association of the Emperor with father-hood can also complicate our relationship with this card if we have a diffi-cult or absent relationship with our own father—just as the association of the Empress with motherhood is similarly complicated. We tend to see the Emperor only through the lens of rulership and forget that he is also protec-tive, supportive, and stable.

The Emperor also represents personal empowerment. He boldly and unapologetically takes up space. His communication is commanding, and he expects to be listened to. He demands respect, and because he demands it, he gets it.

Both the Empress and the Emperor represent archetypes of power, but they wield their power differently. The Empress wields hers in a supportive, nurturing, and receptive way. The Emperor wields his in a firm, demanding, and active way. Both are equally potent.

As a blessing, the Emperor represents authority and responsibility and reminds you that you have more control over your life than you realize. He reminds you that you have a right to define your own boundaries, that "no" is a complete sentence, and that you should stand your ground. The Emperor reminds you that only you can be the ultimate boss of you.

As an obstacle, the Emperor represents the misuse or absence of might and authority. He shows up to indicate that you are dominating a situation that doesn't require as much force as you're applying or to let you know that you've surrendered control to someone undeserving.

I like the word *authority* for the Emperor because it reminds me that the situation involves the use or misuse of one's might. After all, someone in a leadership role can be pushy and overbearing or strong and protective.

Consider what word might work for you if *authority* doesn't fit the bill. Here are a few other words that you may want to consider:

Father/Fatherhood

If you find thinking of the Emperor as the father helps you to understand and engage with the archetype, then the word *father* or *fatherhood* might work great for you. Even a complicated relationship with your father can provide a valuable context for this card if you draw it in a reading. My advice is to be aware of where your relationship with fathers or your understanding of parental energy creates certain biases for you and take that into account when reading the card in this way.

Divine Masculine/God

Looking at this card through the lens of godhood could be a good jumping-off point for you if you have a relatively strong idea of what that would look like and feel it aligns well with the card's meaning. If you're drawn to this aspect of the card, you might enjoy using *divine masculine* or *god* as your keyword.

Control

Control remains one of my favorite keywords for the Emperor because it means almost the same thing as *authority* while focusing on the idea of having the power to direct others (or self). It also has the added subtext of having a limitation, of being a neutral force that you can measure other things against (like with scientific experiments). If you feel the same, *control* may be a good fit.

The Hierophant: Tradition

My keyword for this card is *tradition*. The definition of *tradition* is either a practice or a belief that is handed down from one group of people or a generation to another.

The pope-like figure on the Hierophant card symbolizes an established system or an opportunity to access wisdom from those who have come before, suggesting religious and family systems as well as beliefs and other teachings that are passed down.

This card can be about doing things the way they've always been done, without question, but it's also about having the opportunity to learn from people older, more experienced, or wiser than you.

One of my favorite symbols on the Hierophant card is the crossed keys that lie at his feet. Those are the keys you need to get further along on your path, and the Hierophant has them. In a sense, there's a gatekeeping energy to this card, and I think that is one of the reasons that some of us struggle with the energy of it. No one likes to be told no, or that you're not ready yet, or that someone else knows better than you.

When the Hierophant comes up in a reading, ask who is holding the keys you need to continue your journey. Are they being held by someone (or society) that is dogmatically telling you what you should be or how you should behave? Are they held by a helper or teacher that can lead you in the right direction? Are they held by a system that represents a challenge but a necessary one in order to proceed? Or are they held by a tradition, an opportunity to decide whether you will do things the way they've always been done or challenge the status quo.

As a blessing, the Hierophant is here to help. You have an opportunity to learn or to benefit in some way from those who have come before you. It could be a teacher presenting themselves to you. It could be that the rules you find yourself navigating are there for your greater good. It could even be that you, yourself, have an opportunity to share your knowledge with someone newer to their path.

As an obstacle, the Hierophant is creating a bottleneck in your journey. If you want to get where you're going, you have to get through a carefully guarded gate. Perhaps you're navigating some obnoxious red tape to accomplish your goals. Or perhaps you are allowing a dogmatic social, religious, or political ideal to dictate your actions. If you want to find your way forward, question the status quo and find a way that works for you. Or, if the situation warrants it, grin and bear it. Sometimes, you just have to fill out a bunch of paperwork.

The Hierophant can be a confronting card at times, and I love the word *tradition* because it allows me to hold on tightly to neutrality, to remember that the Hierophant isn't always something I need to push back against. Sometimes, I don't need to buck the system; I need to learn from it! I like the word *tradition* because it reminds me of the beautiful things that can be passed down from one to another. It also reminds me that I can make my own way and create my own traditions.

Consider what word might work for you if *tradition* doesn't fit the bill. Here are a few other words that you may want to consider:

Teacher/Teachings

I like the word *teacher* for the Hierophant because this card often represents a teacher. Remembering that the teacher can show up with uncomfortable or rigid rules, guidelines, systems, or structures can be tricky for me, so I've tended to lean away from it. However, focusing on the idea that there is a learning opportunity can make this card more accessible or relatable.

Dogma

Dogma takes the religious theme that is often hinted at by the Hierophant and runs with it. I tend to avoid it because it leans a little too negative for me. The word *dogma* represents the idea of accepting without questioning.

System

The Hierophant stands for that established set of practices, rules, or traditions being passed down. The word *system* is a reminder that this card is connected to the concept of how things have been done, making this an effective keyword for the Hierophant.

The Lovers: Commitment

My keyword for this card is *commitment*. The definition of *commitment* is an obligation to be loyal to a decision you've made.

It's easy to get caught up in this card's name and pigeonhole the card's meaning into romantic love. However, in the tarot decks that came before the RWS, this card was most strongly associated with a life-changing decision to be made—specifically, choosing whom one was to marry. Whereas the RWS tarot shows a man and a woman overlooked by an angel, the Marseille tarot shows a man choosing between two women. This classic card's meaning centered around choosing to marry for love, beauty, and attraction—or more practical reasons like money, power, or stability.

I never looked at the Lovers card the same after discovering this historical meaning. After all, being faced with the kind of choice that could significantly alter your life path is something we all come up against at one point or another, regardless of our relationship status.

Think of the last time you came to a major crossroads in your life and found yourself faced with the kind of decision that you knew would shape your future not only for the next day or two but for long after. That is what the Lovers card is all about.

I don't mean to imply that the Lovers card is not about romantic love. Of course it is—just not exclusively. In my view, it is first and foremost about choice. Giving your heart to someone, opening to another in such an intimate way is a choice that usually involves at least some measure of commitment, which of course makes it the perfect card to describe a serious romantic involvement.

As a blessing, the Lovers card indicates that you have an opportunity to choose someone or something that will have a positive and lasting impact on your life and will take you where you are meant to go. To make the right choice, let down your guard, take down your walls, and open your heart. Then commit to it with your whole heart. The card can also indicate that you are already connected to the right person or situation.

As an obstacle, the Lovers card represents a commitment to what is not serving your long-term best interest. You may have made the wrong choice long ago and are only recognizing it now. Or perhaps your focus shifted over time to what is not right for you while you neglect what is. Regardless of the reason, you've gotten off track. Making the right choice, now, is the best way to realign with your highest good.

I like the word *commitment* so much for this card because it doesn't minimize the significance of the card, the choices it often represents, or the need for your full buy-in. Frankly, *commitment* is the perfect marriage (forgive the pun, I couldn't resist) between *love* and *choice*: the two most common associations for this card.

Consider what word might work for you if *commitment* doesn't fit the bill. Here are a few other words that you may want to consider:

Love
Some tarot readers prefer to focus on associating the Lovers card with love, whether romantic or platonic. If that's you, then *love* makes an excellent keyword for this card.

Choice
If you resonate most with the crossroads or decision element of the Lovers card, then working with the word *choice* could be the best fit.

Promise
Another word I enjoy for the Lovers is *promise*. *Promise* and *commitment* have similar definitions, but there's something softer and more vulnerable about a promise, which might make it a better keyword for you.

The Chariot: Determination

My personal keyword for this card is *determination*. The definition of *determination* is focused purpose.

It's always bothered me how the Chariot looks absolutely and utterly stationary in the RWS tarot.

The Chariot isn't about staying still. It's about moving forward! It's about focusing on your goal and making steady progress in that direction until you reach it. The Chariot is also about harnessing energy that tries to pull you off course or chaotic energy that threatens to keep you from moving forward. Despite how still it looks, this card has a lot of activity.

Of all the cards in the deck, my keyword for the Chariot has changed the most. I've used quite a few over the years, always searching for the one that would stick. The fact that it's constantly evolving indicates how mutable this card's energy is. It never sits entirely still—at least not on purpose.

My favorite analogy for the Chariot card is driving a car, or at least driving a car well. When I first learned how to drive, I constantly moved the steering wheel as I made micro adjustments to keep the car moving straight ahead. One day, I realized that I always felt like I had to make those adjustments because my focus was not in the right place.

Like many drivers, I would look at the road immediately in front of me to determine my position in the lane and to keep an eye out for possible hazards or obstacles. To drive well, you need to lift your gaze and look further ahead. You want to focus on where you want to go rather than where you are now. By concentrating on the horizon instead of immediately in front of me, I found that I stopped making micro corrections. My driving was smoother, and I had more confidence. In truth, the vehicle is moving fast enough that those minor corrections aren't needed to stay centered in the lane.

That is precisely what the Chariot represents. Life is moving fast all around us. When you have a goal or an objective, you'll go off course if you focus too much on the small things right in front of you. The Chariot reminds us of the importance of focusing on our destination. Concentrating on where we want to go and staying firmly on the course is the work of the Chariot.

I like to see the black and white sphinxes (or horses, lions, etc.) as representations of our internal desires that conflict with our goals. One of them pulls us one way; one pulls us the other. Neither of them is helping us to get where we're trying to go. The work of the Chariot is often about learning how to recognize these desires and find common ground. Instead of letting these desires pull us off course, we harmonize them with the bigger goal we're working toward.

The Chariot reminds you to focus on your long-term objective(s). It isn't always easy to stay on track when so much about life tries to pull you off it.

Let's say you are taking a class. A simple long-term goal would be to do well in the class. You may want to do well in the class because that supports your even longer-term goal of getting a degree. Your Chariot work is keeping your eye on those long-term goals so that you don't end up playing cards with your friends all night (black sphinx) or starting a new creative project (white sphinx) when you should be studying the material so you can pass your test. That doesn't mean you don't play cards with your friends or explore creative outlets when you can (see Temperance for more on moderation), but it does mean that maybe you won't be as likely to self-sabotage your long-term goals by giving in to short-term pleasures if you keep your eye on the prize.

As a blessing, the Chariot reminds you that you have what it takes to reach your goals. All you need to do is keep putting one foot in front of the other and focus on what is most important to you—what it is you're trying to accomplish—and you will get there. Now is not the time to get distracted. Instead, double down on your resolve and do the thing!

As an obstacle, the Chariot lets you know that you are either looking or moving in entirely the wrong direction. Maybe you don't know what you should be trying to accomplish, or maybe you are just unfocused. The point is that no matter how fast you're moving, you aren't actually getting anywhere productive. It's time to re-evaluate your trajectory and get your eyes back on your actual goal.

Determination works well for this card because it taps into the idea that we must stay strong to stay on course. When I think of someone who is determined, I picture someone with their game face on. It's go time.

Consider what word might work for you if *determination* doesn't fit the bill. Here are a few other words that you may want to consider:

Willpower

I used *willpower* for the Chariot for a long time. It's still my favorite. Made up of the words *will* and *power*, this word is a reminder of the power of one's will. Much like determination, our will drives us forward and helps us reach our goals.

Focus

Without focus, how can you know where you're going? *Focus* is an appropriate keyword if you find the idea of not letting distractions interfere with your objectives is what jumps out at you the most about this card.

Movement

Classically, the Chariot card is about going places—literally or metaphorically. The word *movement* is powerful because of its simplicity.

Strength: Fortitude

The best keyword I've found for the Strength card is *strength*. Of all the major arcana cards, the title of this card is the clearest and easiest to understand. However, I also appreciate looking at this card through the lens of the word *fortitude*, a common title for the card in pre-RWS versions of the tarot. The definition of *fortitude* is meeting adversity with courage.

Many readers will find they don't need a keyword to unlock the meaning of this card. Most of us can relate simply by looking at the image of a woman uncomfortably close to a lion but maintaining complete composure and the card's meaning will click immediately.

Lions are symbols of strength, ferocity, and wildness. They're also like animal royalty and are certainly not to be trifled with. Am I right? Why do you think the circus relied heavily on a lion tamer for the wow factor?

Exactly.

This card isn't about physical strength, though it could be if that makes sense in the context of the question. This card is about meeting adversity and overcoming that adversity with grace and confidence.

This card has a message for us all about handling difficult situations gracefully. Strength is not only about facing our fears; it's about learning how to cuddle up to them. Instead of squashing or overpowering what stops us in our tracks, Strength invites us to intimately know ourselves so that we can do the difficult things we need to do in life.

I enjoy the lion as a symbol of what is raw and wild within us. I like how the woman in the card handles the lion gently, not aggressively. In my experience, any attempt to dominate fear fails miserably. On the other hand, if you acknowledge fear, get to know it—befriend it even—you can tame it and, perhaps most importantly, find a way to work with it.

Real courage, as they say, is not about the absence of fear. It's feeling afraid and doing the thing anyway. The Strength card reminds you to find your inner power by believing in yourself.

As a blessing, the Strength card represents that you have within you both resilience and compassion, fortitude and grace. In spite of your fears, or perhaps because of them, you will be able to overcome the challenges you face. Your unwavering resolve will see you through any adversity you face so that you can come out of this situation stronger than you were before.

As an obstacle, the Strength card indicates that self-belief feels out of reach. Instead of moving through adversity with grace, you're pushing too hard or choosing aggression over empathy. You don't need to force your desired outcome to get what you want. Instead, try to understand. Soften your gaze and make room for compassion.

The word *fortitude* can help you think about moving ahead with confidence and vigor. It's not about physical strength but mental and emotional strength. It acknowledges that your situation is difficult, but you can get through it.

Consider what word might work for you if *fortitude* doesn't fit the bill. Here are a few other words that you may want to consider:

Strength

Using *strength* as your keyword for the Strength card makes perfect sense. It captures the meaning of the card perfectly. The only reason I choose another is so that I get the benefit of having two keywords for this card: the title and my chosen keyword.

Resilience

I like the word *resilience* as a keyword for this card, particularly if your approach to working with tarot centers on personal growth and development work. It's a powerful word that references how we can navigate even the most challenging circumstances. The elasticity I associate with this word is a beautiful reminder that a person can bounce back from whatever problem they face.

Soothe

I often think of the action of the Strength card as gentling or taming something wild or challenging. *Soothe* is a word that reminds me of this calming influence. This word can also create more contrast for the card's meaning as a reminder that force is not required here.

The Hermit: Introspection

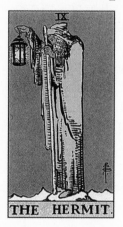

My keyword for this card is *introspection*. The definition of *introspection* is to turn your awareness inward to gain a greater understanding.

The Hermit is one of those cards that can be equal parts comforting and confronting. How you feel about it largely depends on how comfortable you are when alone.

This card is all about turning down the volume on everything but yourself, which sounds so lovely in the hustle and bustle of today's nonstop noise. Still, the kind of self-examination this card indicates can also be intensely uncomfortable. The moment you turn up the volume from within, you find yourself confronted with the full force of your thoughts.

It's easy to romanticize alone time until you find yourself on your own when you don't want to be. While there are benefits to seclusion, it can also be isolating and lonely. And yet, spending time away from others is essential if you want to get to know yourself.

The image of the solitary Hermit, standing on a snowy mountaintop holding a lamp to light his way and a staff to lean upon, makes me think of that *Eat, Pray, Love* journey we take in our lives—literally or metaphorically—to find ourselves. And the Hermit is all about finding and getting to know yourself.

The Hermit represents a gateway to your innermost self and an opportunity to understand yourself more deeply. Even if you find this self-focus uncomfortable, the Hermit will guide you to wisdom by taking you to a place where you can be intensely honest with yourself.

As a blessing, the Hermit represents your inner wisdom and invites you to rely upon it more than you already do. It can also be a reminder that you are enough as you are. You don't need to rely on others to lead the way. You can shine your own light on the path ahead. The Hermit can also indicate that you have wisdom or knowledge worth sharing. You can light the way for others.

As an obstacle, the Hermit advises you that you're relying too much on external sources of information or avoiding spending time alone. You may be avoiding learning more about yourself or fearing what you'll find when you look within.

Ultimately, I like the word *introspection* for the Hermit because that word suggests the act of intentionally looking inward to gain wisdom and knowledge about the self.

Consider what word might work for you if *introspection* doesn't fit the bill. Here are a few other words that you may want to consider:

Self-Knowledge/Self-Awareness/Self-Reflection

The Hermit is, by nature, focused on learning about or becoming more familiar with the self, making *self-knowledge, self-awareness*, and *self-reflection* excellent keyword options for this card about turning one's attention inward.

Wisdom

While the Hermit is focused on the solitary work of self-understanding, it is also about the development of personal wisdom. While broader in its meaning, *wisdom* makes a wonderful keyword if you would like to focus on the search for deep inner knowledge or the desire to share one's earned wisdom with others.

Withdrawal/Retreat

Withdrawal or *retreat* would make a great keyword if you would prefer to focus your interpretation of the Hermit on the concept of pulling out of the business of day-to-day life and seeking the self instead. Either of these words allows for a more practical interpretation but is also flexible enough to expand to deeper meanings.

The Wheel of Fortune: Change

My keyword for this card is *change*. The definition of *change* is the act of one thing or state of being becoming another.

I used to giggle at this card's name, but the Wheel of Fortune is not like the game show of the same name.

Some would say the Wheel of Fortune is aptly named, but I find it a little deceptive. After all, the changes that the wheel of life brings don't always feel fortunate—even when they are ultimately for the best. While the transitions that the Wheel of Fortune refers to can be positive, such as a stroke of good fortune, they can also be intensely challenging.

Visually, this card is often among the least interesting in a tarot deck. That's because the concept it depicts is relatively simple, even though the way it plays out in life can be much more complex.

The wheel pictured on the card represents the cycle of time. Time is always moving. It never stays still. It may seem to slow down or speed up, but it is always moving forward. The three figures positioned on the wheel represent where someone might be on the wheel at any one time.

First, you have the figure that sits atop the wheel. In the RWS, that figure is a sphinx looking comfortable and settled. This figure represents being on top of the wheel or, in more mundane terms, being in the position of good fortune—things are going well for them. Opposite this figure, on the way up from the bottom, is a figure that will eventually replace the sphinx at the top of the wheel. On the reverse side, a snakelike figure descends toward ill fortune.

The concept is simple: the experience you are having right now, good or bad, will not last forever. Time is always moving us on to the next thing. If life is rough at the moment, you have only to wait for the next turn of the wheel to start making your way upward into better times. If you're at the top and everything is hunky-dory, brace yourself for the reality that it won't stay that way forever.

Life is time, and time is change. There is a saying that change is the only thing that stays the same. It sucks, but it's true.

My favorite analogy for the Wheel of Fortune is a carousel—not a carousel with a motor and animals you can ride but the type that used to be common on children's playgrounds. It looks like a flat metal disk with bars to hang on to that only turns when someone on the ground gives it a good spin.

It's my favorite analogy because it beautifully illustrates how your relationship with change affects how it feels.

On this simple piece of playground equipment, kids instinctively choose where to position themselves based on the experience they want to have. The kids who want to feel the ride the most, who want it to be wild and a little scary, position themselves at the edges of the wheel—making themselves big by standing up as they hold on or stretching an arm out. Because they're at the edge of the wheel, the wind resistance makes them feel the ride more. It's more exciting. It feels bigger. The kids who want to ride but don't want to feel it as much move toward the middle, take a seat in the absolute center where the wind resistance is least, and the ride is more peaceful. Then you have the kids who want to be in control and don't ride at all: they push the wheel instead and skip out on the experience entirely.

All of us are one of these kids when it comes to change. We're usually trying to control it, which—unlike with playground equipment—is impossible. If we're not trying to control it, we're either resisting it or making peace with it.

How traumatic or significant a new development feels depends entirely on your position on the wheel. The choice is yours; the wheel will continue to turn regardless. The only thing you can control is how you respond to each turn.

As a blessing, the wheel often indicates a change for the better. Things are looking up, and good fortune is here or on its way to you. Even positive shifts can be uncomfortable, and the desire to resist even the best new developments is incredibly human, but try not to get in your own way. Trust the process and the upside of this turn of the wheel will reveal itself.

As an obstacle, the wheel tells you that things may be taking a turn for the worse. Remember that fighting or controlling this change can make things more challenging. Whatever transition is at hand, know that the wheel will turn again and your fortune will improve. All you have to do is give it time.

Change has always been the perfect keyword for me for the Wheel of Fortune because it beautifully describes pivotal moments in life.

After reading this, what word jumps out at you? Consider what word might work for you if *change* doesn't fit the bill. Here are a few other words that you may want to consider:

Luck

The Wheel of Fortune has strong links to the word *luck*. The Wheel of Fortune is about a change in fortune or, in other words, a sudden stroke of luck—good or bad. *Luck* makes an excellent neutral keyword for this card and reminds you that change is often out of your control.

Time

Arguably the greatest catalyst of the shifts we experience in our lives is time. Using the word *time* as a keyword for the Wheel of Fortune can help you tap into the ways that the relentless march of this force in the universe brings about some of the most impactful transitions in our lives.

Cycles

Cycles makes an excellent keyword for the Wheel of Fortune because a cycle is anything that repeats—seasons, days of the week, moon cycles, planetary cycles, and even the ocean's tides. This word can work well for reminding you that even if things aren't so great now, they'll return to being great again.

Justice: Accountability

My keyword for this card is *accountability*. The definition of *accountability* is the state of being responsible for your actions or decisions.

This card used to confuse me until I realized it wasn't exclusively about the actual legal system or judges on a bench. This card primarily concerns taking responsibility for—or facing the consequences of—previous actions, decisions, and behaviors. The Justice card is about accountability.

Contrary to popular belief, consequences aren't inherently negative but can be positive, negative, or neutral. We often think of accountability as facing the music, but you can also take ownership of the positive results of your actions or behavior. Accountability is the understanding that you are ultimately responsible for how your actions and decisions play out, which means accepting the consequences—no matter what they are.

I get analytical when I think of Justice. I think about the laws of physics and the idea that every action has an equal and opposite reaction. If I throw something fragile at a hard surface, it will break. It was my choice to take that specific action. The moment of accountability comes when I recognize I have a broken object. Similarly, if I help a friend move out of their apartment, their appreciation for my help might be the consequence. When that friend says, "Thank you," I take responsibility by saying, "You're welcome."

My favorite symbols on the Justice card are the sword and the scales. The scales being perfectly balanced reminds me of how actions and reactions work. If I place a heavy stone on one side, an equally heavy stone needs to be placed on the other side for everything to remain even or fair. That is why I prefer to see a sword held straight rather than tilted to either side as an indicator of neutrality and fairness in the Justice card of any tarot deck. The sword also reminds me that Justice can be swift.

Taking accountability isn't about assuming that you are responsible for everything that happens to you, good or bad; it's about looking at your contribution to what you are experiencing in your life and owning where you have played a part.

If I get in a car accident because some jerk side-swiped me, that's not my fault, but if I were texting at the time or fiddling with my radio, then this card would indicate the responsibility I have for my part in it. Similarly, if I get a raise at work, it's partly to do with my performance, and I should give myself some credit for that.

Justice can be that voice of tough love that lets you know that you need to own your part of your current life situation, which isn't always the most fun thing to do. The neutrality of Justice is the point. It doesn't hold any bias, and you shouldn't either. It's the way life is.

Justice says, "You made this bed, so now you must lie in it." My advice? Make your bed nicely with loads of extra pillows and a few squishy stuffed friends as well. You can thank me later.

As a blessing, Justice brings some much-deserved reward for prior decisions, actions, and behaviors. What is coming to you now, you deserve. Take a moment to recognize the ways you contributed to this positive outcome.

As an obstacle, Justice is here to tell you it's time to face the music. Whatever you've done has resulted in something unpleasant that you must now deal with. You may not be entirely to blame, but you've played your part. Take accountability. Learn. Do better next time.

I love the word *accountability* for this card because it immediately puts me in the mindset to look at where I or my querent are responsible for the current situation. I find that helpful for interpreting this card.

Consider what word might work for you if *accountability* doesn't fit the bill. Here are a few other words that you may want to consider:

Consequence

The word *consequence* taps into the analytical way of looking at this card as the reaction to the prior action. This card reminds us of our obligation to take responsibility for prior decisions, actions, and events.

Impartiality

As I pointed out earlier, Justice is non-biased, so the word *impartiality* can work well if you want to focus on this neutrality as the primary energy of the card.

Equity

Using the keyword *equity* for Justice can work well if you resonate with the broader concept of balancing the scales.

The Hanged Man: Suspension

My keyword for this card is *suspension*. Two definitions of *suspension* apply to this card: to pause or take a break from something and to be in a state of hanging.

One of the coolest things about the Hanged Man card is that it has several meanings that complement each other. This is exciting because we, as tarot readers, have several directions to go with it.

First and foremost, given the obvious imagery, the Hanged Man represents being a little tied up, whether voluntarily because of a desire to wait or involuntarily because life has put them into a holding pattern. Either way, the Hanged Man could free themselves but chooses not to. In this state of suspension, the Hanged Man represents a waiting period that offers the gift of personal insight.

The Hanged Man is also about sacrifice. In the RWS version of this card, we see a man hanging upside down in a position that seems terribly uncomfortable. I think we do a disservice to this card when we focus on the Hanged Man's peaceful expression and forget to notice the discomfort. That discomfort is relatable because waiting is uncomfortable. Sometimes, waiting is a sacrifice. And yet, sometimes, waiting is necessary. That discomfort is for a reason.

And finally, the Hanged Man represents a shift in perspective. The Hanged Man views the world through an entirely different lens. This card shifts common perceptions upside down, which allows you to see things in a new way.

I enjoy using the analogy of the cocoon stage in a butterfly's life cycle to illustrate the meaning of this card. When a caterpillar enters its cocoon, it is literally held in a state of suspension. Life pauses for the creature while it undergoes a significant shift; that is the caterpillar's sacrifice. When it emerges, it's changed. It's gained a new perspective and become a butterfly. Boom!

As a blessing, the Hanged Man offers the gift of a new perspective—an opportunity to flip the current situation upside down and look at it in a new way. This opportunity for insight may be uncomfortable, but it's what is most needed for you to move forward. Be patient and look for the insights this situation has to offer you.

As an obstacle, the Hanged Man represents the frustration of having to make sacrifices to move forward. Being forced to wait in stillness can be frustrating. You could be resenting and pushing back against this necessary pause. If so, you are likely doing more harm than good. It's time to surrender control and allow things to unfold. One day, you'll be able to look back at the frustration of this standstill with gratitude for where it led you.

I love the word *suspension* because it describes two of the meanings of this card: waiting and hanging—both of which fit neatly with the idea of a caterpillar in a cocoon. There is also a potent shift in perspective when the caterpillar—now a butterfly—emerges from the cocoon. The word *suspension* allows me to tap into these layers of meaning.

Consider what word might work for you if *suspension* doesn't fit the bill. Here are a few other words that you may want to consider:

Surrender

The word *surrender* is a great option for the Hanged Man. Often, this card points out a loss of control to one degree or another. Acknowledging the necessity of giving oneself over to the experience of surrender can be a powerful way to interact with this card. Reminding yourself or your querent that sinking into the experience can help open the door to insight is also helpful.

Perspective

The Hanged Man's upside-down position certainly grants them a new perspective—a central theme for the card, one that scores of readers lean heavily into. If this part of the meaning resonates in a big way for you, *perspective* could make an excellent keyword for this card.

Sacrifice

While a bit more heavy hitting, the word *sacrifice* fits this card well. Rarely do we choose to wait because it's fun. Usually, this waiting period is uncomfortable at best and often involves a sacrifice to gain further knowledge. There's also that whole story of the Norse god, Odin, hanging upside down for nine days and nine nights—after piercing himself with a spear—and being rewarded with knowledge of the elder futhark rune system to back up this keyword. I highly recommend looking that one up. It's essentially the Hanged Man's origin story.

Death: Ending

My keyword for this card is *ending*. The definition of *ending* is the act of reaching the final part of something existing. It's the act of something coming to an end or ceasing to be.

It sucks when something ends.

You knew this card was coming. We talked about it at the beginning of this chapter, so you know that the Death card is rarely—if ever—about biological death or the ending of a life, which is not to say it never is. I promise you that if I believed that I had a one in seventy-eight chance of drawing a card that predicted an actual death in my life every time I read tarot cards, I wouldn't have been working with them for over twenty-five years.

Death is rarely about physical death, but it is always about endings. Something has reached its final part. Perhaps you're going through a tough breakup or facing a layoff at work or another difficult end. Every conclusion, even the ones that you understand and know are—ultimately—for the best, is painful and requires a grieving period.

We, humans, enjoy holding on to things and people that we've grown attached to. Raise your hand if you've ever held on too long—yeah, me too.

The Death card in tarot is about the inevitability of endings. It's about realizing that nothing is forever and time will keep marching on. Time doesn't care who you are or how much money or power you have. Good things end. Bad things end, too.

It can feel a little like the Wheel of Fortune card in the way that Death signals the inevitability that time will keep marching on. I think that, often, the Death card shows up to remind us that we're holding on too tight when we should be letting go.

I suppose, in that way, Death is about the process of acceptance and learning to let go more than it is about the actuality of the thing ending. It's about recognizing that sometimes in life we don't get a say. That can be hard to swallow.

We learn so much by accepting the inevitability of endings. We learn to value things and people while they're with us. Death teaches us about life. The same is true of the Death card in tarot.

As a blessing, the Death card signals that it's time to let go. You're ready to move on. Allow yourself your feelings about it—good or bad—and then release its hold on you. Look forward. Something else is on the horizon.

As an obstacle, the Death card can indicate you're trying to stop the inevitable. Fighting this ending won't prevent it; it will only make it more painful. Stop holding on so tightly to what is, in fact, already gone. Give yourself time to accept what has ended and then close the door on this chapter so that you can open the door on the next one.

I like the word *ending* because it's punchy but hits a little softer than *death*. I'm aware that sometimes we're grateful for endings—some are wished for and celebrated—while others are fought against and mourned. That is what makes this keyword feel more neutral to me than *death*.

Consider what word might work for you if *ending* doesn't fit the bill. Here are a few other words that you may want to consider:

Transformation

Transformation is one of the most popular keywords for the Death card. One of the most powerful symbols for transformation is the butterfly because of the way this creature transforms from its former caterpillar state. The former form dies so that the butterfly can be born. Isn't it interesting that the Death card arrives after the Hanged Man? Could it be that the butterfly only emerges when it finally lets go of its former self? I think so. *Transformation* does indeed make a beautiful and empowering keyword for the Death card.

Loss

When something ends, we're often left with the realization that there is an empty space that once was filled. That feeling is loss. If you're looking for a more emotive keyword for the Death card, *loss* works beautifully.

Letting Go

I know that *letting go* is technically two words, but who's counting? Anyway, this key phrase works beautifully for Death. It focuses on the action associated with the card. Something is coming to an end, but the action someone takes during that time is the process of letting go, which can make this an excellent key phrase for this card.

Temperance: Moderate

My keyword for this card is *moderate*. As an adjective, something that is moderate (MOD-uh-ruht) is something or someone that avoids extremes. As a verb, to moderate (MOD-uh-rayt) is to lessen the intensity of something or to bring it away from extremes.

Temperance was one of those cards that always felt unreachable and confusing to me. I'd see this image of an angel with two cups and throw my hands up in frustration. It didn't make any sense—until it did.

The figure representing Temperance on the card isn't the point. The point is that Temperance exists outside of any one extreme. Temperance doesn't choose sides; Temperance blends the sides.

Visually, the angel in Temperance has one foot in the water and the other on land, effectively avoiding picking sides! Also, notice that it's either dusk or dawn—neither day nor night. Yet again, it represents the in-between place that Temperance occupies.

Then there are those danged cups. I finally understood when I encountered some trivia about how the ancient Greeks used to water down their wine—tempering its strength. Suddenly, I understood what could be going on with those two cups. The idea of blending to bring something away from its most potent strength and into something more moderate made sense to me.

Temperance is about walking the middle path. It's about the path of moderation versus the path of extremes. Temperance advises us to look at how we can move away from too much and not enough to that beautiful and balanced place in between. It all made sense once I started thinking of Temperance as the Goldilocks principle of the tarot.

The cups are also associated with alchemy, mixing and blending different ingredients to create a final product that is more than the sum of its parts.

As a blessing, Temperance can show you the way through a difficult situation by inviting you to look for the middle path. It invites a measured approach that considers all extremes but doesn't swing wildly between them. This card offers a respite from the back-and-forth and invites blending, not rejecting, opposing viewpoints.

As an obstacle, Temperance highlights the fact that your behaviors, beliefs, actions, or attitudes are imbalanced. It's important to find the moderate point between extremes so that you can balance your approach going forward.

I love that the word *moderate* can be used as an adjective or verb without changing anything about its construction, even though you pronounce it differently (e.g., taking a moderate approach versus moderating your behavior). I love it, also, because it suggests the idea that we are pulling back from an extreme. There's a gentleness to it that encompasses the energy of Temperance.

Consider what word might work for you if *moderate* doesn't fit the bill. Here are a few other words that you may want to consider:

Balance

Temperance holds the energy of balance. Think of two opposites: fire and water, happiness and sadness, silence and noise. Temperance is the point at which these opposites reach equilibrium so that neither overpowers the other. Consider using the word *balance* if looking at Temperance through this lens works best for you.

Harmony

I like the word *harmony* because it makes me think of pulling in two opposing factors and having them work together the way that two different notes can work together in musical harmony. If you like the idea of blending and alchemizing opposites to find the point of balance, *harmony* might make the perfect keyword for you to use for Temperance.

Equilibrium

Equilibrium is the result of having found balance. It's less action oriented than balance and anchored in the present. *Balance* can be a verb, but *equilibrium* is a noun—a state of being. This one could do the trick if you prefer a more still, less action-oriented word for Temperance!

The Devil: Bondage

My keyword for this card is *bondage*. The definition of *bondage* is to be restrained or held captive.

The Devil card is not nearly as terrifying as it looks.

As we discussed earlier in this chapter, the Devil card does not represent a literal devil or demonic influence. Still, it's also not intended to make you feel all comfy cozy.

This card is about being trapped, or at least feeling trapped, in a situation that is harmful to you. The figures in the card are chained here. What I find interesting is that the collars around their necks are large enough that they could slip them right over their heads.

The point is, they could free themselves—if they chose—but they don't believe they can or don't want to. Either way, they remain stuck.

The Devil isn't usually about external influences that trap you but about your own internal beliefs and behaviors that keep you held captive in your life.

But how did you get there in the first place? The answer is simple. You let your temptations lead the way. Most things that tempt us look appealing until we find ourselves stuck in an endless loop of unhelpful behavioral patterns—bad habits, if you will. Most bad habits start off feeling good—procrastination, self-indulgences of all varieties, relationships that we know aren't healthy—and we remain ensnared because they seem better than the unknown alternatives.

Modern decks often lean heavily into either the captive element of the card or the temptation aspect. But in my view, the power the Devil has in a reading has more to do with the ways we consistently choose to stay stuck and the ways we are committed to the things we've bound ourselves to even though we know better.

This card can be incredibly empowering when you remember that you have the power to choose freedom. You don't have to let yourself stay stuck.

As a blessing, the Devil identifies your imprisonment and reminds you that you have the power to free yourself at any time. Your escape route is right in front of you—if you dare to take it. The Devil, as a blessing, can also be a reminder that it's helpful to loosen your inhibitions occasionally as long as you're careful not to let an occasional indulgence become an unhealthy obsession.

As an obstacle, you are avoiding looking at uncomfortable truths and are missing the opportunity to free yourself. There's self-sabotage at play here, or perhaps you're more comfortable being uncomfortable. What unhelpful thing are you clinging to? If you need more clarification, ask yourself where you feel restricted to point yourself in the right direction.

I love the word *bondage* for this card because it has a double meaning. Words like *captivity* or *enslavement* imply an abdication of power. Bondage, on the other hand, can be consensual. It's a word that reminds me that a choice was made to get into this situation and a choice must be made to get out of it.

Consider what word might work for you if *bondage* doesn't fit the bill. Here are a few other words that you may want to consider:

Trapped

Trapped is a great word that reminds you that the primary meaning of this card is about being stuck. If this word reminds you of the meaning of this card without making it too easy to lose sight of the control you have in this situation, this could be a suitable keyword for you.

Temptation

Some folks love the word *temptation* for the Devil, and it certainly applies. I have used this keyword off and on over the years, and I'm still a bit of a sucker for a Devil card that focuses on temptation in the imagery. If you prefer thinking of the Devil as a force of seduction or temptation in your readings, this could be your best keyword.

Toxic

Toxic is a potent word to use if you want the reminder that the Devil often signals unhealthy patterns, behaviors, people, or situations. While *toxic* is a confronting word, it might be the right word for you and your tarot practice.

The Tower: Destruction

My keyword for this card is *destruction*. The definition of *destruction* is the act of breaking something beyond repair.

The Tower card often makes me think of the nursery rhyme about Humpty Dumpty: the egg-like creature that fell from a high place that he probably shouldn't have been sitting on in the first place. When he fell, he broke open, yolk spilling out on the ground, and no one could put him back together again.

It's a gruesome image and an abject lesson that—I assume—was meant to impart to young children that sometimes when something breaks, it stays broken. If you shatter a dish, saying, "I'm sorry" doesn't put it back together.

Tower moments are like that. Something is collapsing (or has already), and you can't fix it now. All you can do is move forward, learn, and build a better Tower next time.

The Tower card shows a tall stone tower, struck by lightning, ablaze with flames, and cracks running down it as people leap or fall from the windows. It's devastating, this image, and that's intentional.

I've always been fascinated by how the lightning blows the crown off of the Tower. It seems like a reminder that sometimes we give away too much power and importance to systems, traditions, and relationships in our lives. We hold them up on pedestals and assume they're perfect. Sometimes, it's ourselves we've put on a pedestal. Hubris, I think you call that. The lightning doesn't care about crowns. Sometimes, that lightning symbolizes the stroke of truth or insight you've had that makes all those preconceived ideas and beliefs tumble down. Sometimes, it's the truth you have seen that you can't unsee that destroys whatever it is that it has destroyed. Sometimes, it's a blessing. Most of the time, it sucks.

We rarely see Tower moments coming. Whether it's a broken dish, a sudden job loss, a relationship falling apart, or your car breaking down—it's not an easy thing to go through.

As a blessing, the Tower card acknowledges that what has been broken is not reparable, but you can start fresh. Perhaps you've even torn that Tower down with your own two hands. Sometimes, you are the lightning, and now you have an opportunity to engage with the powerful energy of the Tower to reclaim your life. Not all Tower moments are harmful. Sometimes, they help us find freedom. This is an opportunity for a new beginning.

As an obstacle, the Tower came down despite your best efforts. You saw the flaws. You knew the foundation was shaky, but you stuck your head in the sand and avoided the truth and now you are left standing in a pile of rubble, undeniably shaken. Tower experiences are intensely challenging and often catch us off guard. There's no real silver lining to this experience, but you will have the chance to build a better tower next time.

I used to work with other, gentler, words for the Tower, but I always come back to *destruction* because I've found, over the years, that the Tower is easier to face when you call it what it is. Destruction doesn't always have to be disempowering. What's come down is staying down, but destruction often comes right before construction.

Consider what word might work for you if *destruction* doesn't fit the bill. Here are a few other words that you may want to consider:

Shake-Up

A shake-up is a dramatic reorganization that usually involves dismantling existing systems and structures in order to facilitate a new way forward. *Shake-up* makes a great keyword for the Tower and can feel less devastating and confronting than a word like *destruction*.

Ruin

If *shake-up* is gentler than *destruction*, then the word *ruin* is harsher, which makes it a practical keyword if you want to bring home the devastation of a Tower event.

Breakthrough

Breakthrough can make a powerful keyword for the Tower as it describes the sensation of blasting through a structure that no longer works to create room to expand and grow. It's the most positive word I've ever used for this difficult card.

The Star: Hope

My keyword for this card is *hope*. The definition of *hope* is the feeling of wanting something to be and trusting that it is possible.

There is something beautifully simple and complex about the Star card.

The Star represents the moment in the Fool's journey when the dust has settled after the destruction of the Tower. The skies have cleared, and you can look up and see that clear night sky and one star shining more brightly than all the others. It is a beautiful and poignant reminder that everything will be okay.

The Star card represents a time of peace, of sanctuary. During this time, you are safe enough to let your guard down. Nothing is lurking around the corner. All is well. The night is still and quiet.

The central figure in the Star card is naked. To me, nakedness implies vulnerability. We are undoubtedly vulnerable after we've been through a Tower situation. Our walls have come tumbling down, like it or not. We're raw and open. We haven't built new walls—yet. It's a precious time full of possibility and hope.

The Star is more than merely a respite, though. It's time to regroup, to take stock of where you've been and set your sights on where you're going. More than knowing where you're going, you trust that it's the right direction this time. That's what the Star feels like.

Hundreds of years of stories and lore speak about following the guidance of the stars, especially the North Star. The Star card reminds us that we will be okay and have guidance to follow now. We have a sense of direction. We are realigning with our true purpose.

As a blessing, the Star is a much-needed balm on open wounds and the calm after the storm. This card predicts peace, tranquility, and an opportunity to reconnect with your purpose. It reminds you to have hope. Things are improving. Imagine that the future you've always dreamed about is truly possible and you will make it possible.

As an obstacle, you might be struggling to feel a sense of hope for the future. Perhaps you're feeling negative or defeated. You might need help knowing which direction to move or feel out of touch with your inner compass. Remember your purpose and then head in that direction. You can find your way, again.

Hope isn't always easy. If you struggle to see the barest hint of a silver lining, faith can feel like a real reach. The fantastic thing about stars is that even when you can't see them, they're always there. Hope is the same way, which is why it makes the perfect keyword for the Star.

Consider what word might work for you if *hope* doesn't fit the bill. Here are a few other words that you may want to consider:

Healing

The Star card represents a time of healing. This card arrives as a welcome respite after some of the most difficult experiences depicted in the tarot: Death, the Devil, and the Tower. The Star indicates a time of rest, recovery, and recalibration to prepare you for moving forward once again. *Healing* is a powerful keyword for this card and is one that I come back to now and again.

Navigation

The power of the stars to help us find our way is indisputable. If you like working with the Star as a card that represents following your true path (your personal North Star), then the keyword *navigation* could be a great choice.

Peace

Sometimes, the best keyword for the Star is simply *peace*. Peace invites a sense of calm and of stillness or reflection, which are all feelings that tie directly into the meaning of this card.

The Moon: Illusion

My keyword for this card is *illusion*. The definition of *illusion* is a misleading image or something that may not be perceived accurately.

The Moon in tarot represents the discomfort or distress we experience when we cannot see the path ahead clearly, when whatever is going on is coming from a wild place—the unknown.

It took me a long time to reconcile my love of the moon—its beauty, magic, and feminine power—with the representation of this card in the tarot. In tarot, this card represents discomfort, illusions, fears, and the wild inner self that lives deep within our unconscious.

It all began to make sense when I considered the qualities of moonlight. Moonlight has always been a mysterious sort of light. It casts things in interestingly shaped shadows and gives enough light to move forward but not enough to fully illuminate the path. The shadows lurk deeper around a moonlit path than a sunlit one. You could say that moonlight tends to highlight our fears, insecurities, and projections. It shows us where our view may be distorted or the ways in which we lack clarity and truth.

The Moon also opens up a liminal space within. The moonlit path pictured in the RWS version of this card represents the solid ground of the conscious mind. The dark water represents the deep mysteries of the unconscious mind. A crawfish emerges from the water—a symbol of a connection forming between the two. The towers in the distance represent the gates we walk through when we're ready.

The Moon presents an opportunity to make the unconscious conscious—to explore the inner wild. I also see this connection between the conscious and the unconscious in the dog and wolf who flank the path. The domesticated dog reminds me of the conscious mind, tamed by life experience. The wild wolf reminds me of the untamed unconscious.

It takes courage to journey the inner wild, to face one's fears and the illusions that seem to be everywhere, and to continue to put one foot in front of the other in search of truth. For this reason, I appreciate a Moon card that makes me a little uncomfortable.

As a blessing, the Moon is an invitation to explore the depths of a situation and uncover the truth and reminds you that there is more than meets the eye. There is an opportunity for learning and personal growth here. All you need to do is look beneath the surface to find the profound, underlying truth.

As an obstacle, the Moon presents you with your fears and assumptions, the illusions you take on as truth, even when some part of you knows better. You need to see clearly and could make unhelpful choices if you take things at face value. Instead, question what you see and experience. Ask yourself what filter you may be viewing the world and your interactions through.

I've always found it challenging to pin the Moon card down to only one keyword. I settled on *illusion* because, most often, when I'm working with this card in real time for myself or my querents, this meaning is the most applicable and resonant. When I think of illusion, I also think of the Buddhist concept of Maya—a veil made up of all our externally reinforced beliefs and ideas through which we view the world. That is how I feel about the Moon and the strange, wild, and beautiful light it casts.

Consider what word might work for you if *illusion* doesn't fit the bill. Here are a few other words that you may want to consider:

Mystery

Mystery is a beautiful word for the Moon card. It feels more welcoming than *illusion* and keeps the magic and otherworldly nature of the card close to the front of the mind. If this feels right based on the card's meaning, try it out and see what you think.

Wildness

There are hundreds of myths and stories about the magic of the moon and the associated wildness it brings out in us. The wolf on the Moon card is directly connected to the wildness of the moon. If the Moon card makes you think of how we all get a little wilder under the full moon's light, then *wildness* could be a perfect word match for you.

Unconscious

Those of you who enjoy leaning more into the psychological aspects of the Moon card might enjoy using *unconscious* as a keyword. This card brings things up from the depths of the unconscious mind, which makes this word an excellent way to work with this card.

The Sun: Radiance

My keyword for this card is *radiance*. The definition of *radiance* is to be lit from within or without and full of joy.

My understanding of the Sun card has evolved so much over the years, and I can't wait to tell you all about it.

The Sun sits in counterpart to the Moon. Where the Moon highlights shadows, fear, hesitance, and insecurity, the Sun offers illumination, confidence, freedom, and joy.

The RWS tarot image gets a lot of flack. Tarot collectors lovingly make fun of it as the card with the naked baby on a horse. Admittedly, I was one of them for a time. Then it dawned on me (See what I did there? Dawn? Sunrise?) that the naked baby on the horse in the sun's bright light is precisely the point.

Nakedness, particularly under bright light, is a powerful symbol of vulnerability and authenticity. You're being seen for who you are. Nothing, not even shadows, can hide who you are. We see the wall of a garden behind the child. We know that there is safety in this space. There's also freedom. The horse carries the naked child away from the security of the wall.

Wow.

Wouldn't we all like to feel like that? Free to be who we are while being completely visible? What a feeling, what freedom that would be.

The Sun card is strongly associated with positivity and joy, but—more than that—it symbolizes clarity. Everything is bathed in bright light. Everything is visible. What you see is what you get. The Sun card is arguably the most positive card in the deck, but more than happiness, this card is about being filled up with joy and self-fulfillment. There's a realization of worth that this card is now strongly associated with for me. I love that about it.

As a blessing, the Sun is happiness, joy, the ability to be authentic, freedom, and truth. There's an invitation to make space for joy from a place of authenticity and clarity about who you are. Trust the radiance within. Believe in yourself. You can trust what you see.

As an obstacle, the Sun can highlight that you feel blocked from joy or authenticity—or both. Perhaps you're worrying too much about what others think about you. Perhaps you are wearing masks instead of revealing your true self. Where are you hiding in the shadows? How can you step more fully into the light?

My favorite word for the Sun is *radiance* because it immediately makes me think of the idea of being lit from within, so full of joy, life, and vibrance that you shine outward for others. That is what this card means to me—authenticity, joy, and light rolled up in one shiny ball: the Sun.

Consider what word might work for you if *radiance* doesn't fit the bill. Here are a few other words that you may want to consider:

Illumination

Illumination was my favorite keyword for much longer than *radiance*. It works beautifully for this card. It sets a nice contrast against the Moon (*illusion*) and can remind you that all is cast in the light of truth.

Joy

While hardly neutral, the word *joy* does capture so much of what the Sun card is all about and, therefore, makes an excellent keyword for it—as long as you remember that if it shows up as an obstacle, it likely represents a blockage to joy.

Authenticity

I've often been tempted to make the word *authenticity* my primary keyword. I love how this word reminds me of the joyful, naked child—fully illuminated by the light of the sun, so unburdened. I regularly lean into this part of the

Sun card's meaning. If this quality of the card jumps out at you, then you might prefer *authenticity* as your keyword.

Judgement: Evolution

My keyword for this card is *evolution*. The definition of *evolution* is a process of permanent change.

In the RWS version of this card, a trumpeting angel calls souls up to heaven. I'm honestly not a fan of this imagery. It just feels very … judgey. (Yeah, I know. I honestly couldn't help it.) And because I didn't like the way this card was depicted, I struggled to connect with it. Frankly, the image of people rising out of their tombs, called up by some angel feels way more Bible-y than I'm strictly comfortable with. It took some internal gymnastics to get to the point where I had truly befriended this card and what it meant.

To do that, I had to put the imagery in its place and remind myself that tarot was heavily influenced by the religions that dominated society at the time of its creation. Once I integrated that understanding, I stopped avoiding this card and really took the time to understand it. As I did, I began to understand that it was the imagery, and not the meaning, that I was struggling with.

Contrary to its name, the Judgement card isn't about being judged by others. If anything, this card is about judging or evaluating yourself. That's because Judgement represents an opportunity to evolve. Evolution is tricky because, to evolve, you must completely let go of one version of yourself so that you can embrace another.

Every time you've taken a big step forward in your personal growth, you were answering the call of Judgement. Every time you look back and realize that who you are isn't who you were, you are looking back from the other side of Judgement.

Have you ever heard of a calling? That's what the trumpet-blowing angel on the card is doing: calling you. Whether you follow that call, though, is entirely up to you. There's no forced change here, like we see in the Wheel of Fortune, and the evolution you are invited to is not inevitable, as depicted with the Death card.

In Judgement, you're invited to make a choice: to continue as you have been or to step up and do better. It's time to evolve, but no one will make you. Evolution is a choice, not a promise, and it demands your cooperation and commitment to the process. When Judgement sends you an invitation, it's the part of you that knows your worth and what you're truly capable of that RSVPs with yes.

The truth is that evolution is often painful. Stepping into a better version of ourselves requires us to let go of the version of ourselves we have held dear for a long time. You may not be ready. But do you need to be? While it's true that you can refuse the call of Judgement and remain where you are, the opportunity to evolve that Judgement presents isn't necessarily the kind of opportunity that waits forever. If you choose to remain where you are, as you are, that opportunity may pass you by. But, really, no pressure.

I kid, of course. There's definitely some pressure.

As the second to last card in the major arcana of the tarot, I see Judgement as the doorway we have to walk through if we ever want to reach our own personal Happy Ever After. Before we can reach that joyous place of true completion, we have to grow, and we have to evolve. So, yes, evolution is a choice. To languish, though? That is also a choice.

As a blessing, Judgement acknowledges all you've accomplished and learned. You're ready now. You're ready to step into the next phase in your life. It will be a little uncomfortable, and you'll have to grow into this new skin, but the rewards are well worth it. Say yes to your personal evolution.

As an obstacle, Judgement points out your resistance to growth. You're clinging too hard to the way things always have been, even though you know better. There are signs everywhere that it's time to change. Are you going to keep your head in the sand? Are you going to refuse to grow forever? If you don't make a change now, when? Maybe you don't feel ready. Maybe you never will. You can still say yes.

I love the word *evolution* for this card because it indicates stepping up, moving forward, and doing better. It's a serious and powerful card. And it's also a card I can't think about without also thinking of Pokémon. If you're familiar with the adorable creatures from the game of the same name, you'll understand that Pokémon are an excellent analogy for Judgement. Throughout the Pokémon game, you train adorable creatures who evolve into stronger (and often cooler!) forms as they gain experience. It's simply too perfect an analogy for what the Judgement card is all about, not to mention it.

Consider what word might work for you if *evolution* doesn't fit the bill. Here are a few other words that you may want to consider:

Progress

The point of the Judgement card is that you are invited to make progress, and *progress* makes a good keyword for this card. *Progress* has a grounded, everyday feeling that could make this high-vibe card more accessible and relatable.

Rebirth

I love the word *rebirth* for the Judgement card. That's what it feels like. We are born anew, having fully shed what no longer served us from the past. It draws a clear dividing line between then and now and makes an excellent keyword for the Judgement card.

Ascension

Ascension ultimately means moving in an upward direction, like ascending a mountain. In that way, it's an apt keyword for the Judgement card. It could hold a profound double meaning for those who want to retain the more religious association of the Judgement card.

The World: Completion

My keyword for this card is *completion*. *Completion* means to have reached a state of wholeness, to be finished.

When I pull the World, I often think, "Well, that's a wrap!"

The World card—the culmination of the major arcana—signals that this part of your journey is finished. This is the culmination of everything that has come before. You've done it! What will you do next?

Visually, this card feels joyous. An uninhibited, naked figure is dancing in the center of the card. An oval wreath surrounds the figure, creating a boundary. There's something mystical about this card in that the central figure seems to be floating in space, entirely off the ground. It feels like a moment of connection to the universe. This card is more than wholeness; it's Wholeness—with a capital *W*. Sometimes the World represents an internal feeling of completion, of recognizing that you've come home to yourself and are at home in your skin.

The World signifies completion and, more specifically, successful completion. The last puzzle piece has fallen into place, and you can now look at what you've done with the satisfaction of someone who has truly put in the work to get to this point. And now, it is finished.

While the World is generally seen as a positive, congratulatory card, you may not feel like celebrating. Recognizing you've done all you can (or should) do can feel a little bittersweet. When you raise children, for example, there comes a point when they reach adulthood and are ready to go out and live life on their own. You're done raising them, but you may not feel ready to be done parenting them (and maybe you never will). Closing out a chapter of your life can be both immensely satisfying and a little sad.

Your work here is done. That's what the World card is all about. And yet, except on the rare occasion that something is genuinely concluded—like the final draft of a writing project submitted and approved—things we complete may linger a little, and that's okay.

The World card is a little like the apple that falls, ripe, from the tree. It fell because it was done growing, at least in that form. And as the flesh melts into the earth, its seeds will grow new roots and shoots and one day become a new apple tree. The World is completion, but every end leads to a new beginning. We see this theme again and again in the major arcana of the tarot. What goes up will come down, and what falls will rise again. The Fool, the Wheel of Fortune, Death, and the Moon also speak to this never-ending cycle of life.

As a blessing, the World signals the successful completion of this part of your journey. Don't rush off so fast to the next thing. Take time to pause and recognize all you've accomplished. There's time enough for the next thing. Until then, be present with this experience.

As an obstacle, the World can indicate a fear of being finished. Sometimes, this can show up when we hesitate to take those last few steps across the finish line because we're afraid of the unknown new adventure that awaits us on the other side.

Completion has always felt like the most comprehensive keyword for this complex card. This card asks that you be aware of what is now complete, accept it, recognize your accomplishments, and then prepare yourself for the next journey.

Consider what word might work for you if *completion* doesn't fit the bill. Here are a few other words that you may want to consider:

Accomplishment

You may find *accomplishment* a more accessible word than *completion*. Accomplishment can feel more grounded and approachable and might be easier to recognize than completion. For example, when you are working on a painting, it can be hard to identify the point when it's fully complete and easier to recognize that you've accomplished something by painting it.

Integration

I love *integration* for the World because that's a huge part of the underlying lesson of the card. Not only have you reached the end of the journey, but you've integrated the lessons along the way. If you hadn't, you wouldn't be finished yet! *Integration* is a wonderful word for remembering every step that led you to this place.

Wholeness

The word *wholeness* feels more person-centered than *completion*, though you could use *completion* and *wholeness* interchangeably. There's something, though, about wholeness that feels more introspective and less attached to the circumstances that may surround this card.

You now have your own keywords for each of the twenty-two major arcana cards, so where they're concerned, I guess you could say, "That's a wrap!"

Getting to Know Your Major Arcana Keywords

Now that you have a complete set of major arcana cards, each labeled with a keyword, it's time to put them to work so you can get to know them better.

There's no better way to test-drive your new set of keywords than by doing some readings for yourself (or willing friends and family) with them.

How to Read Tarot in Five Easy Steps

You may have been expecting a detailed how-to on how to read your tarot cards, now that the time has come to jump in and practice, but it's honestly not complicated at all. Let me break it down into a few simple steps.

1. Determine what you would like to know.

Before you start shuffling and drawing cards, it's helpful to have an idea about what it is you would like to get information or answers about from your cards. This can help you focus, but it can also help you choose a spread.

2. Choose a tarot spread (optional).

If you're new to reading the tarot, I strongly suggest starting with a tarot spread because it provides context for each card you pull and can act as a guide. However, you can totally skip this step and go right to step 3!

3. Concentrate on the subject of the reading or say it aloud as you shuffle the deck.

Intention matters. How you shuffle your cards doesn't. Some people shuffle tarot cards like playing cards. Some people mush them around on a table (this actually has a name; it's called "washing" your cards). Some people deal out a bunch of piles and then mix the piles. Some people fan out the deck and choose cards at random. No matter how you choose your cards, putting all your attention on the purpose of the reading will help you be attentive to the answer. At a minimum, this step is a great tool for tuning out the other thoughts and worries cluttering your mind so you can read your cards clearly. If you also believe that there is something unexplainable about how the cards work, then tapping into the power of your intention is also a wonderful energetic boost for your reading, helping to ensure that the cards most needed in a particular reading are drawn.

4. Lay out your card(s).

Lay your cards out in the same order the spread indicates. If you aren't using a spread, lay out the number of cards you feel you need to answer the question (it's usually best to decide the number ahead of time, or it may be tempting to keep laying cards down until you see what you want to see). When you put the cards down, you can lay them face down or face up. When I was new to tarot, I laid them face down and turned each card up one at a time as I interpreted it. I found this method helped me not get overwhelmed by all the cards. As I got more comfortable, I began laying all my cards face up so that I could look at the reading as a whole as well as interpret the cards one at a time. Either method is valid. If you're not sure which you might prefer, try it both ways to see what feels right.

5. Interpret each card using your personal keyword and the spread position.

The heart of reading tarot is the act of interpreting the cards. Using your chosen keyword as the jumping-off point for each card, consider what that card could mean when combined with the spread position (if you're using a spread). For example, a card that lands in the obstacle position of the three-card layout I share below would be interpreted as a roadblock in your path or a hurdle you must leap over. Share your interpretations of each card as you go or the reading as a whole with your querent if you're reading for someone else. If you're reading for yourself, reflect on or write down your interpretations.

That's it! Easy. Trust me. You've got this.

The following are a few spreads to try out with your marked-up majors. Try each layout a couple of times to see how working with your own set of keywords feels. If any of your keywords don't hold up throughout these exercises, revisit that card and try a different one.

Once you're satisfied with the major arcana cards and the keywords you've chosen for them, you're ready to move on to the next chapter!

One-Card Reflection Spread

A single-card tarot reading is a powerful way to work with the energy of the cards. This past-focused spread is meant to help you look back at your day and reflect upon an important lesson or message of the day.

CARD 1: Key lesson or message of the day.

Two-Card Personal Growth Check-In Spread

This simple two-card spread is grounded in the present time and designed to help you check in with your personal growth.

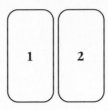

CARD 1: What should I be working on?
CARD 2: What can help me do better?

Three-Card Week- or Month-Ahead Spread

One of the simplest prediction or future-based tarot readings to practice is a week-ahead or month-ahead spread. With this simple three-card spread, you'll practice using the cards to get a sort of forecast of what is coming up for you.

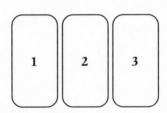

CARD 1: What is the primary theme of the upcoming week/month?
CARD 2: What to avoid this week/month?
CARD 3: What to embrace this week/month?

Four-Card Guidance Spread

One of my favorite ways to use tarot cards is to help me process a current situation so that I can understand it better. If something is weighing on your mind, you can use this spread to get at the heart of it so that you can determine your next best steps.

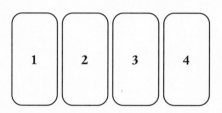

CARD 1: What lies at the heart of the issue?
CARD 2: Internal influences.
CARD 3: External influences.
CARD 4: Key to a favorable outcome.

Chapter 4
The Everyday 40: The Numbered Minor Arcana

N ow that you've had a little time to get to know the major arcana, it's time to talk about the numbered minor arcana, what I like to refer to as the "everyday forty."

Like playing cards, the minor arcana of the tarot contains four suits. Instead of clubs, hearts, spades, and diamonds, we have wands, cups, swords, and pentacles. You'll find numbered cards from ace through ten and four court cards within each suit.

We'll handle the court cards in a later chapter. I treat them as a unique part of the tarot because we approach them differently than the numbered minor arcana cards.

Within the numbered minor arcana cards of the tarot, we find reflections of our everyday struggles, triumphs, celebrations, conflicts, and activities.

One of the quickest ways to learn to interpret the minor arcana is to familiarize yourself first with the elements and numbers, the essential building blocks of these cards.

The Elements

Each of the four minor arcana suits is associated with an element. Wands are typically associated with fire. Cups are associated with water. Swords are usually associated with air. Pentacles are associated with the element of earth.

If you want to understand the role each suit plays in a reading, it's helpful to build some personal associations with each element—and yes, assign an individual keyword for each as well.

The Element of Fire: Passion

The suit of wands is associated with the element of fire.

My keyword for the element of fire is *passion*. Passion is a spicy enthusiasm for something.

When I think of fire, I think of heat, intensity, and how fire behaves. It can smolder, or it can rage wildly. It can warm, or it can burn. Since fire is associated with the wands suit, it tells me that the wands suit is a suit of intensity and passion. We can be passionate about our hobbies, our work, our interpersonal relationships, our goals in life, or our purpose.

Fire creates action or movement. When I think of what creates movement, I think of will, drive, purpose, intention, and—especially—passion.

Understanding the wands' association with fire lets me know that the cards of this suit will involve a lot of energy, heat, or intensity. Whether it's the push of inspiration, the exploration of possibilities, the drive to try something new, the will to finish what we've started, or the exhaustion of having bitten off more than we can chew—the wands suit is incredibly dynamic. It has so much to teach us about what is beneath our actions and choices.

In many ways, this suit is about the energy that lies beneath or behind our actions and choices.

Why are we doing what we are doing? What pushes us forward? Why do we keep going? Why are we committed to this path? What old beliefs are we burning away? In what ways are we stepping into our power?

Fire is bright but can also be fast. What makes us feel motivated one day can overload us the next. Fire is a mutable element—constantly changing, always moving. Fire creates, destroys, heats, and burns. It's a force to be reckoned with.

I love the word *passion* for fire because passion can inspire us and drive us forward to make positive changes, but it can also get us in trouble. We can be passionately joyful or full of passionate rage, and it's precisely that mutable quality that makes this keyword work so well.

After reading this, what word jumps out at you for the element of fire? Consider what word might work for you if *passion* doesn't fit the bill. Remember not to use a word you've already picked for a different card. Here are a couple of other words that you may want to consider:

Enthusiasm

Much like *passion*, *enthusiasm* can work well for the element of fire. While this word tends to lean more positive than neutral, enthusiasm is a force that can drive us forward when we need a push and keep us going when we're running out of steam.

Intensity

I also enjoy the word *intensity* for the element of fire. We can feel good things intensely—like love. We can feel bad things intensely—like jealousy. It gives a lot of wiggle room for interpretation.

The Element of Water: Feeling

The suit of cups is associated with the element of water.

My keyword for the element of water is *feeling*. I define *feeling* as both an emotional state and a type of intuition, both of which are strongly associated with the element of water.

When I think of water, I think of the way that water supports, shapes, heals, soothes, and flows, but it is also a powerful force that erodes and destroys. Since water is associated with the cups suit, it tells us that the cups suit is about the forces in our daily life that have these same qualities—primarily, our emotions. Our emotions support us, help us heal, and move us through difficult situations. When out of balance, they cause disharmony in our lives, erode our relationships, and isolate us. Water also acts like a mirror, one that reflects who we are back to us but also allows us to peer into its depths to gain access to deeper wisdom—much like our inner voice does.

Understanding the cups' association with water lets me know that the cards of this suit will involve feeling, emotions, and intuition—and will be about how we emotionally engage with the world around us, how we feel our way through situations in our life, and how our feelings are affected or affecting our life.

What draws us to someone else? What keeps us there? How do we move on? How do we learn to love where we are instead of only where we want to be? How can we tap into love or joy? What does happiness look like?

Water connects us to our humanity and to our soul. Water reminds us of our softness, and also of our strength.

I love the word *feeling* for water because it helps me remember that sometimes we have feelings (emotions), and sometimes we have a feeling (intuition). Our emotions and intuition help us understand the most profound truths of what we are experiencing and teach us about what matters most to us. How we engage with our emotions and inner knowing can largely dictate how we experience our relationships with others—which is incredibly relevant to the suit of cups.

After reading this, what word jumps out at you for the element of water? Consider what word might work for you if *feeling* doesn't fit the bill. Remember not to use a word you've already picked for a different card. Here are a couple of other words that you may want to consider:

Emotion

While I enjoy the flexibility to interact with the element of water by seeing it as either emotion or intuition (or both), in truth, this suit and this element are mainly connected to the realm of emotions. *Emotion* makes a powerful keyword for this element.

Relationships

Another great keyword for this element, particularly concerning the cups suit in tarot, is *relationships*. It's important to remember that this suit is about the ways we connect with others and with ourselves.

The Element of Air: Thought

The suit of swords is associated with the element of air.

My keyword for the element of air is *thought*. I define *thought* as the process of thinking, considering, or exploring ideas. It's entirely a mental process.

When I think of air, I think of the mind, the intellect, psychology, and all the ins and outs of how the mind works! *Thought* is such a great word for capturing the essence of the mind for me.

Since air is associated with the swords suit, it tells me that it is the suit of the mind: how our mind works, thinks, or processes situations or problems in our lives.

The suit of swords is primarily associated with the workings of the mind and the connection between our thoughts and actions or decisions. The mind is a complicated and challenging place and some of life's greatest challenges involve our mental processes and perceptions about the events we experience.

The suit of swords teaches us about how thought influences action. What helps us decide? How do we learn and grow from our mistakes? Can we choose a different path in the future to be even better versions of ourselves? What can we change? How can we improve?

The qualities of air remind me of the qualities of different states of mind. Like the mind, air can be calm, active, or influential. It can move slowly or quickly or not at all. The air stirs things up.

Using the word *thought* for the element of air, as it pertains to the suit of swords in the tarot, works well for me because it reminds me of how strong of an influence conscious reasoning has on our day-to-day reality—in the same way that clouds can dramatically change the state of the sky. A clear sky with only a few fluffy white clouds is calm and serene—but when dark clouds roll in ahead of a storm, we can see and feel the disturbances in the air. The suit of swords is about recognizing what is happening in our minds with our thoughts.

After reading this, what word jumps out at you for the element of air? Consider what word might work for you if *thought* doesn't fit the bill. Remember not to use a word you've already picked for a different card. Here are a couple of other words that you may want to consider:

Intellect

Intellect is an excellent word for the element of air and the suit of swords. This word is about thinking and comprehension, which can open it up to different types of interpretation and is a reminder of the suit's connection to the workings of the mind.

Learning

The swords suit brings us face-to-face with situations that challenge our thinking and encourage us to learn and grow in new ways, which makes *learning* an excellent keyword for this element and the suit of swords.

The Element of Earth: Resources

The suit of pentacles is associated with the element of earth.

My keyword for the element of earth is *resources*. I define *resources* as the source or supply of anything that is regularly relied upon—like money or personal energy.

When I think of the earth element, I think of the tangible ways I engage with what is around me through my senses. Earthly things can be seen, touched, smelled, tasted, and experienced. I think of our resources, the stuff we engage with, the things we grow and build upon. Money is a resource, but we have less quantifiable resources as well, such as skills, knowledge, or our personal energy.

Since earth is associated with the pentacles suit, it tells me that the pentacles suit is the suit of resources and the responsibility to maintain, acquire, or divest ourselves of those resources. This suit is also about how we engage with and take care of what we have and are responsible for in our lives.

The suit of pentacles is primarily associated with how you handle your resources and build skills in life. From working your way up to establishing a legacy you can pass on for generations, earth and the pentacles suit relate to everything you rely on to feel safe and secure in the most tangible ways.

The suit of earth teaches us about our relationship with the material world and our responsibilities. How do you juggle work and pleasure? How do you work with others? Do you have a lack mentality or tend to run fast and loose with your resources? Who relies on you, and can you be relied upon?

Using the word *resources* for the element of earth works well for me because it reminds me that not all resources are things we can hold in our hands. Money is entirely tangible, but physical or emotional energy is not. Yet, we rely on both heavily, not only to survive but to thrive.

After reading this, what word jumps out at you for the element of earth? Consider what word might work for you if *resources* doesn't fit the bill.

Remember not to use a word you've already picked for a different card. Here are a couple of other words that you may want to consider:

Assets
If you prefer to focus on the financial or currency correspondence with the element of earth, *assets* is a fantastic keyword for this element.

Responsibilities
Using *responsibilities* as a keyword allows you to associate the element of earth with what keeps us grounded and creates stability in our lives.

The Significance of Numbers

Once you wrap your mind around the elements, the next step in learning the numbered minor arcana is building an association with the numbers. It took me years to settle on keywords that really resonated for these numbers, and to be honest, they're still evolving. But I'll walk you through my current favorites.

While I invite you to choose alternate words if my choices don't resonate with you, it may be difficult to determine the keyword that would work best for you for a particular number without knowing the associated tarot cards very well. For that reason, if the keywords I share with you are good enough for right now, I'd encourage you to start with them.

As you get more comfortable with tarot, revisit your view of the numbers now and again and see if they are still working for you. If they're not, switch them up. As always, remember rule #2: You're the boss!

One (or Ace): Potential
My keyword for the number one is *potential*. The definition of *potential* is something, as yet, unrealized.

The number one is a powerful number, often underestimated. The number one contains the potential of all the numbers that follow. Without the first step, there is no second or third step. We stand still. We go nowhere.

The number one is more than the beginning. It contains all the possibilities and potential of what could come after.

Remember the Magician from the major arcana? That card also is number one. Within it, we learn that all the potential to manifest anything we dream or desire is already contained within us.

I like to think of the number one and the ace of each minor arcana suit as a seed that, if put under a microscope, would visibly contain the entirety of the suit within it.

The number one is pure potential.

Two: Choice

My keyword for the number two is *choice*. The definition of *choice* is the act of selecting between two or more options.

Whenever there are two of anything, we either see partnership or opposition. Both require a conscious choice. We choose to partner with someone or something. Or we choose between two opposing ideas, people, or situations.

When you list the pros and cons, you're fully in the energy of number two. When there are two paths in front of you and you're trying to decide which to take, you're experiencing the number two. When you buddy up with someone for a project, you're experiencing the two.

The High Priestess is a two that reminds us that we have an inner voice full of wisdom, but we get to choose to listen to it or not.

I visualize the two as two open doors, each glowing with possibility. There is so much power in the ability to choose, and choosing is the quintessential energy of the two.

Three: Growth

My keyword for the number three is *growth*. The definition of *growth* is the process by which something increases in number, size, knowledge, skill, wisdom, or any other quality.

There are a number of unknowns in the one and the two, but the three is when whatever we engage with has taken shape. We know our direction, good or bad, and are well underway.

Three is the number of creation, expansion, and growth. New life often comes from the combination of two of something. Two people choose each other and take their relationship to the next level when they create a third in their likeness. The two grows or expands into the three.

It's not always so on the nose. When you choose to undertake a path of study, you grow and expand into a new version of yourself—one with greater knowledge and understanding. This kind of learning is also an example of the choice in the two leading to growth and expansion in the three.

The Empress is a three and is often depicted as pregnant, full of life, or in some way nurturing other creatures, plants, or beings as they grow.

Whether the growth is literal or metaphorical, every three in the tarot contains a lesson about growth.

Four: Stability

My keyword for the number four is *stability*. The definition of *stability* is the state of being unchanging or resistant to alterations or fluctuations.

When you have four of something, you have something solid and reliable. There is a moment when everything stabilizes. The two is a teeter-totter of choice; the three is the process of growing and expanding. The number four creates that first sense of solidity in the journey.

I often imagine the four as a sturdy wooden platform. It's not necessarily the end goal, but something is complete enough to build upon. It can be relied upon to hold fast. The four is when everything stops moving for a moment, and we can catch our breath.

The Emperor is a four, and we can see the stability in how that card is illustrated. The Emperor represents reliability and solidity. The Emperor isn't running off somewhere but takes care of all within their domain.

The four is stable.

Five: Disruption

My keyword for the number five is *disruption*. The definition of *disruption* is an interruption or disturbance.

Change is the only thing that stays the same. The five comes in to stir up the stability we were experiencing in the four. Now, there's a new element, some energy, that is shaking up the reliability of the four. For good or bad, things are shifting, and we'll have to deal with it.

When you have a stable surface—like the four—and some new element emerges, it draws your attention. The table is still the table, even while you're wiping up the red wine that spilled all over it—but it won't be the same. That red wine will probably leave a mark, and the table will be different because of it.

The nature of disruptions is that they challenge us to be more than what we are. The Hierophant is a five and disrupts the status quo by asking us to investigate our beliefs and decide how we will engage with established ways of thinking. Will we follow in kind or rebel and go another way?

The five invites us to face the challenge of disruption head-on.

Six: Harmony

My keyword for the number six is *harmony*. The definition of *harmony* is the blending, arrangement, or cooperation of two or more unique elements.

The six brings an opportunity to regroup and rebalance. It's a significant energy shift, and it's what we need after the disruption of the five.

The six is made up of three plus three—growth plus growth. It's the kind of growth you can only get after being challenged. It's not growth despite challenge; it's growth because of challenge.

You can also make six by adding one to five or, put another way, finding potential after a disruption.

In the six, we find a way to harmonize life's ups (potential, growth, and stability) with the challenge of disruption. It's an opportunity to find your footing again, to come up for air, and to look at things in a new way.

The Lovers card is a six, and with that card, we are faced with the sort of choice that will require a long-term commitment, one that will change the shape of our life in the future.

The six has a significant effect on our trajectory. It reminds us that it's not how you fall that matters—it's how you rise. The six offers us an opportunity to grow, not by ignoring difficulty, but by integrating it.

That's the harmony of the six.

Seven: Predicament

My keyword for the number seven is *predicament*. The definition of a predicament is a troublesome, perplexing, or challenging situation that lacks an obvious solution.

The seven presents a predicament, a sticking point, where the energy we're dealing with feels muddy and heavy. The seven represents a time when we see how much we've learned and what we will do when faced with difficulty. Nothing about the seven is easy.

The seven is a bridge from the harmonizing action of the six to the established structure of the eight (more on that in a moment). The seven represents a period where time moves slowly. We can reflect on our chosen path and either continue as we have so far or make a change. There's a feeling of determining whether we will shake things up or double down on continuing to do what we always have.

The Chariot is a seven and invites us to stay the course, to hold on to what matters to us with determination, no matter what threatens to pull us off course. In the numbered cards, you'll see that every seven presents a predicament in the form of a test, temptation, or opportunity.

That is the predicament of the seven.

Eight: Discipline

My keyword for the number eight is *discipline*. The definition of *discipline* is maintaining focus or control over a situation or circumstance through the application of acquired skills or knowledge.

The number eight speaks to the kind of discipline born of experience. It is only because of the earlier numbers' growth, challenges, and tests that you can do what you need to do now. There is more than book smarts in the eight; there's life smarts.

You know what to do, and you're going to do it. You may need a minute. You may need to remind yourself of what you're made of. When the eight comes around, there's an opportunity to step up your game and do what you know you can do. That's the discipline this card speaks to.

Discipline isn't about doing what feels good; it's about doing what needs to be done. It's not always glamorous, and sometimes it can feel like you're stuck, but that is what progress looks like.

Strength is an eight, which should tell you so much about the quality of this number. You have the fortitude you need to keep going despite the odds. You've gone through the challenges and passed the tests of the numbers that came before, and you're so ready now.

You know what to do. Buckle up, stay the course, or step on the gas because that's the discipline of the eight.

Nine: Fulfillment

My keyword for the number nine is *fulfillment*. The definition of *fulfillment* is the point of completing or achieving something that is sought, expected, anticipated, or promised.

The nine is the point of fulfillment. It's the moment when the work done, the choices made, and the opportunities taken (as well as those squandered) bring one to a result.

In the nine, you'll find the results of prior efforts (or lack thereof). You've ended up where you've ended up, but you're still learning and growing in the process. The nine isn't the end. It's the near end, the place of deep wisdom and incredible growth.

The Hermit is a nine. That card teaches us about looking within and profoundly knowing and understanding ourselves. There's a little Hermit in each of the nines in the tarot: opportunities to understand yourself at a deeper level and be better for it.

The fulfillment of the nine is the fruition of all that came before.

Ten: Realization

My keyword for the number ten is *realization*. The definition of *realization* is the moment of having brought something into form or awareness.

Ten is an exciting number. It's the point beyond the fulfillment of the nine when we realize the point of it all. As soon as you understand the point and have that deep knowledge, it's time to begin again.

Numerologically, the ten is usually reduced down to one (1 + 0) instead of treated as its own number. There's something powerful about that quality to this number. The ten is both the end (10) and the beginning (1), which is exactly the point of how this number applies to the tarot.

The Wheel of Fortune is a ten. It's the moment of the shift, the change, the turn of the wheel of time. What is ending is also fertilizing the soil to plant a new seed. The nine resulted from everything that came before; the seed we planted bore fruit in the nine. In the ten, we finally understand how we got here, for good or bad. We can take those lessons with us into the next journey.

The realization of the ten returns us to the one.

Putting It Together

Now that you've studied the elements and the numbers, it's time to combine them. To do that, we'll take the base meaning of each number and its associated keyword, connect it with the base meaning of each element and its keyword, and come up with an essential meaning. Let's get started.

The Wands, Ace through Ten

The wands suit is the suit of passion. It's adventures and pursuits. There's a dynamic energy to the entire suit. It's full of stops and starts, ups and downs. This suit represents our personal vision and the goals we pursue. Consider the nature of fire and how volatile and exciting it is. That is the nature of the suit of wands.

Ace of Wands: Inspiration

My favorite keyword for the Ace of Wands is *inspiration*. The definition of *inspiration* is the feeling of being prompted to take action or pursue something.

Numerologically, the ace is about potential; elementally, the suit of wands is the suit of passion. Inspiration is a driving force that helps us explore the potential to attain whatever (or whomever) we are most passionate about.

You can't have a fire without a spark, and the Ace of Wands is that spark. The moment depicted by the Ace of Wands is the moment that initiates everything that follows in the wands suit. This ace kicks you in the butt and gets you off the couch so you can do the darned thing—whatever that thing is.

In the RWS tarot, a glowing hand emerges from gray clouds to offer a wooden wand alive and speckled with tiny green leaves reminiscent of the first bits of spring growth. A castle sits on a hill in the distance. The castle seems far away and challenging—but not impossible—to reach.

There's an element of a divine gift to all the aces, and in the Ace of Wands, that gift is the first spark of the inner fire that you can tend. It's the excitement of the starter gunshot at a race and the sulfur smell of the match alighting as it's struck. It's the potency of the kind of sudden, naked desire that sets your heart racing.

As a blessing, this card is a green light, a *YES* in all capitals. It's the sign you've been waiting for to go for it! It's the invitation to listen to your inner fire; your muse is calling you. It's time to initiate a new project, journey, or venture.

As an obstacle, inspiration can feel out of reach, as if your muse has turned its back on you. It's writer's block, creative frustration, and that stuck feeling you get when nothing seems to catch your interest and you feel overwhelmed by the mundanity of daily life.

I love the way the word *inspiration* helps me tap into the creative power of the Ace of Wands and all the potential of the passionate suit of fire.

After reading this, what word jumps out at you? Consider what word might work for you if *inspiration* doesn't fit the bill. Remember not to use a word you've already picked for a different card. Here are a couple of other words that you may want to consider:

Spark

Spark is an excellent keyword to use for this card. It brings to mind that match-strike spark of energy I mentioned earlier. It's not uncommon to hear folks refer to a spark of inspiration or of the sparks that fly between lovers.

Influence

The word *influence* suggests the kind of intangible power that the Ace of Wands can represent. Whether it's creative influence, divine influence, or some other unseen force that propels you forward, influence is undoubtedly at play in the Ace of Wands.

Two of Wands: Possibility

My favorite keyword for the choice of passion is *possibility*. The definition of *possibility* is the opportunity to take action or pursue something.

Numerologically, the two is about choice. When it comes to the fiery suit of passion, the Two of Wands is the card of options and possibilities!

The Two of Wands is what comes after the inspiration of the ace. The Two of Wands asks, "Now what?" It's time to decide what you'll do next. You know where you want to go, but now it's time to think about how you'll get there and whom, if anyone, you want to get there with.

In the RWS tarot, you see a man looking out over a vast landscape, the whole world held in one hand. It gives that "the world is your oyster" vibe to this card, which creates a sense of incredible freedom.

There's an expansiveness to the Two of Wands. In this card, we have not yet committed to the path we're going to take because we're still exploring options. We are unfettered by expectations—ours or anyone else's. Our path forward is still unpaved, and anything is possible.

As a blessing, this card lets you know that the world is at your fingertips. Zoom out on the idea you're considering and look at the big picture. Consider what opportunities hover at the edges of your comfort zone and consider all the routes you might take to reach them. Open yourself up to all the possibilities in front of you.

As an obstacle, you may be trying to avoid venturing into unknown territory and your hesitance prevents you from making any progress. Your comfort zone is closing in on you and preventing your access to exciting opportunities in your life. You may also be procrastinating by overplanning, perhaps because you don't feel ready to take the next step—yet. Open yourself up to discovering new possibilities.

I love the openness of the word *possibility*. It brings to mind a vast open landscape, a blank canvas, or an unwritten story. Once you begin the thing, it starts to take shape, and the vast array of options grows more limited as you choose a path, paint your first stroke, or introduce the first character. Along with the "anything's possible" vibe of this card, you also get the worry that comes with imagining what might go wrong, considering possible pitfalls or obstacles you might face. After all, while all the good things are possible, so are the bad. If you're prone to worry or risk averse, the Two of Wands can represent how having such a wide-open range of possibilities can almost paralyze you.

Consider what word might work for you if *possibility* doesn't fit the bill. Here are a few other words that you may want to consider:

Planning

I often use the word *planning* alongside the word *possibility* for the Two of Wands because that is genuinely the tangible action of the Two of Wands.

Intention

The word *intention* is such a magical word. Whereas planning involves deciding how we want to do something, intention taps us into why we want to do it. Both are important to consider before you begin a new venture.

Three of Wands: Commencement

I LOVE the word *commencement* for the Three of Wands. To commence is to begin, to undertake something while looking ahead to the future.

Numerologically, the three is about growth, and what better way to grow your passion than to commit to a course of action and start getting those irons in the fire?

In the Three of Wands, you're past the planning stage of the two and are fully committed to a course of action. That course may shift and change as you progress, but now you are energetically invested in the journey or undertaking.

In the RWS tarot, you see a man with three staves high on a cliff overlooking the sea where some ships sail in the distance. We get the idea that the journey has officially begun. Perhaps the man sent out some ships to gather information or deliver goods or, in some other way, take tangible action toward the end goal, and he is waiting for them to return. Or perhaps he will be boarding one of those ships and heading to the next stop on the journey.

Regardless of how you view the scene on the card, it's clear that things are happening. The man on this card is no longer safe in his castle. The Three of Wands illustrates the moment in an undertaking when we have committed to moving forward and have taken tangible steps in that direction. We've taken the risk, and no matter how it plays out from here, we will have an opportunity to learn something and grow from the attempt. We've stepped outside of our comfort zone.

As a blessing, this card can indicate that you've begun, and your first few steps are already yielding rewards and your journey is underway. You may not know exactly how it will turn out, but you are progressing well. Keep your eyes on the prize because you'll surely succeed if you continue taking steps like these. You're manifesting your desires. You're going places!

As an obstacle, you may be struggling with self-doubt and tempted to retrace your steps back to safety. Not knowing how everything will turn out can be frightening, and you may feel like you've gotten in over your head. You don't need to know your precise destination just yet. You only need to move in that general direction. Remember that the hardest steps are always the first ones. Confidence comes with time.

What's so fantastic about the word *commencement* is that it captures the feeling of being at the beginning of the journey. We're underway, but it's still exciting, new, and fresh. We're enthusiastic, full of energy and anticipation, and confident we can make things work. There's a solid entrepreneurial vibe to commencing a new venture.

Consider what word might work for you if *commencement* doesn't fit the bill. Here are a few other words that you may want to consider:

Manifest

I like to visualize the Three of Wands as pulling or drawing toward yourself what you are seeking. You're taking real action to achieve your desired result, which is why the word *manifest* can work nicely.

Action

The Three of Wands is definitely about taking tangible action after the inspiration of the ace and the potential or planning of the two. The three is when action begins, which makes *action* an excellent keyword for this card.

Four of Wands: Milestone

My keyword for the Four of Wands is *milestone*. A milestone is a particularly significant stage in a broader journey or undertaking.

Numerologically, the four is about stability, and when it comes to a journey or pursuit of passion, reaching a point of equilibrium is the point at which your purpose has taken shape. You have reached a point where you can pause, take everything in, and commemorate how far you've come.

In the Four of Wands, you're well underway. Your project or pursuit is in progress, and you've reached a point when you can recognize a smaller goal reached in pursuit of the larger one, and that is cause for celebration.

In the RWS tarot, four tall staves make up a structure decorated with a floral garland and ribbons. A man and woman, holding hands, approach as if they are celebrating a special occasion together while others mill about. There is a large solid building in the background as well. This image is reminiscent of a party or celebration, perhaps even a wedding.

A wedding is a significant milestone in a couple's time together. Stereotypically, two people will experience a period of friendship, courtship, and eventually marriage. The wedding itself is a moment to pause and recognize the point they've reached and share that joy and happiness with others before they continue their life's journey, together.

At the same time, let's not limit this card's meaning to marriage and instead think of it as a broader metaphor for the type of experience illustrated by the card: one of celebrating how far you've come and allowing yourself to soak up the joy of that moment while being fully aware that there is more yet to do. This card represents stopping long enough to consider the progress that has been made—and to celebrate that progress—before continuing.

As a blessing, this card asks you to look back and recognize how far you've come. When your ultimate destination is still ahead of you, you might fool yourself into believing you haven't accomplished much, but you have. Look behind you and see what you've already done! Toast to your achievements and soak this moment in, but don't stay here too long. There is more to be done.

As an obstacle, the Four of Wands suggests that you might be enjoying the stability of the moment a little too much. When you reach a particular milestone, it can be tempting to stay there a little too long. Don't put down roots and establish a new comfort zone before you've gotten far enough away from your previous one. It's important to stay mobile, now, so you can get where you wanted to go in the first place.

What I enjoy most about the word *milestone* for this card is how it can apply to an event or celebration that might come up—a special day—but it can also signify that you've reached a mini goal on the way to your bigger goal. In a more mundane sense, a milestone is a literal marker of distance—a sign that you have traveled a particular distance. This word helps me expansively interpret this card.

Consider what word might work for you if *milestone* doesn't fit the bill. Here are a few other words that you may want to consider:

Celebration

A celebration is a party with a purpose. It's people gathering to take note of something that has occurred or is occurring, something they feel joyful about and grateful for. In that way, *celebration* can work just as well as *milestone* as a keyword for the Four of Wands.

Success

Some might find it helpful to use *success* as a keyword for the Four of Wands. Since success is fleeting, this word can remind you to notice the smaller successes that stack up on your way to accomplishing your goals.

Five of Wands: Competition

My keyword for the Five of Wands is *competition*. Competition is the experience of multiple people trying to win or gain something by proving themselves stronger or better in some way than others.

Numerologically, the five is about disruption. Disruption within the suit of passion can be quite the experience of headbutting and one-upping.

The Five of Wands challenges the confidence gained after celebrating the milestone of the Four of Wands. That challenge may come from another person, a group, or an event. It can be a conscious and good-natured competition like a sporting event, a game people play to prove themselves or others. It can also be unhealthy and damaging, like when two people shout over each other in a verbal sparring match.

In the RWS tarot, you see five young men playing a game or fighting with long staves. Some hold their staff with two hands, some with one; some look up to be aware of where they are pointing their staff, and others make eye contact with each other instead.

In the ace through the Three of Wands, there's an apparent movement forward in thought or action. In the Four of Wands, you pause to take in the journey thus far. You hit your first real challenge or hiccup in the Five of Wands. There's an obstacle in your path, and you need to face it and figure out how to go around (or through) it before you can proceed.

Have you ever heard the phrase "too many cooks in the kitchen"? That phrase refers to what happens when too many people with strong ideas about how things should be or how they should proceed feel like they need to win their point. Suddenly, progress halts while the cooks try to agree on the correct method for cooking the potatoes. While they're trying to figure it out, the potatoes are still sitting on the counter, uncooked. Progress is halted. That's one way to look at the Five of Wands.

As a blessing, this card lets you know it's time to test your skills and put your hat in the ring. If you've been waiting for a sign to appear before you step up, the Five of Wands is your sign. You've made too much progress to give up now, so jump in and demonstrate to yourself that you can do this.

As an obstacle, this card represents a roadblock in your path. Are you the roadblock? Are other people? Instead of trying to sidestep the issue, face the challenge head-on. If you're being combative to prove yourself, pull back a little. You don't need to compete with anyone or anything else. Your only true competitor is your own inner voice. If the people around you are being combative, remind yourself that you don't have to match their energy. Sometimes, it's best to look for the reasonable or diplomatic approach.

The word *competition* makes a great keyword because competition can be friendly or hostile. It can be good, or it can be bad. It can be something that helps you grow or stops you in your tracks.

Consider what word might work for you if *competition* doesn't fit the bill. Here are a few other words that you may want to consider:

Test

You're certainly being tested in the Five of Wands, so the word *test* is a great keyword to remind you that what is in your path isn't insurmountable, but it won't necessarily be easy to move through.

Friction

Life gets a little sticky in the Five of Wands. *Friction* is a good keyword to use for this card if you want to lean into the idea that this card represents bumps in the road or hiccups that could be interpersonal or not.

Six of Wands: Recognition

My keyword for the Six of Wands is *recognition*. Recognition is the experience of being acknowledged as valid or worthy.

Numerologically, the six is about harmony. In the fiery suit of passion, this harmony is the peace that comes with recognizing your success. If the three is growth, then the six is growth plus growth (three plus three), and that kind of progress is hard to hide from. There's no denying how far you've come now. Even those who don't know you well will be able to see it.

I've always found it interesting how the suit of wands seems to be made up of this push-and-pull pattern of success and challenge. When it comes to what we are passionate about, that's exactly how it feels. We flip between feeling like we're making progress and feeling like we're being tested. It's like a couple in a heated relationship that fights and makes love with equal enthusiasm. That is, after all, the nature of fire. We see that pattern here as the competition of the five leads to the recognition of the six.

In the RWS tarot, you see a man riding a horse, wearing a laurel-leaf crown, carrying a crowned staff as five others watch and cheer with their staves from the sidelines. It feels like you're looking at a conquering hero returning from battle.

There's a validation to the Six of Wands. The smaller milestone reached in the Four of Wands was more of a private moment, one shared only with those closest to you (if with anyone), but in the six, your success is on full display, visible to anyone in proximity to you. You can't keep your progress a secret anymore, nor should you. Remember that the journey still isn't over. You've got a long way yet to go, so it's important not to get complacent.

As a blessing, the Six of Wands shows up to let you know that you've successfully surmounted the challenges you faced earlier in your journey and are making big, successful strides. You've earned the recognition of your peers. You've also earned the right to take pride in your accomplishments. Just be careful not to let it go to your head.

As an obstacle, this card is a warning that you may be relying too much on other people's opinions of you when the only validation you need is your own. It can also be a reminder not to be overconfident and complacent about your victories. Remember the laurel wreath hanging from the staff in the RWS version of the Six of Wands? In ancient Greece, laurel wreaths were awarded as a symbol of success, and the phrase "don't rest on your laurels" is a warning not to stop making strides forward while you sit around patting yourself on the back. It's important to keep going.

The word *recognition* works well for the Six of Wands because it serves as a reminder that with success comes acknowledgment, whether from within or without.

Consider what word might work for you if *recognition* doesn't fit the bill. Here are a few other words that you may want to consider:

Victory

The word *victory* makes a fantastic keyword for the Six of Wands as it brings to mind the idea of being recognized as having won or succeeded at something, which is certainly aligned well with the meaning of the Six Wands. This keyword might work better for you if you want to focus on the wins this card speaks about and not necessarily others' reactions to them.

Recognition

Recognition can come in all forms, but giving praise is an action-oriented way to show appreciation for someone. The word *recognition* may work best for you if you want to focus on the idea that others are noticing and acknowledging the success you've attained.

Seven of Wands: Defense

My keyword for the Seven of Wands is *defense*. To defend something is to stand up for something or someone.

Numerologically, the seven is about predicaments, and in the fiery suit of passion, what you are most passionate about is faced with direct opposition. What you believe is being challenged, and it looks like you're outnumbered in this. If you want to get out of this predicament, you must decide whether you will surrender and go with the flow or stand up for what you believe in.

Again, another challenge comes after the acknowledgment and recognition of the six. Perhaps you were resting on your laurels, or perhaps you are just walking on the edge of what is currently deemed acceptable, but this card is all about being directly challenged—and outnumbered.

In the RWS tarot, you see a man standing on an embankment wielding a single staff defensively against six attackers wielding staves of their own. Visually, two elements to this card always jump out at me: first, that this man is outnumbered, and second, that he clearly has the high ground.

The Seven of Wands is all about being in a situation that demands you hold your position on higher ground. You're elevated above the majority. Is that because you're right? Or is it because you're being stubborn?

How do you know which it is?

To answer that question, you'll need to take a moment to reflect on everything that led up to this point and ask yourself if this is the hill you want to die on. If it is, stand your ground and fight. If it isn't, then perhaps it's time to climb down from there and consider another perspective.

As a blessing, the Seven of Wands indicates that you are on the high ground—or at least are reasonably confident you are. If you believe in yourself and what you're fighting for, then stand tall and defend your position. Whether or not you are outnumbered is irrelevant when you believe in what you are doing.

As an obstacle, this card could indicate that you are stubbornly holding on to something out of habit or because you haven't considered other perspectives. Are you on the high ground, or are you on your high horse? If there's a chance you're wrong, it may be worth it to stop being defensive, climb down, and get on equal footing with those who are challenging you to see what you can learn.

I love using the word *defense* for this card because we can protect what is important to us, which is essential work, but we can also be defensive, which is often harmful, and break down communications in situations that could be easily resolved.

Consider what word might work for you if *defense* doesn't fit the bill. Here are a few other words that you may want to consider:

Frustration

The Seven of Wands certainly illustrates frustration. Instead of moving forward with your plans or pursuits, you have to stop and deal with the conflict in front of you. It's a nonconsensual pause in your journey; how you handle that frustration will determine how you can move ahead. If this part of the card's meaning stands out to you, you may appreciate the word *frustration* for this card.

Courage

Another great word to use for the Seven of Wands is *courage*. This card presents you with a situation where you feel outnumbered or as if the odds are stacked against you, but you're being asked to stand strong in the face of all that adversity. That is the definition of *courage*.

Eight of Wands: Momentum

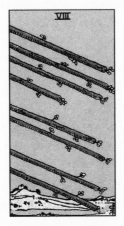

My keyword for the Eight of Wands is *momentum*. The definition of *momentum* is strength gained by motion or from a series of events. As a force, momentum tends to continue growing or developing and can become less likely to be stopped.

Numerologically, the eight is about discipline. It's the stability of the four on top of the stability of the four (four plus four). When you are passionate about something and doggedly pursue it despite all obstacles, you become a powerful force for productivity that knocks everything and everyone out of your way.

The Eight of Wands is powerful, and it's fast. It's a force that grabs you and drags you along with it until you run the risk of losing track of where you were headed in the first place. This card represents what it feels like when a project or pursuit has taken on a life of its own.

In the RWS tarot, you see eight wands pointed at a downward diagonal, as if they are speeding toward the earth like comets, all in a neatly aligned row—like eight arrows released simultaneously.

Every move made until this point in the journey of the suit of wands has established this powerful trajectory. If your aim was true, you're speeding toward success. If not, all those arrows are probably speeding along toward the wrong target. Either way, things are moving quickly.

The fact that the wands are pointed down to the earth, coming from the sky, also makes one think of a powerful force of the universe, intervening for good or ill. It can also speak to a powerful download, a productive flow state, or a moment when your creativity feels channeled. It's as if those wands are spurring you on, providing you the momentum you need to get where you want to go. The Eight of Wands can also feel like a burst of new energy or renewed passion.

I have often experienced the Eight of Wands as a powerful burst of momentum experienced after enduring a creative block, like writer's block. It's as if there's a powerful charge of new information or inspiration that finds me typing madly away on my keyboard as if my fingers are on fire. In those moments, I feel unstoppable.

As a blessing, the Eight of Wands signifies that you're going somewhere—and fast! Take in whatever inspiration or messages are raining down on you, and use this burst of momentum to propel you forward. As long as you ride the power of your passion, you'll get where you need to go.

As an obstacle, the Eight of Wands could indicate that you've gotten swept up in what you're doing and have lost track of the need for caution or an eye for the details. While keeping your gaze on the big picture or final goal is important, you don't want to aim your arrows all willy-nilly and hit the wrong target. This might be a warning to slow down—at least a little—and adjust your aim.

The word *momentum* works well for me for this card because it captures that feeling of being swept up in something. For good or for bad, the Eight of Wands sweeps us off our feet and carries us forward.

Consider what word might work for you if *momentum* doesn't fit the bill. Here are a few other words that you may want to consider:

Progress

I also enjoy the word *progress* for the Eight of Wands because it clarifies that you're moving forward. The Eight of Wands is all about progress!

Speed or Swiftness

Both *speed* and *swiftness* are keywords that effectively convey the feeling of the Eight of Wands. Whatever is going on in this card, it's going quickly, so words about speed work very well for this card.

Nine of Wands: Tenacity

My keyword for the Nine of Wands is *tenacity*, the state of being tenacious. To be tenacious is to hold on tightly to something, someone, a belief, or a value in the face of any challenge.

Numerologically, the nine is about fulfillment. In the suit of passion, this card represents the dedication to the fulfillment of one's purpose. There's no giving up now!

The Nine of Wands represents the moment you realize the cost of passion. You've gotten knocked down repeatedly, and yet you keep getting back up. This card represents what it feels like to constantly encounter a little success and a little failure while never having a moment to get comfortable with either.

In the RWS tarot, you see a wounded man standing guard with eight staves behind him and one held close to his body while he stands watch. The way that he holds that staff is telling. He isn't going anywhere. He is staying right here because he believes in—and is committed to—his path.

The Nine of Wands represents holding on tightly to what you are most passionate about. Despite the challenges and the hits taken along the way, you will not allow even one staff to fall. There's a dogged determination and commitment to your purpose found in this card. You will not give up—no matter what.

When you think about it, it's little wonder that the guy in the Nine of Wands is practically daring anyone to try to take that stick from him. Think of all he must have been through! The wands suit is a wild ride of ups and downs, and it's tiring as hell. In this card, you realize how committed you are. There's been no turning back for a while in this suit, but the nine is that ride-or-die moment.

As a blessing, the Nine of Wands lets you know that you can face whatever anyone tries to throw at you and come out standing strong. You've gotten this far for a reason. You have earned those bumps and bruises, and now you are a force to be reckoned with. Stay strong and stay connected to the reason you're doing this in the first place.

As an obstacle, your tenacity has become a futile form of resistance. You're holding on way too tightly to something that is no longer useful, or you're holding on for the wrong reasons. Don't abdicate your power by waiting for someone to take something from you that you aren't even sure you want anymore.

I've gone back and forth about the best word to use for the Nine of Wands over the years, but when I landed on *tenacity*, it was like fireworks going off in my mind. Finally, I'd found a word that could speak to the strength and conviction of this card—and its obstinance.

Consider what word might work for you if *tenacity* doesn't fit the bill. Here are a few other words that you may want to consider:

Obstinance

Whereas *tenacity* suggests forward movement, *obstinance* is stickier. The Nine of Wands can represent a standstill, and *obstinance* may work better as a keyword if you want to tap into that energy.

Stamina

The scene on this card certainly speaks to stamina. The man pictured on this card still stands strong where others may have crumbled, which makes *stamina* a good choice for the Nine of Wands.

Ten of Wands: Burden

My keyword for the Ten of Wands is *burden*. A burden is a heavy load or oppressive force. It weighs you down. That is the state of affairs in the Ten of Wands.

Numerologically, the ten is about realizations. In the fiery suit of passion, the ten is the realization that the responsibility you've taken on is more than you can bear alone.

In the Ten of Wands, the pressure that has been mounting throughout the suit finally comes to a head, and it's reached the point where it's all just too much. Now what you're carrying feels like a heavy burden.

In the RWS tarot, a man struggles to carry a large, awkward bundle of staves. You can see that he has nearly reached his destination, but his back is bowed from the weight of his load. It's the heaviness of what he's carrying that stands out the most to me in this image. The destination is so close—only a few more steps and he'll reach it. Or maybe he'll simply collapse in the attempt.

While the Nine of Wands feels tired but committed, the Ten of Wands feels impossible. The burden you carry—expectations, responsibilities, goals, tasks, or whatever else is in the pile—feels heavier than any sane person could possibly manage. It feels like there's no way you can keep going, no matter how committed or passionate you are. It's unmanageable. Or is it?

It always strikes me how alone this guy is in the RWS image. Does he really have to carry all those sticks by himself? Or could he ask for help? I've often felt like him: overburdened and burnt-out but still putting one foot in front of the other.

It's easy enough to congratulate yourself for your hard work when you've struggled and strived and finally reach your destination, but what if you didn't have to struggle so hard in the process? What if you were struggling under a burden that you didn't have to carry? The Ten of Wands presents us with an opportunity to ask ourselves if we're doing something all by ourselves because we have to, or because we think that's what we're supposed to do.

Just because you can do something—or everything—all by yourself doesn't necessarily mean that you should.

This burden you're carrying didn't show up overnight. If you look back at the Nine of Wands, you can see a little foreshadowing to the Ten of Wands. You can feel the obstinance of the wounded defender in the nine. If you listen closely, you'll be able to hear the transition from the Nine of Wands to the Ten of Wands. It sounds like a foot-stomping, pouty exclamation of: "I'll do it myself!"

Regardless, it's important to remember that you don't have far to go before you can lighten the load. The question is: How you will take those last few steps? Will you take them alone, or ask for help? Will you carry all those staves to the end, or will you lay down those you don't need? The choice is up to you.

As a blessing, the Ten of Wands is a reminder that, while the load may be heavy, you are strong enough to carry it. You don't have much further to go. You could make the journey more comfortable, though, with just a few minor changes. You could change how you're carrying your load, you could set down what is least important, or you could ask for help from someone else to ease your burden. You can do this.

As an obstacle, the Ten of Wands is a reality check. You've bitten off more than you can chew and are carrying far too much. Ask yourself if what you're carrying is even yours. Are you carrying other people's burdens? Did they even ask you to? Either way, you're going to need to put something down. If push comes to shove, could you make it to your destination as is? Absolutely. Is that what's best for you? Certainly not.

Over the years, I've found other keywords for the Ten of Wands, but I always come back to *burden*. No other word has covered as much ground as *burden* does for me.

Consider what word might work for you if *burden* doesn't fit the bill. Here are a few other words that you may want to consider:

Burnout

I like the word *burnout* for the Ten of Wands because it brings a modern-day relatability to the card's meaning.

Fatigue

You'd better believe that the man pictured in the Ten of Wands is tired as hell and wants nothing more than to drop all those staves on the ground and take a nap. I think *fatigue* is a very fitting keyword for this card.

The Cups, Ace through Ten

The cups suit is the suit of feeling. It's emotions, relationships, and human connection. There's a flowing energy to the entire suit. It's full of joy and sadness, heartbreak, and deep love for others and ourselves. This suit represents how we form bonds with others, give and receive emotionally, and experience love. Most of all, this is the suit that teaches us how strong we are. Consider the nature of water. It's soft and fluid but also incredibly powerful.

That is the nature of the suit of cups.

Ace of Cups: Blessing

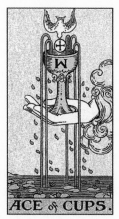

My favorite keyword for the Ace of Cups is *blessing*. The definition of *blessing* is something that brings a great deal of joy or happiness.

Numerologically, the ace is about potential; elementally, the suit of cups is the suit of feeling. What better potential for feeling than a blessing—something that comes into your life and brings with it a sense of joy and happiness?

In the RWS tarot, another glowing hand offers something up. This time, it's an overflowing cup over a lake dotted with lotus flowers and lily pads like an ever-flowing fountain. A dove drops a wafer into the cup. The dove is reminiscent of the peace that comes with true happiness and joy, and the lotus flowers hint at the healing required to be open to the offered blessing.

The Ace of Cups represents the moment you find yourself face-to-face with something or someone that fills your heart with joy. Your cup is full to the brim—overflowing even—with happiness, possibility, and hope.

The cup's contents are not still or stable but moving, spilling out over the rim of the cup to the waters below—a visual reminder that the happiness we seek isn't something that stands still but is constantly in motion. Moments of bliss are fleeting. You cannot grasp them tightly in your fist or put them in your pocket. It's a reminder to be present and to fill your cup when you can.

As a blessing, this card represents an opportunity to open your heart to someone or something that could be a source of joy for you, but it isn't going to simply land on your lap or be handed to you on a silver platter. You'll need to keep your eyes open. Pay attention so you don't miss it.

As an obstacle, the Ace of Cups represents a blessing that is passing you by, and you may not even be aware that it's happening. You could be taking someone, or something, for granted. You could be so preoccupied with what doesn't matter that you have little time left for what does. Remember that a blessing with the potential to bring you a lifetime of happiness can be lost in a moment.

I love the word *blessing* because it signifies things, people, and experiences that bring goodness to your life. Whether that goodness is there for a moment or a lifetime, it changes you—even when things don't turn out exactly as you hope. Sometimes, the biggest blessings in our lives are the ones we don't recognize until long after they've left us again. And sometimes the most difficult experiences set us on the path to realizing our dreams, events we refer to as "blessings in disguise." All of these are represented by the Ace of Cups.

Consider what word might work for you if *blessing* doesn't fit the bill. Here are a few other words that you may want to consider:

Love

In the suit of emotion, *love* is a powerful keyword to associate with the ace; it represents the force that initiates so much of the joy we experience in life. We can also wall ourselves off from love, preventing us from accessing the Ace of Cup's blessings.

Delight

The word *delight* has an unabashed openness to it that works beautifully for the Ace of Cups. When we are in alignment with all the Ace of Cups has to offer, there is no attempt to hide from the joy we feel. Delight is an expression of love, wonder, or joy—all of which could be contained within the cup on this card.

Two of Cups: Connection

My favorite keyword for the Two of Cups is *connection*. A connection is any link between two things or people.

Numerologically, the two is about choice. When it comes to the watery suit of feeling, this card is about what happens when you choose to form a connection with the blessing offered to you in the ace.

The Two of Cups represents the "Yes!" of the early stages of a relationship, romantic or platonic, when everyone is full of hope and optimism and the future remains a vast expanse of possibility. It is the card of chemistry and connection, usually between two people who have chosen each other.

In the RWS version of this card, a man and a woman raise their cups to each other, or perhaps we see the moment they each offer their own cup to the other, which is how I prefer to view it. Between the two cups, you see a caduceus—a symbol of two snakes intertwining along a staff topped with a winged lion head. The intertwining symbolism of the caduceus shows us that there is a strong link between these two individuals.

One of the things I love most about the RWS Two of Cups is the way that both people are on equal footing. Neither seems to wield power over the other, and they hold their cups at heart level, indicating that both are offering something to the other from the heart and neither gives or takes more than the other. There's a beautiful, balanced energy to this card that demonstrates the way that two people can maintain their unique qualities and identities while also forming something new: a connection.

As a blessing, the Two of Cups represents the hope, optimism, excitement, and attraction of the beginning stages of a powerful connection between you and someone else. The future seems bright, even if it is a little too soon to know, for sure, how it will turn out. For now, you're both equally invested in this connection and are choosing each other.

As an obstacle, this card can indicate a magnetism drawing you to someone, but this person may not be in your best interest. Alternatively, this card could represent an opportunity for connection that you are choosing to ignore or avoid. If so, ask yourself if you are letting your insecurities or doubts get in the way of that connection.

I love the word *connection* for the Two of Cups because it speaks to choosing to form a unit of two. It feels neutral and could easily apply to personal, romantic, or professional relationships.

Consider what word might work for you if *connection* doesn't fit the bill. Here are a few other words that you may want to consider:

Promise

I appreciate the word *promise* because it can have a double meaning. It can be the actual act of making a promise to another person, or it can be that feeling of optimism when you feel like you've met someone you see a future with; something about it feels so right! This word works very well for the watery two.

Attraction

The word *attraction* works well for the Two of Cups because it is the feeling that leads to forming a bond with another person or an idea.

Three of Cups: Support

My favorite keyword for the Three of Cups is *support*. The definition of *support* is the act of providing assistance, either emotionally or materially, in order to improve someone else's happiness or well-being.

Numerologically, the three is about growth. In the realm of water, that growth is in the relationships surrounding you. You don't have one friend—you have several, and those friends are people you can rely on to be there for you, and they can rely on you as well.

You have grown a circle of friends around you, people you can celebrate with or grieve with. These are your chosen family, community, and confidants.

In the RWS tarot, three women raise their glasses as they cluster together in a tight circle. Around them, a ripe pumpkin and other foliage suggest harvest, but the focus is on merriment. It's a party!

One of the things that has always struck me about the Three of Cups is that each woman is different. It's their differences that I focus on the most because it reminds me that the strongest bonds between people are bonds that appreciate and benefit from each other's unique qualities. Each brings different strengths and struggles to the group, allowing them to support each other.

The Three of Cups show us a type of friendship that is special and intimate. This card represents your people: your inner circle, your chosen family, and your support system.

As a blessing, the Three of Cups reminds you that you're not alone. You have people you can trust, people you can rely on. It can also indicate that you've gotten good news or are experiencing something joyful. You should do something to recognize the moment and share it with your support network.

As an obstacle, this card can indicate discord in your inner circle that you want to address so it doesn't fester and sour the relationships that are important to you. It could also suggest that you don't want the party to end. While it's important to let yourself experience the joys in life, you don't want to linger here so long that you overlook your responsibilities. It may be time to pack the party up.

I like the word *support* because it speaks to the relationships you've nurtured and grown over time and can now rely on and lean into.

Consider what word might work for you if *support* doesn't fit the bill. Here are a few other words that you may want to consider:

Friendship

The Three of Cups is about friendship among a group of people who know how to show up for one another in joy and in sorrow, which makes *friendship* a fantastic choice for this card.

Community

I like the word *community* for the Three of Cups because it brings to mind a group of people who can offer support and encouragement to one another.

Four of Cups: Stagnancy

The word that fits the Four of Cups best is *stagnancy*. The definition of *stagnancy* is the state of being dull, unmoving, or lifeless.

Numerologically, the four is about stability, and in the watery suit of cups, it's important to remember that water is usually at its best when it's flowing or moving, even if gently. Water that stays still too long tends to stagnate.

There is a comfort to the stillness of this card. Life is still and unchanging, but not necessarily bad. It's a bit lackluster. Nothing seems shiny and new. Nothing is tugging you outside of your comfort zone. It's more of the same, over and over.

In the RWS tarot, you see a man looking discontent as he stares absently at three cups, all of which are full but unchanging. Out of view of his peripheral vision, a spiritual hand offers a fourth cup (almost like a miniature Ace of Cups). All he has to do is turn and look to see the blessing awaiting him. He just needs to get off his butt and accept it.

The Four of Cups represents the rut of complacency you can find yourself in when you take life's little joys and gifts for granted.

This card also highlights the effects of staying within your comfort zone. The stability of the Four of Cups represents that things are staying the same. This kind of emotional stability can be a gift and a joy. If you take it for granted and stop seeing the shine and sparkle of what you have in front of you, it can turn into discontentment and stagnancy. You can begin to feel like you're settling. You may be settling. Or you may simply be settled. Part of the dynamic nuance of this card is exploring which of those is true for you.

When I look at the sullen guy in the Four of Cups, I imagine he thinks the grass is greener on the other side. In reality, the grass is greener where you water it. With that in mind, the hand offering the cup may not be offering something new but reminding you what it felt like to feel that ace, that newness.

Sometimes, the solution to stagnancy isn't to chase after something new but to appreciate what you have.

As a blessing, the Four of Cups acknowledges that your emotional and relational world is stable and healthy. Sometimes, a lack of excitement is a signal that things are exactly as they should be, at least for now. Recognize all that you have to be grateful for.

As an obstacle, this card suggests that you're in a rut. The boredom of the same old routines is bringing you down and making it hard to get motivated to accomplish anything or make the changes you know you need to make. Instead of marinating in your discontent, look around. An opportunity for joy is within your reach.

I'm particularly drawn to the word *stagnancy* because it is a quality that water develops when it becomes still. The elemental association is too good to pass up. I also appreciate that stagnant water is not necessarily bad; it only needs a little freshening up—a little zhuzh, if you will.

Consider what word might work for you if *stagnancy* doesn't fit the bill. Here are a few other words that you may want to consider:

Boredom

When emotions become too still, boredom is the natural result, making the word *boredom* an effective keyword for the Four of Cups.

Comfort

I used the word *comfort* for a long time for the Four of Cups, and I still appreciate it as a keyword for this card. The Four of Cups can represent being comfortable—maybe even too comfortable—or being stuck in your comfort zone.

Five of Cups: Grief

I've not yet found a word more apt for the Five of Cups than *grief*. The definition of *grief* is the emotional distress caused by loss.

Numerologically, the five is about disruption, and in the feelings suit, there is a sense of upset. Our feelings are overwhelming and spilling out all over the place.

In the RWS tarot, you see a person wrapped in a black cloak—an image that, to me, symbolizes the way we wrap ourselves up in and cling to our grief—with their head bowed over three overturned cups. The contents of the spilled cups slowly soak into the ground. Behind this person, two upright cups remain. In the background, there is a flowing river and a bridge leading from this mourning place to a building or village.

The Five of Cups is often linked to the adage "don't cry over spilled milk," but I don't think that's fair. It's okay to cry over the spilled milk. It's just that, at a certain point, you need to accept that you can't get the milk (or, in this case, wine) back into the cup. What's gone is gone. It's important to recognize that there are still two cups that remain.

To me, the river signifies the ever-moving state of our emotions. Grief, pain, anger, joy, and love are not static. They are constantly in motion, like the water that moves in the river in this card. We move from feeling to feeling. Even when you try with all your might to hold on to a particular emotion, you'll find that—eventually—it will slip between your fingers.

As a blessing, the Five of Cups is a reminder that, while you may be struggling with difficult emotions, this experience is temporary. Try not to get so wrapped up in what you're feeling right now that you lose track of the good that remains.

As an obstacle, the Five of Cups warns that you are dwelling too much—or for too long—on these difficult emotions. There is a difference between processing your feelings and refusing to move forward. You may have lost sight of the future that is still ahead of you. Look for the bridge that will help you transition from the difficulty you've been experiencing to all the good that still awaits you.

There's no question that the Five of Cups represents grief. There are countless things we grieve in life besides people. We grieve missed opportunities, failures in life and work, and choices we could have made, which makes *grief* an excellent keyword for the Five of Cups.

Consider what word might work for you if *grief* doesn't fit the bill. Here are a few other words that you may want to consider:

Sorrow

The word *sorrow* may be a good choice if you find that *grief* feels too connected with death. The word *sorrow* encompasses the overwhelming difficulty of painful emotions.

Regret

The word *regret* works well for the Five of Cups because what often keeps us stuck in this place of not wanting to move forward is a sense of guilt or regret over things we could have, should have, or wished we would have done differently.

Six of Cups: Nostalgia

The keyword I keep coming back to, again and again, for the Six of Cups is *nostalgia*. The definition of *nostalgia* is a yearning or wistfulness for simpler times from the past.

Numerologically, the six is about harmony, and in the feelings suit, we seek to harmonize the present with the past. Looking back at what came before can provide context to what we're facing in the present. Failing that, reminiscing can provide some much-needed escapism that can give us the peace we need to regroup before continuing our journey.

It isn't that simple. Nostalgia is like hunting through an attic. You might uncover sweet memories that provide for some delightful escapism and reminiscing. You might also find reminders of wounds you buried from a difficult time in your past that you now need to deal with. Either way, you risk losing your grip on the present.

In the RWS tarot, an older child gives a flower to a younger child—or perhaps receives flower from the younger child. A guard makes his rounds in the background. There's a sense of both safety and innocence in this image.

The scene in the Six of Cups feels like a fond memory. Everything about this scene seems right—maybe even too right. There is this tender and private moment between the two children where one gives and the other receives a gift. The white flowers feel like symbols of purity and innocence.

It's easy to overlook the challenging side of the Six of Cups. Sweeter memories are easier to focus on, but the past isn't always sunshine and white lilies, safety, and sweetness. A dip into the past could be nourishing and joyful or jarring and difficult. Either way, there is a risk of losing yourself to the past.

Imagine finding a box of old photos, letters, and memorabilia from long ago in your life. Then, consider how it might feel to look through those things. That is the energy of the Six of Cups.

As a blessing, the Six of Cups lets you know that the past is seeking your attention or acknowledgment. It might be time for some reminiscing, or you may need to work on healing a buried wound. Either way, the past has a role to play in the present. On the other hand, if you're struggling in the present, this card could be reminding you that it's okay to spend a little time recalling simpler and sweeter times in order to process or move through the difficulties of the present.

As an obstacle, this card could indicate that you are getting caught up in romanticizing your past and are unfairly comparing your present to this idealized view. It could also suggest that a not-so-happy time from your past impacts your present. Be careful not to paint the present with the brush of the past because to do so is to project outdated expectations on a present full of possibility.

The Six of Cups represents an escape, of sorts, from the worries and stresses of the present. It's important to remember, though, that as sweet or as difficult as the past may be, it is in the past.

Consider what word might work for you if *nostalgia* doesn't fit the bill. Here are a few other words that you may want to consider:

Memories

In truth, *memories* is a more neutral word than *nostalgia* and could work much better for you if your past is more sour than sweet or you want to maintain a more careful neutrality for the card's meaning. It can also be an evocative keyword if you want to recall the visual of looking through a box of things from the past.

Wistfulness

I like the word *wistfulness* for the Six of Cups because it brings to mind that feeling of yearning for a simpler, sweeter time. Instead of focusing on what you're recalling, the word *wistfulness* implies you are drawn explicitly to simpler or happier times from your past.

Seven of Cups: Fantasy

The keyword I use to represent the energy of the Seven of Cups is *fantasy*. A fantasy is the product of imagining improbable things.

Numerologically, the seven is about predicaments. In the watery realm of feelings, you find yourself trying to avoid your current predicament by fantasizing about what *could* be possible rather than focusing on what actually is possible.

The Seven of Cups is what dreams are made of. It's that feeling you have when imagining what you would do if you won the lottery, or if you found out you were secretly royalty, or if you could have a superpower. When you picture castles in the sky, you're in Seven of Cups territory. This card asks, "What would I do if I could do anything?"

In the RWS tarot, the imagery shows a person looking up at a dreamy, cloud-filled array of options. Seven cups float in the clouds, each offering something different: riches, power, victory, adventure, and more.

The Seven of Cups represents what it feels like to dream of a better future, to imagine what could be. It's the pipe dream card.

The transition from the Six of Cups to the Seven of Cups feels like emotional whiplash as you fling yourself from the past to the future. In both the cards, it's clear that we want to be anywhere but here.

There is also an element of indecision in the Seven of Cups. Instead of dreaming up one possible future, we're dreaming up seven. We are spoiled for choice, and the idea that we could pursue any of these dreams can lock us up in daydream territory where we remain stuck. Sometimes, that's the point. We're avoiding the difficult work of changing our circumstances and daydreaming our time away instead.

As a blessing, the Seven of Cups invites you to dare to dream! Imagine what could be possible. Ask yourself, "What if …?" There are so many possibilities in front of you. Now is the time to dream, so dream. Then, plant your feet on the earth and be honest with yourself about what course of action is truly best for you.

As an obstacle, the Seven of Cups warns that you are engaging in pie-in-the-sky thinking. In this daydreamy state, it's difficult to determine what is possible for you—let alone what is best for you. You may be avoiding a real predicament in the present by fantasizing instead of being realistic. It's time to come back down to earth.

Dreaming is a powerful way to play with possibilities and imagine the future. Just remember not to get so lost in your dreams that you leave yourself ill-equipped to deal with reality.

Consider what word might work for you if *fantasy* doesn't fit the bill. Here are a few other words that you may want to consider:

Imagination

Whereas *fantasy* brings to mind the idea of making up concepts and ideas out of thin air, *imagination* is sometimes a little more contained. We sometimes imagine something before we do it. *Imagination* can have a more grounded feel and, thus, make a better keyword for some.

Distraction

Daydreaming, fantasizing, and even imagining can be distractions from reality. The Seven of Cups represents the feeling of being disconnected from present reality. The fact that there are a myriad of options in the Seven of Cups can also adequately illustrate what it feels like to be distracted, so the word *distraction* makes a practical keyword for this card.

Eight of Cups: Divergence

The keyword I use for the Eight of Cups is *divergence*. To diverge is to break off from the primary path, to depart and go in a new direction.

Numerologically, the eight is the card of discipline. In the watery suit of feeling, it's time to apply that discipline to take control over the future you deserve, rather than the one you were headed toward. Choosing yourself requires strength of character and the discipline to know how to make the decisions that will serve you best in the long term.

The Eight of Cups represents the moment you realize you can't change how you feel. No amount of wishing for the past or daydreaming about what could have been will change your circumstances, so it's time for you to change your circumstances.

In the RWS tarot, we see eight neatly stacked cups in the foreground. Behind the stack, a person turns their back on the viewer as they slowly climb uphill in the dark toward a new future. Overhead, the moon lights their way.

In the Eight of Cups, we realize it's time to recognize that the path we're on, or the situation we're in, is not serving our greater good—if it ever has. It's the moment we realize that all the time and emotional energy we've invested in this situation has not gotten us what we truly wanted: happiness. And so, we diverge from our current path and depart for something better.

The fact that this departure takes place at night is telling. Typically, journeys would begin in the light of the morning sun. The fact that this person seems to be setting out in the middle of the night speaks to the jarring nature of this kind of understanding.

The neatly stacked cups in the front speak to the time, effort, and emotional energy spent in this relationship or situation. In the Eight of Cups, you're diverging from a lifestyle you've heavily invested in emotionally. You're taking a new approach because you recognize that the path you've been on is no longer the right path for you. It's painful and difficult to allow this truth to rest in your heart, and once you do, you know there's no turning back.

As a blessing, the Eight of Cups arrives to confirm that it's time for you to break away from the path you thought you were on and seek new horizons. No matter how much time and effort you've put into someone or something, the time has come to choose yourself. Walking away may be hard, but it is also an act of empowerment.

As an obstacle, the Eight of Cups could be a warning that you put others' wants before your needs. It can indicate that you are sticking it out in a situation you know isn't right for you because of all you've invested in it. You may be settling. Perhaps it's time to re-evaluate your situation more honestly.

The Eight of Cups is an empowering card but can also be deeply sad. You'd chosen the path you were on. You had put your whole heart into it. Diverging from that path, now, means acknowledging that it's no longer for you, and that's difficult and painful. Take time to recognize that, despite the pain, this divergence is a gift to yourself.

Consider what word might work for you if *divergence* doesn't fit the bill. Here are a few other words that you may want to consider:

Departure
The Eight of Cups is the card of leaving what no longer serves you. I love the word *departure* because it reminds me of boarding a plane. Once the plane takes off, you know there's no turning back. That feeling of liftoff? That's the universe letting you know you've chosen well.

Boundaries
The Eight of Cups represents when you say, through word or deed, "Enough is enough!" You decide what is no longer right for you and go after what is. In the same way, when you establish or hold your boundaries, you also choose

yourself over the status quo. That's what makes *boundaries* such a good keyword for this card.

Nine of Cups: Contentment

My keyword for this card is *contentment*. The definition of *contentment* is to be in a state of satisfaction and happiness.

Numerologically, the nine is about fulfillment, and in the suit of feeling, we're feeling fulfilled emotionally. The Nine of Cups represents a time of pleasure and contentment.

Of all the cards in the tarot, I think the Nine of Cups is my favorite—not the RWS image, necessarily, but the meaning. The Nine of Cups signals emotional comfort that we find within ourselves, a sense of personal fulfillment and gratitude for all we have. When you look around yourself and think, "This is good," you're in Nine of Cups territory.

In the RWS tarot, nine cups are neatly arranged on a semi-circle cloth-draped table. A man who looks incredibly pleased with life sits in front of this neat row of cups. This image makes one think of simple pleasures, but honestly, I'm not a fan. I have a habit of referring to the RWS Nine of Cups as "just a dude with a bunch of wine" because I feel so strongly about what this card represents that I want more from the image. In fairness, this card shows a man who knows what makes him happy and has surrounded himself with exactly that. I think my frustration stems from how strongly I believe that this card is about finding fulfillment from within, rather than from external things.

There's something so powerful about the fact that this card arrives after the Eight of Cups, where a difficult choice was made to walk away from what wasn't working. This card is so validating, as it affirms that you made the right choice. In the Nine of Cups, you can look around yourself at the life you've begun to build and recognize that this is what you really wanted all along.

There's nothing fancy or over-the-top about the pleasure in the Nine of Cups, but there's also nothing lacking. This card represents that feeling you get when you know you've landed at a beautiful place in life, which might look somewhat mediocre to others but is what you've been wanting.

There's a rightness to the feeling in the Nine of Cups because this is when you realize you've come home to yourself. You know what you want out of life, and you have sought exactly that for yourself and no more, at least not yet. For now, all you want and need is this.

The Nine of Cups is often called the card of wishes fulfilled. For me, this is the card of reality fulfilled. You have what you deserve in this card. You're not settling, and you're not overreaching. It's just enough. It's peace, calm, and tranquility. It's contentment.

As a blessing, the Nine of Cups represents emotional fulfillment, contentment, and gladness, all of which bloom from within. You have enough. You are enough. Come home to yourself.

As an obstacle, the Nine of Cups indicates that you've become disconnected from the little joys in your day-to-day reality or have been looking for happiness in all the wrong places. If you find yourself constantly chasing more or better, it may be time to slow down and look within. You may already have all that you need to be content. Remember that you are responsible for finding (or creating) your own pleasures in life.

The Nine of Cups is, indeed, wishes fulfilled—when those wishes are made realistically and from a place of personal empowerment and self-worth.

Consider what word might work for you if *contentment* doesn't fit the bill. Here are a few other words that you may want to consider:

Gratitude

I like the word *gratitude* for the Nine of Cups because it brings to mind the idea that you have much to be grateful for. I even use a representation of this card on a gratitude altar I keep in my home because it so beautifully aligns with the practice of counting your blessings.

Self-Love

There is no better card in a pack of tarot cards than the Nine of Cups to represent self-love. In particular, because you choose yourself in the Eight of Cups, the enjoyment of the Nine of Cups is all for you. You have learned to fill your own cup, making *self-love* a beautiful keyword for this card.

Ten of Cups: Bliss

What could be better than the sweet contentment of the Nine of Cups? The bliss of the Ten of Cups! *Bliss* is my personal keyword for this joyous card. The definition of *bliss* is a state of perfect happiness.

Numerologically, the ten is about realization, and in the suit of feeling, you have realized a state of perfect happiness and joy in your life.

In the RWS tarot, we see a young family. Two small children play together, holding hands, while a couple, clearly in love, hold one another beneath a rainbow's arch decorated with ten cups. The scene is idyllic and almost unbelievable in its perfection.

This scene is straight out of a fairy tale. Nothing is out of place in the image of the Ten of Cups. Everyone is happy and getting along. The weather is perfect. There's even a rainbow! Nothing could be better.

Could it?

The Ten of Cups is deceptive in its perfection because life, as we know, isn't perfect. I am an intensely optimistic person who likes to see the good in every situation, and even I must admit that the scene depicted in this card can feel unattainable. It's one of the (countless) reasons I love the Nine of Cups so much more than this card.

The Ten of Cups represents the kind of happiness you experience when you look at a loved one, child, or pet and realize that you are perfectly, blissfully happy. The trouble with this is that happiness is rarely perfect, and even when it is, it's short-lived. The truth is that perfection is never truly sustainable.

We get glimpses of this pure, untarnished bliss throughout our lives. We snatch it up in tiny sips like the tiniest taste of the most decadent dessert. If we're smart, we savor those sips, but we don't hold on too tight or try too hard to find them because they'll never fill our cup to the top. They're too scarce.

If the Nine of Cups is a delicious, satisfying, heavenly cupcake—fully iced of course; no one would suggest you should be content with an uniced cupcake—then the Ten of Cups is the sprinkles on top. You can eat delicious cupcakes without sprinkles and be happy all your life, and yet it's nice to indulge, occasionally, in that dash of extra sweetness. That's what we're talking about here when we talk about bliss. Like all the tens, the Ten of Cups is extra, and in this case, that means extra happy.

Here's the thing: Chasing bliss is a recipe for dissatisfaction in your life. When you strive for perfect joy, you'll never feel fully content with all the good-enough happiness and contentment in your life. You'll always compare the pleasure of the day-to-day with the unattainable perfection of bliss and feel disappointed.

As a blessing, the Ten of Cups represents a precious and rare time of perfect happiness. Enjoy it while it lasts, but try not to become too attached to it and definitely don't measure the rest of your life against it.

As an obstacle, you may be missing out on life's day-to-day pleasures while you chase an idealized version of happiness that is mostly unattainable. Instead of holding yourself and those around you to an unreachable standard of perfection, settle back into contentment instead. Don't chase bliss—it tastes the sweetest when you wait for it to find you.

Consider what word might work for you if *bliss* doesn't fit the bill. Here are a few other words that you may want to consider:

Delirium

If *bliss* doesn't feel quite right for you, consider using *delirium*. While you can be deliriously happy, you could also just be delirious. This word invites you to enjoy the over-the-top joy of the moment but to make sure you stay connected to reality. Yes, it's perfect happiness … but it could also be an unrealistic expectation, making *delirium* an excellent keyword for the precarious happiness of the Ten of Cups.

Ideal

I like the word *ideal* or *idealized* for the Ten of Cups because it reminds me that the seeming perfection in this card is an ideal but not necessarily attainable reality. The word *ideal* helps you tap into this card's lesson about keeping your expectations realistic.

The Swords, Ace through Ten

The swords suit is the suit of thought. It's about how we think, perceive, and process information about the world and our experiences. Because this suit exists entirely within the realm of the mind, the cards within this suit encompass a lot of difficulty. It's not easy to navigate the mind and the many places our thoughts can take us, but recognizing what is happening with our thoughts can also empower us.

There's an ethereal and intangible quality to the suit of swords. This suit contains doubt, fear, and confusion but also peace. This suit is the quest for self-knowledge. Consider the nature of clouds in the sky and how quickly they can morph and change. That is the nature of the suit of swords.

Ace of Swords: Discovery

My favorite keyword for the Ace of Swords is *discovery*. The definition of *discovery* is the process of becoming aware of a thought or a situation.

Numerologically, the ace is about potential, and in the airy suit of swords—the suit of thought—the ace is all about the seed of a big idea or thought process.

Sometimes, a discovery is something we find while searching for an answer. In this case, the Ace of Swords can represent the ah-ha moment of figuring something out. Other times, a discovery is something you happen upon that sets off a domino effect of thoughts and choices that take you to some more significant revelation.

In the RWS tarot, a glowing hand emerges from gray clouds to offer a shining silver sword that pierces a golden crown from which hangs a palm branch and olive branch.

There's a triumphant feel to the Ace of Swords. It's reminiscent of the exhilarating feeling of having a big realization, epiphany, or, as I like to call it, a clue-by-four because of how it seems to hit you upside the head.

The discovery is the truth. It's undeniable.

The moment of clarity you discover in the Ace of Swords is pure and uncluttered by competing ideas, fears, and doubts. Within that discovery lies the entirety of the journey to come. Remember that the ace contains the rest of the suit within it. Because of that, you know that there is more than meets the eye in this moment of truth.

As a blessing, this card confirms that what you think is true is true. You've discovered new information and have the clarity you didn't have before. Knowledge is power.

As an obstacle, you may have uncovered something you wish you didn't and might be tempted to ignore the truth or convince yourself you're wrong. Try not to give in to that impulse. It's a futile effort. You cannot unknow what you now know.

There is a heaviness to the Ace of Swords. With knowledge comes responsibility. You can't pretend you don't know what you now know—and that's a big responsibility.

I love the word *discovery* for the Ace of Swords because it makes me think about how it feels to be suddenly faced with truth, clarity, or knowledge about something. It's like a light bulb suddenly goes off, and we now understand.

Consider what word might work for you if *discovery* doesn't fit the bill. Here are a few other words that you may want to consider:

Idea

You have a new idea, or you've come around to a new way of thinking about an old idea when you encounter the Ace of Swords. The word *idea* works well for this card.

Clarity

The Ace of Swords is about how truth brings clarity to whatever situation we find ourselves in, which makes *clarity* an excellent keyword for this card.

Two of Swords: Indecision

My favorite keyword for the Two of Swords is *indecision*. The definition of *indecision* is to be stuck wavering between two or more options.

Numerologically, the two is about choice, and in the swords suit—the suit of thought—the Two of Swords is all about what goes on in the mind when trying to make a decision, particularly a difficult one.

The Two of Swords is the card that represents that quintessential concept of being stuck between a rock and a hard place. It's not clear what the right decision is. When this card comes up, there's a good chance neither option feels right.

In the RWS tarot, you see a woman seated on a stone stool before a restless sea dotted with stones. She is blindfolded and wearing a long gray gown, almost the same color as the stone she is sitting on. Her arms are crossed over her heart as she rests two long swords against her shoulders.

The Two of Swords is so relatable. Most of us have experienced the discomfort of trying to make a choice when neither option feels right. It always strikes me how frozen the person in this card appears to be—as if the tiniest twitch would tip her into one decision or the other.

Beneath her calm countenance, this woman's mind is agitated as her thoughts race, considering the pros and cons of either choice. All her mental energy is being spent on trying to figure out the best way out of the conundrum she's found herself in. The way she crosses her arms over her heart reminds me of someone who is trying to protect themselves. Perhaps she is guarding her heart from other people's opinions or advice so she can hear herself think.

It's as if she knows that she won't be able to make this decision until she can be still and quiet enough to hear her own inner voice. There's a call back to the High Priestess in all the twos of the tarot, but this is the card where it is the most obvious. The blindfold is a reminder that the answer lies within.

As a blessing, the Two of Swords shows up to remind you that, even though none of your options seem particularly pleasant, there is a part of you that knows the right move to make. You may be hesitating to trust yourself, but you are trustworthy. No decision is perfect, but the decision you make from your heart is the right one. Tune out all the voices in your head that are not your own and listen to your heart. Then trust yourself and make your choice.

As an obstacle, the Two of Swords highlights your immobility. You're trying so hard to avoid making a mistake that you're doing nothing. You might also be spending too much energy listening to other people and ignoring your own inner voice. You can't go on this way forever—it's time to make a choice.

What trips us up with the Two of Swords is that we feel torn between this or that, option A or option B. Remember that sometimes the best choice is option C.

I love the word *indecision* for the Two of Swords because that word homes in on the feeling of needing to make a decision but thinking that you're incapable of making the call. It highlights the insecurity and stuckness of the moment, which I find helpful in interpreting this card in a reading.

Consider what word might work for you if *indecision* doesn't fit the bill. Here are a few other words that you may want to consider:

Self-Doubt

When you trust yourself, decisions are much more manageable. The reason the Two of Swords presents a dilemma is because you doubt yourself, either your abilities or your instincts. *Self-doubt* is a fantastic keyword for this card.

Stuck

The Two of Swords is immobile. You're frozen in place, unable or unwilling to move forward because to do so represents making a decision or picking a side. You're stuck when this card comes up, so *stuck* works well as a keyword for this card.

Three of Swords: Reckoning

My favorite keyword for the Three of Swords is *reckoning*. To reckon with something is to face the reality of how something has impacted you and to process and integrate the lessons from that experience.

Numerologically, the three is about growth, and in the suit of thought, that growth is a burst of personal and mental development brought about through a painful or heartbreaking experience.

While unfortunate, we learn the most from life's biggest disappointments, mistakes, and hurts. When we reckon with those difficult experiences, we can learn powerful lessons about ourselves, others, and life.

In the RWS tarot, you see a gray and stormy sky streaked with rain. In the foreground is a simple red heart pierced by three swords.

The Three of Swords is contentious among tarot readers because the image immediately makes one think of heartbreak, and what does heartbreak, an emotional experience, have to do with the suit of thought or the growth usually depicted by the number three? Some readers ignore the card's symbology and read this card numerologically as the growth of the mind. Others choose to ignore the elemental association of the suit with the mind and instead focus on the emotional experience of heartbreak and betrayal that the swords stabbing through the heart make them think of.

I, however, want to have my cake and eat it, too. Both things could be true. This card could represent heartbreak, betrayal, or disappointment—and still be about what's going on in your mind. All I had to consider was what those experiences were like. When you're hurt in a way that involves your feelings, your emotions (typically the realm of the suit of cups), you have the initial feeling about it. What follows is what you think about it—and what you learn from it. That is the reckoning that the Three of Swords represents.

As a blessing, the Three of Swords is a lesson you are learning the hard way. Though you've been through a difficult or painful experience, there's an opportunity here, so don't squander it. Dust yourself off, recognize what you can take away from this challenging experience, and take stock of what you've learned or how you've grown.

As an obstacle, the Three of Swords can indicate that you're so focused on the pain and emotions of the experience that you can't see the light at the end of the tunnel. You risk losing yourself to the emotions instead of learning from what occurred.

Think of the last time you felt hurt, betrayed, or stabbed through the heart. Did you learn something from that experience? I'll go out on a limb and say yes, you did. That's what the Three of Swords represents. It's the lesson learned from the experience.

I love the word *reckoning* for the Three of Swords because it bridges the gap between the two most common ways to interpret the card.

Consider what word might work for you if *reckoning* doesn't fit the bill. Here are a few other words that you may want to consider:

Heartbreak

The word *heartbreak* works well as a keyword for the Three of Swords—as long as you remember to tie this meaning back into the mental processes associated with that heartbreak. It might be easiest to remember this keyword, as it closely aligns with the card's imagery.

Lesson

The Three of Swords asks you to recognize and acknowledge something painful but true so that you can grow. The word *lesson* can help connect you with the process of understanding and growth from difficult experiences.

Four of Swords: Respite

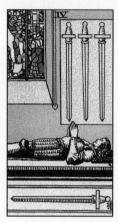

My favorite keyword for the Four of Swords is *respite*. The definition of *respite* is a pause or break, relief from something difficult or unpleasant.

Numerologically, the four is about stability, and in the suit of thought, the Four of Swords is about experiencing a moment of stability or calm in the mind.

The Four of Swords signifies that "I need a break!" energy. It's what you need when life has been kicking your butt up one side and down the other or you've been surrounded by chaos, drama, or conflict.

In the RWS tarot, you see a man who seems to be cast in stone on a flat stone surface. It seems as though he is a part of the statuary, or perhaps we are looking at a tomb. A horizontal sword is engraved on the side of the stone structure, and three other swords hang on the wall. To the left is a stained glass window that shows a religious figure with a halo granting a blessing to a supplicant.

Some time ago, I discovered in my studies that there is a fun little Easter egg in the Four of Swords. In the stained glass window, the golden halo on the spiritual figure contains three letters: *PAX*. *Pax* is Latin for peace. The supplicants are being granted a blessing of peace. This card offers a moment of peace, rest, and recovery, a respite from the mental turmoil of the cards that come both before and after the Four of Swords.

The way I like to describe what you see happening on the Four of Swords is that this person, a knight, has stepped away from an ongoing battle or campaign to rest and recover his mental and physical energy before re-engaging once again. It's a pause in the action. It's a moment to get clear and to get your wits about you.

As a blessing, the Four of Swords confirms that for now the realm of the mind is stable and calm. It's time to relax. You may be tempted to push ahead, but you will get more accomplished in the long run if you're well rested. While you take some time to clear your mind and recover your energy, remember to stay present. It could be easy to let your much-needed rest morph into avoidance.

As an obstacle, the Four of Swords can indicate that you're pushing yourself too hard and not resting when you know you should be, in which case: be careful. Life has a funny way of making you take a break if you refuse to take one on your own. On the other hand, the Four of Swords can suggest that you're resting a little too long, delaying your return to your responsibilities. It feels wonderful to step away from chaos or conflict, but make sure you're not sticking your head in the sand if you know it's time to return to the battle of your day-to-day life.

The Four of Swords is a calm and pleasant card, but it also comes with a warning. If you neglect to take a necessary mental or physical break, circumstances will line up to force you to take one anyway. The Four of Swords can come up when both your body and your mind need to rest. This card can indicate a period of healing.

I love the word *respite* for the Four of Swords because it reminds me that this is a pause, not a complete stop. If it were sleep, the Four of Swords would be a nap. It's essential to take advantage of the opportunity to rest and recover, but it is equally essential to ensure that rest doesn't become procrastination.

Consider what word might work for you if *respite* doesn't fit the bill. Here are a few other words that you may want to consider:

Recovery

The Four of Swords, especially as it comes right after the incredible difficulty of the three, is certainly a period of recovery and healing, which makes *recovery* well suited as a keyword for this card.

Peace

This card represents a time of peace. Since the word *peace* in Latin is placed intentionally in the artwork of the original RWS tarot, you can be confident that this is a well-aligned keyword for the card.

Five of Swords: Tyranny

I love the word *tyranny* for the Five of Swords. The definition of *tyranny* is the cruel or unreasonable use of power.

Numerologically, the five is about disruption, and in the suit of thought, the disruption represented by the Five of Swords is happening in the mind as a result of a battle that's likely not been a fair one.

In the RWS tarot, you see a young man sneering at the bowed heads of his defeated comrades as he holds three of the five swords, the other two at his feet. Stormy gray clouds streak across the sky.

The person in the foreground of this card is being a jerk. You can see it in the look on his face. He knows that he cheated or used unnecessary force to win the battle. The people in the background are beaten down and defeated, likely feeling terrible.

There's a sense of failure and defeat for the losing party and nothing but a shallow victory for the winner. But what does this have to do with the suit of thought? Mentally, we pay a heavy price when we don't play fair. Guilt, regret, or fear plagues the mind instead of the pride that comes with winning a fair fight. When we're defeated, especially by someone who used their power inappropriately to beat us, we can feel unworthy, self-conscious, weak, or helpless.

Nobody wins in the Five of Swords, even though it looks like someone does.

Whether you identify with the winner or the losers in the battle depicted in the Five of Swords, you've paid a heavy price.

If you've won, ask yourself what price you paid to win. Perhaps you didn't consider how your actions would impact those you defeated. Or maybe you cut corners or betrayed your morals or ethics to come out on top. If that's the case, you should course correct, and soon.

If you were defeated, ask yourself if you lost fair and square or if someone took advantage of your kindness or trust to win. It's important to learn from the experience and to hold yourself accountable for mistakes you've made. It's equally important that you don't take responsibility for others' misuse of power or their errors in judgment.

As a blessing, the Five of Swords is a tainted one at best. You may have won the battle, but at what cost? If you haven't played fair, there is an opportunity to make amends. If you've lost, you'll get back up again, but you risk becoming jaded and untrusting. You don't have to let this be the event that defines you or your life going forward. You have the power to do things differently next time. Remember the Three of Swords and learn what you can from this experience.

As an obstacle, the Five of Swords warns that your focus is in the wrong place. If you're the winner, you've won by only thinking of yourself and what you want without consideration for others, and now you have to decide what to do about that. If you're the loser, you're focusing too much on feeling sorry for yourself rather than figuring out what is next for you and need to shift your focus.

The Five of Swords is an unpleasant card, no matter how you look at it. The trick with this card is not to let it become who you are. Pick yourself up or drop those extra swords you don't need and begin again.

I love the word *tyranny* for the Five of Swords because, in this card, whoever wins without considering the cost to others is a tyrant. Humans are flawed. Sometimes, we behave in selfish, harmful ways. Occasionally, we're the recipients of selfish, harmful behavior. That's what this card is all about.

Consider what word might work for you if *tyranny* doesn't fit the bill. Here are a few other words that you may want to consider:

Defeat

Some readers prefer to focus on either the characters in the back or the one in the front. If you prefer to narrow down the focus of this card to the ones who have been defeated, then the word *defeat* is an excellent one to work with.

Selfishness

If you prefer to focus on the poorly behaved person in the foreground, *selfishness* can make an excellent keyword for the Five of Swords. The person in the foreground cared more about winning than anything else. What is more selfish than that?

Six of Swords: Escape

For the Six of Swords, my favorite keyword is *escape*. To escape is to get away from something or to break free.

Numerologically, the six is about harmony, and in the suit of thought, the Six of Swords is about finding a point of balance or harmony after the experience of the five.

The Six of Swords is when you choose to turn your back on the drama of the five.

In the RWS tarot, you see a person standing and rowing a boat, ferrying two vulnerable passengers: a cloaked person who is elderly or unwell and a small child. Six swords sit in the boat as well. The water behind the boat is rough, and the water ahead is smooth. Some small tranquil islands are visible.

This card reminds me of the old Calgon commercials: "Calgon, take me away!" If you know, you know. At its core, the energy of the Six of Swords is one of getting the heck out of Dodge, either by putting the drama behind you or by choosing to turn your mind and your attention away from the rough time you've been through and to focus on a smoother, better future.

I find it interesting that the swords are in the boat—point down, no less. I don't know about you, but if I'm in a boat, I don't want sharp, pointy things stuck into the bottom of it. That seems like a sure way to sink. And that's exactly the point (forgive the pun) of the card. You are getting out of a bad situation, but you might be bringing baggage along with you that could sink the boat if you're not careful. You'll travel more lightly and get where you're going quicker and without any surprise leaks in your boat if you leave those swords behind.

As a blessing, the Six of Swords is the sign that you are putting some discomfort behind you, and as you do, you're changing your way of thinking. You're not going to let anyone hold you back from learning and growing. This card could also indicate an opportunity to escape from the everyday stresses of life by taking a vacation or engaging in a pleasant activity as a bit of a palate cleanser for your life. Either way, there are smoother waters ahead.

As an obstacle, the Six of Swords could be warning you that you're bringing a little too much extra baggage with you as you get out of this situation. Time to do a baggage check. If you are carrying a few too many souvenirs from recent unpleasantness, consider chucking them overboard so you don't set yourself up for a repeat occurrence of the very thing you're escaping from.

I love the word *escape* for the Six of Swords because it conveys that you're getting away from one experience or way of thinking and heading toward something new and better. This type of change and growth can only happen when you leave behind what doesn't serve your greater good. In a literal sense, the Six of Swords can also indicate physical movement over water or vacationing, which is another way to think of escape.

Consider what word might work for you if *escape* doesn't fit the bill. Here are a few other words that you may want to consider:

Transition

The Six of Swords represents movement from one state to another, which is the essential meaning of *transition*. The word *transition* might also be more expansive and more neutral than *escape*.

Healing

This card represents mental healing and processing of difficult situations, so *healing* works well as a keyword for this card and ties in nicely to the idea that things are improving.

Seven of Swords: Rebellion

My favorite keyword for the Seven of Swords is *rebellion*. To rebel is to resist or defy the current status quo.

Numerologically, the seven presents a predicament, and in the suit of thought, the Seven of Swords presents the predicament of being faced with a person, possibly yourself, who is not following the rules.

I like to call the Seven of Swords the "sneaky sneak card" because it often seems someone is doing something they shouldn't be—something they could get in trouble for and that they'd likely prefer they not be caught doing. However, this card can also represent our assumptions. Sometimes, our eyes or our minds deceive us and not the people we're observing or interacting with. Therefore, the warning of this card is to be wary of making assumptions. That evidence might be circumstantial.

In the RWS tarot, you see a young man clutching five swords close to his body while he looks over his shoulder at the camp he seems to be running from. Two swords remain stuck in the ground. Those two remaining swords often catch my eye when I draw this card. Seems like he left some evidence of his actions behind. Oops.

At its core, the Seven of Swords is about breaking the rules, whether one's intentions are honorable or dishonorable. It's easy to make assumptions about the image or the person involved and assume ill intent. You might be right; they might be up to no good. But there could also be more to the story.

The word *rebellion* gets to the heart of the meaning of this card. The person who decides to push back against the status quo is definitely a rebel. Thieves are rebels. But so are activists, revolutionaries, entrepreneurs, whistleblowers, outlaws, artists, and—let's be honest—most teenagers. While it certainly appears that someone is sneaking around or stealing, there could be more going on than meets the eye here. The Seven of Swords signifies that someone is behaving in a way that is not in alignment with what society expects of them. It could be that they're doing something underhanded. However, it could also be that they are taking some sort of empowered action.

As a blessing, the Seven of Swords may be indicating that the time has come for you to step outside what is expected from you, buck the system, and take inspired action. It could also indicate that someone's intentions are better than you think. What you see is not necessarily the truth. Ask questions and avoid the temptation to make assumptions.

As an obstacle, the Seven of Swords could indicate that you're sabotaging yourself. Watch out for the temptation to behave in dishonorable or unethical ways. It could indicate that someone doesn't have your best interests at heart. It can also indicate that you're the one who is behaving in ways that would not be considered socially or morally acceptable. If that's the case, make sure the prize is worth the cost.

The word *rebellion* works well for the Seven of Swords because it reminds us that the Seven of Swords is about someone who is not behaving the way someone or society says they are supposed to, and while it could be deceptive or dishonorable behavior, there could be more to the story than what we see at first glance.

Consider what word might work for you if *rebellion* doesn't fit the bill. Here are a few other words that you may want to consider:

Assumptions

I like the word *assumptions* for the Seven of Swords because assumptions can be true or untrue. When we make assumptions, there is always the chance to get it wrong, and this word reminds us that if we are in doubt, we should probably get an outside opinion or ask an important question.

Deception

I used the word *deception* for a long time for this card. It works well because deception can be about another person deceiving you, your eyes deceiving you, or a situation or society deceiving you—all of which work well for the Seven of Swords.

Eight of Swords: Overwhelm

I love the word *overwhelm* for the Eight of Swords. To be overwhelmed is to be overcome by thoughts or feelings.

Numerologically, the eight is about discipline, and in the suit of thought, the Eight of Swords shows us what happens when our thoughts become undisciplined, keeping us from focusing on the careful consideration of our options.

In the RWS tarot, you see a woman in a long red gown, loosely bound with wide ribbon or fabric, and with her hands behind her back and a blindfold covering her eyes. Eight swords are stuck into the ground around her, creating a sense of enclosure—except there seem to be no swords directly in front of her. She seems to be standing in some muddy water.

What often stands out to me about the RWS Eight of Swords is that there is a clear and easy escape route. It's apparent that this woman could quickly and easily free herself, but she doesn't, which begs the question: Why doesn't she?

The answer is simple: she doesn't know that she can.

The eight swords clustered around the woman in this card each represent an idea, an opinion, a thought, a possible way forward. There are so many swords that the woman in this card remains stuck in her situation, seemingly surrendering to the onslaught of thoughts, opinions, or perspectives.

This card visually captures the concept of being unable to see the forest for the trees. When we are in an Eight of Swords situation, we're so focused on all the tiny details—and so overwhelmed by them—that we feel unable to move forward. That's why I call this card the "analysis paralysis card" because it so beautifully illustrates that concept. We can't seem to think our way out of the trap we've found ourselves in, either because we're giving others' opinions or suggestions far too much weight or because we simply are overthinking our situation.

In truth, we have the power to change our circumstances. We simply need to shed the ties that bind us, rip off that blindfold, and look at what is in front of us. We need to look at the big picture.

I find it interesting that in the RWS version of this card the woman wears a red gown. Red is a color we associate with strength and sovereignty in the tarot. It feels like a nod to the Emperor card. It tells us that she has the power to change her circumstances. She only needs to believe in herself!

As a blessing, the Eight of Swords is a reminder of your power. Sure, this situation is overwhelming, but you don't have to stay stuck here. You can get yourself out of this, so take off that blindfold and look at the big picture. Find the gap between the swords and get the heck out of there.

As an obstacle, the Eight of Swords lets you know that you're spinning your wheels because you're too focused on all the details, or you're paying too much attention to other people's opinions and advice. You need to stop trying to make everything work, attempting to please everyone, or accommodating every thought and idea. Stop surrendering to overwhelm. Get focused so you can find a clear path forward that works for you.

I love the word *overwhelm* for this card because, when it comes to the realm of the mind, we often feel more paralyzed when we have too many options than when we don't have enough. It's like what you felt in the Two of Swords—quadrupled.

Consider what word might work for you if *overwhelm* doesn't fit the bill. Here are a few other words that you may want to consider:

Restriction

When you feel like no move is correct and that you're trapped right where you are, that is the feeling of the Eight of Swords. *Restriction* is a good word for how the Eight of Swords can feel like your thoughts are closing in on you.

Trapped

The word *trapped* works well for the Eight of Swords. It certainly can feel as though there's no where you can turn without ending up right back where you are.

Nine of Swords: Anxiety

Anxiety has been my go-to word for the Nine of Swords for as long as I can remember. Anxiety is the experience of being painfully fearful or uncomfortable about anticipated unpleasantness.

Numerologically, the nine is about fulfillment, and in the suit of thought, we find ourselves blocked from personal fulfillment, rest, and peace because of our fears.

In the RWS tarot, you see a person sitting up in bed, burying their face in their hands. Nine swords hang horizontally beside and above them, creating a barrier between them and the blackness in the background. The bed has a carving of two people locked in a battle, and the quilt on the bed is a checkerboard pattern of red roses on yellow and astrological glyphs.

This card represents the kind of fear and anxiety that wakes us up in the middle of the night or keeps us from falling asleep in the first place. Fear presses down on us like the oppressive blackness in the background of this card and prevents us from getting anything done or even getting a good night's sleep.

The nine swords that hang overhead in this image represent the way that our fears and worries weigh down over us. Another way to look at these swords is that they are representations of the truth that protects us from the blackness of our fears. Either way, this is a deeply unsettling card.

In the Nine of Swords, your fearful thoughts run the show, filling your mind with what might go wrong and keeping you from any sense of peace.

As a blessing, the Nine of Swords reminds you that your fears are unfounded. Whatever you're afraid of is a product of the mind, not reality. Soothe your troubled mind by reminding yourself of your ability to navigate difficult situations. You will find a way through.

As an obstacle, the Nine of Swords indicates that you are caught in an unhealthy cycle of fear that is disrupting your peace. Don't dismiss your fear—it's warning you about something you need to pay attention to—but stop letting it rule you.

The word *anxiety*, for me, perfectly describes the feeling of the Nine of Swords because it taps into the idea that what we are experiencing is fearful thoughts, not necessarily true thoughts or accurate representations of reality.

Consider what word might work for you if *anxiety* doesn't fit the bill. Here are a few other words that you may want to consider:

Worry

Anxiety may feel a little too clinical or specific, in which case *worry* is a great word to use to convey a similar meaning, perhaps softened a bit, for this card.

Fear

You could also use *fear* as a keyword for the Nine of Swords. The word *fear* can give you more flexibility. When this card comes up, fear is undoubtedly at play, whether or not that fear is founded.

Ten of Swords: Finality

For the Ten of Swords, my favorite keyword is *finality*. The definition of *finality* is an ending that cannot be altered or undone.

Numerologically, the ten is about realization, and in the suit of thought, you've realized that you've hit rock bottom and can go no further in actuality or with a particular idea or train of thought. It's the end.

In the RWS tarot, you see a man lying face down in the dirt, the back of his body stabbed with ten swords. The sky is black, but the sun is rising. His red cloak drapes over him, blending in with the blood pouring out onto the earth from his wounds.

Well, this is a dramatic scene, now isn't it?

This card is so intensely over-the-top that I have to admit I get foot-stomping tantrum vibes over it. Not only have you reached a point where you can go no further, but you have lots of thoughts and opinions about how awful everything is. It's a good bet that anyone in your vicinity knows how you feel about it.

This card seems to illustrate someone or something's death. One sword would have done the trick, yet here there are ten. Talk about overkill.

But wait! What's going on with this guy's right hand?! That's the question I found myself asking while writing this book. I'd never noticed it before, but his visible hand is formed into what appears to be a very intentional shape: two fingers extended, thumb curled in. The Hierophant holds his hand in a similar position as a symbol of blessing. To me, this is the evidence we need that not ALL is lost in the Ten of Swords.

While the Ten of Swords is a very final card, it's important to remember that the end of something isn't the end of everything. The sun is rising. There's something new around the corner. Instead of giving in to despair and making the situation worse by dramatizing an already difficult moment, maybe you should pluck those swords out of your back, get up, and decide which way you will go.

As a blessing, there is hope despite the difficulty. This situation is still terrible, but you're being reminded to focus on the sunrise and what comes next. There is a new beginning on the horizon. You will find peace. It may just take a little time.

As an obstacle, the Ten of Swords is confirmation that you've come as far as you can and can go no further. You can kick and scream all you want, but it's over. You're entitled to have your feelings about that, but you're spending too much energy lamenting about something you can't change. Work on acceptance so that you can use that energy to focus on the future instead.

The word *finality* works well because it describes the absolute end that this card depicts. There is no negotiating. There is no redo. There is only: do something else.

Consider what word might work for you if *finality* doesn't fit the bill. Here are a few other words that you may want to consider:

Wallow

The Ten of Swords is about more than the thing that ended. It's about the way we respond to the thing ending. It can speak to how we curl up in defeat, convinced that this one thing ending means there's no point to anything.

To wallow is to choose helplessness over empowered action, which is what is often going on in the Ten of Swords. That is why *wallow* can work so well as a keyword for this card.

Betrayal

It's hard to ignore this card's "stabbed in the back" visual. Ten swords in the back is a powerful symbol for betrayal, which makes *betrayal* an effective keyword for this card. This card can also be about how you betray yourself when you surrender to the feeling of defeat and refuse to get up and start again.

The Pentacles, Ace through Ten

The pentacles suit is the suit of resources. It's finances, physical energy, health, and other tangible and intangible ways we maintain our lives and livelihood. There's a stable, grounded energy to the entire suit. It's full of work, responsibility, and the pressure of the quest for success. This suit represents how we use, spend, and share our resources. It speaks to how we handle responsibility and build skills. Consider the nature of the earth and how sturdy and reliable it is. That is the nature of the suit of pentacles.

Ace of Pentacles: Opportunity

My favorite keyword for the Ace of Pentacles is *opportunity*. The definition of *opportunity* is a favorable condition or set of circumstances that make it possible to do something.

Numerologically, the ace is about potential. In the earthly suit of resources, the Ace of Pentacles is about the potential for advancement and success that can lead to increased resources.

In the RWS tarot, a glowing hand emerges from gray clouds to offer a sizable golden coin engraved with a pentacle. Below the hand is a beautiful garden adorned with roses and lilies.

Hey, wait a second. Didn't the Magician also have roses and lilies around him? Why, yes. Yes, he did. Since I'm confident that Pamela Colman Smith put everything on the card for a reason, I can't shake the feeling that the opportunity presented in the Ace of Pentacles is something you can manifest for yourself (or perhaps already have).

It's easy to look at the opportunity that the Ace of Pentacles refers to as something like luck, but those roses and lilies are there to remind you that while luck may have played a part, so have your own efforts. It's you who laid the groundwork for this opportunity. Give yourself some credit!

As a blessing, the Ace of Pentacles is like a door opening to a golden shining light. This could be a chance to learn a new skill, pursue a new job prospect, start a business, tackle a new project, or any other kind of opportunity that could result in more physical or energetic resources for yourself. Say yes.

As an obstacle, an opportunity is slipping through your fingers. You may be distracted, careless, or so afraid of success or change that you are subconsciously self-sabotaging whatever threatens your comfort.

The Ace of Pentacles is usually a positive card full of potential. Good things await you if you are open to them.

I love the word *opportunity* for the Ace of Pentacles because it reminds me of job offers, promotions, investments paying off, receiving unexpected help to move a project forward, and other doors that open.

Consider what word might work for you if *opportunity* doesn't fit the bill. Here are a few other words that you may want to consider:

Ambition

Ambition works for the Ace of Pentacles because the acts of an ambitious person often preclude new opportunities. This keyword implies that you are opening your own doors and are focused on the opportunities that come your way.

Solidity

The Ace of Pentacles is also about the opening of the kinds of doors that promise comfort and solidity, a chance to feel solid ground beneath you, metaphorically speaking, which makes *solidity* a word that works great for this card.

Two of Pentacles: Priorities

My favorite keyword for the Two of Pentacles is *priorities*. The definition of a priority is something that is more important than other things or should go first.

Numerologically, the two is about choice. In the earthly suit of resources, the Two of Pentacles is about needing to choose what you will prioritize.

In the RWS tarot, you see a person who appears to be on a stage, juggling or balancing two golden pentacles using a ribbon shaped like a figure eight (also known as a lemniscate). In the background, you see ships being tossed about on big waves.

There's a precarity to the Two of Pentacles. You get the idea that one wrong move and one or both pentacles will crash to the ground. Not only is the person in this card trying to keep the pentacles moving, but they appear to be trying to dance or balance on one foot simultaneously. It's a lot to keep track of—maybe too much. It's a juggling act.

I'm sure that I look like that person in the Two of Pentacles when I'm multitasking, or at least when I think I'm multitasking. In truth, I'm juggling tasks and responsibilities back and forth, choosing what will take priority at any given moment. That's life, though. We have personal responsibilities, professional responsibilities, and a responsibility to look after ourselves, practice self-care, and pursue our hobbies and interests. Those are a lot of balls to try to keep in the air, and the Two of Pentacles highlights exactly that.

As a blessing, this card is like your own personal cheerleader, congratulating you on how well you manage your different responsibilities, but it also warns you that you're likely at capacity and probably shouldn't take on anything else at the moment.

As an obstacle, you are managing for the moment, but there is a high probability that you'll drop something. It might be a good idea to re-evaluate your priorities and see what you can back off on so that you can better manage what is left. Your position is far more precarious than you realize.

The word *priorities* works well for the Two of Pentacles, a card of being in a constant state of juggling where the only thing that keeps your feet on the ground is the ability to decide what needs to come first in any given moment.

Consider what word might work for you if *priorities* doesn't fit the bill. Here are a few other words that you may want to consider:

Balance

While I think of the Two of Pentacles as a card of juggling responsibilities, the word *balance* has a more positive and empowered feel and works well as an expansive keyword for this card. *Balance* recalls the precariousness of this card and the need to walk a fine line to manage all that is on your plate.

Adaptability

When the Two of Pentacles shows up, it's a sure bet that you're good at thinking on your feet and switching focus to ensure you get what you need done. This kind of flexibility is a sign of adaptability, which makes *adaptability* a good choice for the Two of Pentacles.

Three of Pentacles: Collaboration

My favorite keyword for the Three of Pentacles is *collaboration*. The definition of *collaboration* is to work together in a coordinated manner.

Numerologically, the three is about growth. In the earthly suit of resources, the Three of Pentacles is all about work—not working alone but in collaboration with others, where you can grow together by sharing your resources, skills, and efforts to achieve a common goal.

In the RWS tarot, a person with an apron stands on a bench, holding a stonemason's mallet beside a stone archway featuring three pentacles. Beside them, two other individuals hold up what appear to be plans for the arch.

In the Three of Pentacles, you're working hard and growing your skills by practically applying them. You're not doing all this hard work by yourself, though. You have help.

I like that the three people on the card are not all doing the same thing. One person does the stonemasonry work while the other two help by holding up the plans. It's a simple but powerful illustration of collaboration. They all have an equal say in how things go, but their roles differ. It's the working version of the Three of Pentacles. Each person brings unique experience, skills, and personality to the whole.

As a blessing, this card is about recognizing the resources available to you, especially human resources. This is a time to do practical work and get things done by working collaboratively with others. Work to your strengths, but also recognize where you can benefit from the help of others. Teamwork!

As an obstacle, your ego is getting in the way of practical work. You might be thinking your skills are more advanced than they are and could end up biting off more than you can chew. Take a step back and remember there's nothing wrong with admitting you would do better if you had help.

I love the word *collaboration* for the Three of Pentacles because it speaks to the active process of working with others. It lets me know that this card isn't about assigning individual duties to everyone but about working organically together to collectively grow your skills and resources.

Consider what word might work for you if *collaboration* doesn't fit the bill. Here are a few other words that you may want to consider:

Work

At its foundation, the Three of Pentacles is about working to build your resources and skills. With that in mind, the word *work* functions well as a keyword for this card.

Development

The Three of Pentacles is about skill building, whether you work alone or in a group. You are developing skills that will serve your future progress. I am a fan of the word *development* for this card.

Four of Pentacles: Security

My favorite keyword for the Four of Pentacles is *security*. The definition of *security* is to feel protected against theft or loss.

Numerologically, the four is about stability. In the earthly suit of resources, the Four of Pentacles is about holding on tight to the resources you rely on for stability.

In the RWS tarot, you see a man wearing a crown, sitting on a stone seat, clutching a golden pentacle close to his chest. Another pentacle rests on his crown, and two more sit on the ground, each secured by a foot.

The Four of Pentacles is a card about protecting the resources you rely on—perhaps a little too much. You're afraid to risk losing anything, so you hold your resources close to you, where they may not do you much good. Your fear of loss also creates a strong distrust in others, so you isolate yourself.

The thing about working hard to build your resources is that when you finally feel you have enough, you can become so afraid of losing any that you fail to reap the benefits of having built up a sense of security for yourself in the first place. You can be so risk averse that you also prevent the possibility of growing your resources. This is a lot like gathering seeds from the fruits you've harvested but refusing to plant them because you're afraid they might spoil. When you do that, you keep your seeds safe and dry but also prevent the possibility of growing more fruit!

As a blessing, this card lets you know that your hard work has paid off and your resources are stable. You have enough. You may not have everything you want, but you have everything you need, and it is good enough.

As an obstacle, you are being too protective of your resources and it's not necessary. Your overattachment to security is creating walls around you that cut you off from others. This kind of attachment to your security also prevents you from making progress in your life. Progress demands a degree of risk.

I love the word *security* for the Four of Pentacles because security can be interpreted in a wide variety of ways. You can be very secure in a home with ten-foot-high barbed wire fencing, a guard dog, and seven locks on the door. You can be just as secure in a home with a locked door and a dead bolt. Imagining the wide variety of home security options is a helpful way to conceptualize this card.

Consider what word might work for you if *security* doesn't fit the bill. Here are a few other words that you may want to consider:

Greed

Greed may not be my favorite keyword for the Four of Pentacles, but it works well for some readers because it effectively describes what it looks like when you are guarding your resources so fiercely that you're unwilling to share with anyone else.

Caution

A primary theme of the Four of Pentacles is caution. Being cautious is not necessarily bad, but it is certainly possible to be overly cautious, which makes *caution* a great fit.

Five of Pentacles: Hardship

My favorite keyword for the Five of Pentacles is *hardship*. The definition of *hardship* is suffering or poverty.

Numerologically, the five is about disruption. In the earthly suit of resources, the Five of Pentacles is about a resource loss, representing a material disruption in our lives.

In the RWS tarot, you see a wounded woman and a disabled man outside in the snow. Both feel underdressed for the harsh winter conditions and what clothes they do wear are shabby. One person looks down at their feet as they walk, and the other looks toward the foreground. Neither seems to notice they are walking by a well-lit stained glass window decorated with five pentacles that could indicate a welcoming sanctuary is close.

The Five of Pentacles shows what happens when we lose resources. When you experience the loss of your material resources, you might have difficulty taking care of your basic needs like food, shelter, or health care. Your health is also a resource, and when life kicks your butt health wise, you will struggle to take care of your needs. You may feel isolated and alone.

Often, when we experience a loss of resources, we can feel suddenly powerless and alone because we don't feel worthy of having what we once did. There's an ego hit that accompanies loss, even when that loss is through no fault of our own. Too often in society, we value people for what they can do or what they have. When either is compromised, you can feel like you don't have value. That response of our ego also cuts us off from the same people and situations that could offer us solace or assistance if we let them.

In most Five of Pentacles cards, you'll see a hint that help of some kind is readily available to the people in the card who seem to be suffering, and yet they don't see it. This is much like the Five of Cups, where we're so lost in our grief and sadness over the emotional loss we've experienced that we don't see the two cups that remain upright.

As a blessing, the card's emphasis is on the aid being offered to you. Your situation isn't easy, but all you need to do is admit you need a helping hand and help will be there for you. Things are going to be okay. Reach for hope.

As an obstacle, you're stuck in a lack mindset. You assume things will never improve, and if you continue to behave as if that's true, things won't improve. This situation is temporary—unless your refusal to seek help or access nearby resources makes it permanent.

The word *hardship* works well for me for the Five of Pentacles because, in life, we experience all kinds of hardships. They aren't always material or tangible, but they can be, and this word is flexible enough to allow for that.

Consider what word might work for you if *hardship* doesn't fit the bill. Here are a few other words that you may want to consider:

Loss
You've experienced a loss of resources in the Five of Pentacles. The word *loss* works exceptionally well if you look at resources primarily financially, as the Five of Pentacles speaks to material loss, not necessarily emotional or mental upset.

Isolation
There is a feeling of being outcast, shut out, or left out in the Five of Pentacles. *Isolation* can be a good keyword to work with if you want to focus more on the ways that hardship isolates you from others.

Six of Pentacles: Reciprocity

My favorite keyword for the Six of Pentacles is *reciprocity*. Reciprocity is a state of giving and taking equally.

Numerologically, the six is about harmony. In the earthly suit of resources, the Six of Pentacles brings harmony between those whose resources overflow and those who don't have enough. This harmony is brought about through intentional acts of generosity and reciprocity.

In the RWS tarot, you see a well-dressed man, holding a scale, dropping coins into the outstretched hands of people in need. Six pentacles are shown at the top of the card: one in the center, three on the left, and two on the right.

The Six of Pentacles is about the redistribution of resources. Balance and harmony are achieved when those who have more offer help to those who have less. This requires cooperation from both the giver and the receiver. The giver provides and the receiver accepts. When everyone participates consciously with this process, everyone wins.

As a blessing, the Six of Pentacles indicates that you are successful in life and have more than enough. You've worked hard to get to this point, but it's very likely that you also had support or assistance along the way from others who shared their resources, knowledge, or skills. Now, it's your turn to pay it forward.

As an obstacle, the Six of Pentacles gently points out that you may be struggling and suggests you consider being willing to accept the help offered, which can be difficult when you want to do it all yourself. Remember that if you receive help now, you'll be better positioned to help others in the future. Don't let your pride get in the way of a chance for improvement.

The word *reciprocity* works well for me for the Six of Pentacles because it highlights the cyclical nature of give and take. We receive, but we also give. We give, but we also receive.

Consider what word might work for you if *reciprocity* doesn't fit the bill. Here are a few other words that you may want to consider:

Generosity

A common word for the Six of Pentacles is *generosity*. The Six of Pentacles highlights your relationship with generosity and how you handle being on either the giving or receiving side of the experience.

Sharing

Sharing is a keyword that works well if you'd like to move away from the more material aspect of this card and, instead, focus on the broader implication of sharing knowledge and skills or other gifts—or having them shared with you.

Seven of Pentacles: Evaluation

My favorite keyword for the Seven of Pentacles is *evaluation*. To evaluate something is to determine the value or significance of something.

Numerologically, the seven is about predicaments. In the earthly suit of resources, the predicament you are in is that you are at a point in your efforts where you don't know whether your endeavors will pay off. You have no choice but to wait to see if the seeds you've planted will bear fruit.

In the RWS tarot, you see a man leaning on a shovel as he evaluates a grapevine with seven pentacles on it. He seems pensive, maybe even a little worried, as he frowns at the state of his grapevines. There's no way to know what type of harvest he will get. All he can do is reflect upon the actions he took to nurture the crop and hope for the best.

There's a tension to the Seven of Pentacles because we are at the point where it's too late to completely change what we're doing, but we also can't yet tell if we're going to be successful. It's like baking a cake. You can measure your ingredients carefully and follow all the directions, but you won't know how it will turn out until it's out of the oven and cooled. While you wait for it to bake, all you can do is mentally go back over the steps you followed in hopes that you can predict the outcome. The Seven of Pentacles perfectly portrays that period of waiting nervously for the results of your efforts. The time to make significant changes has likely already come and gone.

As a blessing, the Seven of Pentacles lets you know that you have done all you can to ensure an excellent result! Trust what you've done so far and try not to hover too closely over the outcome. The parts of this process you have control over are in the past. Believe in yourself and let time do its thing.

As an obstacle, the Seven of Pentacles warns that you are creating unnecessary stress by worrying about things you can no longer change. Everything may be fine, and you're worrying for nothing. If you know you made mistakes, learn from them to ensure a better outcome if you need to start over. Otherwise, have confidence in the steps you've taken so far.

The word *evaluation* functions well for the Seven of Pentacles because it reminds me of what it feels like to critique the work you've done until this point. The evaluation stage that this word signifies is a necessary part of improving your skills, but that doesn't mean it's easy or comfortable.

Consider what word might work for you if *evaluation* doesn't fit the bill. Here are a few other words that you may want to consider:

Waiting

The Seven of Pentacles is a card about waiting when you sure wish you didn't have to. There's a conscious release of control with this card that the keyword *waiting* captures well.

Reflection

The Seven of Pentacles often involves reflecting on the past. While you wait to see how events will play out, you reflect on everything you have or haven't done that may have impacted the outcome. That's what makes *reflection* a good keyword for this card.

Eight of Pentacles: Mastery

My favorite keyword for the Eight of Pentacles is *mastery*. Mastery is the quality of being excellent at something.

Numerologically, the eight is about discipline. In the earthly suit of resources, it is discipline that allows you to repeat your efforts over and over again to produce consistent exemplary results.

In the RWS tarot, you see a young man using a hammer and chisel to engrave a pentacle into a golden disk. Seven other completed disks are arranged around him, some displayed on a wooden board and two at his feet.

The Eight of Pentacles speaks to the point in life where you can repeat your successes consistently because you've built the skills you need to succeed and can rely upon those skills. The result is that you can be relied upon to produce superior work or to spend your resources responsibly and effectively.

Mastery is an excellent quality, but it does have its downsides. Being the master of something can sometimes lock you into a path that you don't necessarily want. Additionally, being the master can cause you to become your own worst enemy, as your standards for your work or life can be so strict that even the slightest perceived flaw in your actions or work can cause you to feel like an abject failure.

As a blessing, the Eight of Pentacles acknowledges your expertise. You've worked hard to build your skills and it shows, as you are able to repeat your successes. The mastery you have achieved allows you to be consistent in the caliber of your work, and it may even come quite easily to you. Be careful not to get too comfortable or complacent, though. Even the master can—and should—continue to learn.

As an obstacle, the Eight of Pentacles suggests boredom or monotony. You can be highly skilled in something you take no pleasure in. Consider whether continuing to do the same thing again and again still feels right. Alternatively, this card could indicate you are too hard on yourself. Others may readily see your skills and abilities, but you struggle to see them yourself and may be slipping into a state of perfectionism where nothing you do could possibly be good enough. This can be impostor syndrome or simply an exceptionally pushy inner critic. Either way, it's probably best to get some perspective because you're better than you think.

The word *mastery* is effective for the Eight of Pentacles because it accurately conveys the level of skill being brought to the table. The Eight of Pentacles is sometimes called the journeyman card. I think the reference gets lost sometimes, but in skilled trades, journeymen are people who have passed their tests and logged a great deal of time in their profession. Mastery isn't simply being good at something; it's the state of having proven yourself.

Consider what word might work for you if *mastery* doesn't fit the bill. Here are a few other words that you may want to consider:

Consistency
One of the most significant qualities of the Eight of Pentacles is the ability to repeat your successes. Being consistent is a telltale indicator of mastery, but

it also reminds you that this card is about doing the same thing over and over again. I am a fan of the word *consistency* for this card.

Perfectionism

The problem with becoming highly skilled in something is that you are constantly trying to prove to yourself and others that you know what you're doing and can do it well. *Perfectionism* is an effective keyword for those who see the Eight of Pentacles as the practice of perfecting their work.

Nine of Pentacles: Luxury

My favorite keyword for the Nine of Pentacles is *luxury*. The definition of *luxury* is significant comfort or extravagance.

Numerologically, the nine is about fulfillment. In the earthly suit of resources, fulfillment is the evidence of having reached a point where you can enjoy your resources instead of spending all your time working to acquire them.

In the RWS tarot, a woman stands before a lush trellis or wall with ripe grapes. She rests one hand on one of the nine pentacles that adorn the garden wall while a hooded falcon perches on her other, gloved, hand. The woman in the card has the time and resources to enjoy her life (grapes, wine) and pursue her hobbies (falconry).

The Nine of Pentacles is the card of luxury and attainment. It beautifully illustrates what it is like when you have accumulated enough resources to be able to pursue what fulfills you while remaining comfortable and secure within the home you've built for yourself. There's an ease to this card that represents the hard work that got you here in the first place.

Some readers jokingly read this card as the "treat yourself card." While I don't disagree, it also goes deeper than that. The Nine of Pentacles is about enjoying the resources you've worked hard for, but it's also about feeling safe enough and comfortable enough to put down roots. You don't need to chase more. You have enough. You have enough to feel safe and to stretch your wings.

As a blessing, the Nine of Pentacles confirms an outstanding harvest or yield for your efforts. All your efforts have paid off and the worry of the Seven of Pentacles and the pressure of the Eight of Pentacles are behind you. Allow yourself to enjoy your success.

As an obstacle, the Nine of Pentacles could indicate that you're taking comfort or luxury to a place where it's no longer helpful. Be wary of squandering your resources, taking them for granted, or abandoning all work if you want to hold on to this success and benefit from it for the long term.

The word *luxury* works well for me for the Nine of Pentacles because it makes me think of the point where you have more than enough to relax and enjoy life for a while.

Consider what word might work for you if *luxury* doesn't fit the bill. Here are a few other words that you may want to consider:

Pride

The Nine of Pentacles involves reaching a point where all that work has paid off, and some much-deserved preening is in order! Using *pride* as a keyword reminds you to be proud of your accomplishments but warns you to beware the pitfalls that accompany too much pride.

Indulgence

If the word *luxury* feels too tied to finances or financial success, the word *indulgence* may work better for you. It ties in beautifully with the idea of treating yourself and often describes doing so because it feels as though it's been earned.

Ten of Pentacles: Legacy

My favorite keyword for the Ten of Pentacles is *legacy*. The definition of *legacy* is having something you leave behind to share with future generations, such as an inheritance, knowledge, or a lasting impact.

Numerologically, the ten is about realization. In the earthly suit of resources, there is no greater realization than having enough resources to live securely and comfortably and ensuring the comfort and security of those dear to you.

In the RWS tarot, you see a family. In the center of the card, under a stone archway, a man and woman gaze at each other, a small child at their feet reaching for the tail of one of two dogs you see in the foreground. An elderly man sits in the foreground, patting the other dog on the head. In the distance, there is a large complex featuring towers and tall walls. Ten pentacles overlay this scene.

Three generations are visible on this card, giving the sense that this is a well-established home. The addition of dogs adds a cozy and settled energy to this card. This place has both physical and sentimental roots and is an example of the legacy you leave behind—a loving family, safe and comfortable.

The Ten of Pentacles represents the apex of achievement. While the Nine of Pentacles represents the ability to indulge in one's personal interests and pleasures, the Ten of Pentacles represents the point at which you have secured long-term stability for you and yours. What you've realized in the Ten of Pentacles will continue beyond your lifetime. Whether it's physical resources, like money or a home, or something harder to quantify, like knowledge or skills, you have something you can leave behind for those who come after you. You've established something strong enough to be built on in the future—the strongest of foundations. As with all the tens, the Ten of Pentacles lays the groundwork to return to the ace.

This card isn't only about inheritance. After all, one's legacy isn't only the sum of money you pass on to your beneficiaries—if it's that at all—but rather the mark you leave on the lives of the people you've met. Your legacy is what people will remember you for.

There is a completeness to the Ten of Pentacles. In a way, it represents the result of all four suits of the minor arcana. The inspirations you follow in the suit of wands, the relationships you form in the suit of cups, and the mental growth you experience in the suit of swords all support and enhance the success you achieve in the Ten of Pentacles. Look closely at the Ten of Pentacles and you will see the rewards of a life filled with passion, love, wisdom, and hard-won prosperity. As the last of the numbered minor arcana, it shows the pinnacle of success in all these areas.

As a blessing, the Ten of Pentacles indicates long-lasting achievements and reaching the summit of accomplishment. You have put in time and effort to get to this point. It also suggests that you have accumulated a vast wealth of resources (financial, intellectual, or spiritual) that you can share with others.

As an obstacle, the Ten of Pentacles could suggest that you're counting your chickens before they're hatched. Don't assume success or achievement is guaranteed. This may not be a good time to take unnecessary risks. Your foundations might not be as solid as they seem.

The word *legacy* works well for the Ten of Pentacles because it brings the concept of time to the forefront. This isn't merely achievement but the outward ripple effects of that achievement and how it impacts the people around you.

Consider what word might work for you if *legacy* doesn't fit the bill. Here are a few other words that you may want to consider:

Satisfaction

The word *satisfaction* also works well for the Ten of Pentacles. This cozy card conveys the feeling of laying back in your favorite recliner with a full belly after a wonderful meal with your loved ones. It's not exclusively material security and success. However, it can be the satisfaction of knowing you've built a life for yourself and one you can share and—eventually—pass on to your loved ones.

Home

Home is a great keyword for the Ten of Pentacles because it encompasses the satisfaction and success accompanying this card and provides a helpful analogy for what you might be leaving behind for those who come after you. For loads of people, owning a home is the absolute realization of achievement and security, which makes *home* a memorable keyword for this card.

Getting to Know Your Numbered Minor Arcana Keywords

Now that you have a complete set of numbered minor arcana cards, each labeled with a personal keyword, it's time to put them to work so you can get to know them better.

There's no better way to test-drive your new set of keywords than by practicing doing some readings for yourself (or willing friends and family) with them.

In the following sections, you'll find a few spreads to try out with your marked-up numbered minors. Try each spread a couple of times to see how working with your personal set of keywords feels. If a keyword doesn't hold up throughout these exercises, revisit that card and try a different one. Once you're satisfied with these cards and the keywords you've chosen for them, you're ready to move on to the next chapter!

One-Card Focus Spread

Let's revisit the one-card focus spread. In the major arcana, I suggested you pull a card at the end of your day to reflect on it. For this one-card spread, shuffle and draw a card near the beginning of the day, focusing on something you should keep in mind, focus on, or be aware of for the day ahead.

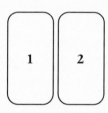

CARD 1: Focus for the day.

Two-Card Situation/Advice Spread

The two-card situation/advice spread is a great one for getting quick insight to help you navigate a situation that has come up, whether good or bad. The first card focuses on providing you more context or information about what is happening. The second card provides advice for the action you should take.

CARD 1: What do I need to know about this situation?
CARD 2: What action should I take?

Three-Card Wants vs. Needs Spread

Sometimes what you want is also what you need, but often that isn't the case. You might want to take a nap but you need to meet a deadline, for example. The three-card wants vs. needs spread is designed to assist you in becoming aware of your current want and need and how to bridge the gap between the two. This is a great spread to pull for a general reading or to apply to a particular predicament in your life.

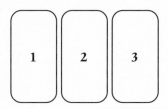

CARD 1: What you want.
CARD 2: What you need.
CARD 3: How to bridge the gap between the two.

Four-Card Life Learning Spread

I really enjoy this fun play on a past/present/future spread. The four-card life learning spread is designed to bring your attention to important lessons from your past and present, give direction on where to focus for the future, and help you integrate all the above.

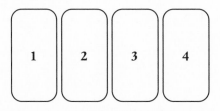

CARD 1: Something you can learn from your past.
CARD 2: Something you can learn from your present.
CARD 3: What you need to learn next.
CARD 4: How to integrate this knowledge.

Chapter 5

The 16 Faces:
The Court Cards

I t's time to meet the sixteen faces, or personalities, of the tarot: the court cards.

Ask anyone who has ever attempted to learn the tarot, and they will tell you that the court cards are the most challenging. It certainly took a long time for me to build a strong connection with each of them.

My breakthrough came when I stopped trying to see them the same way as all the other cards, because they aren't the same, and they aren't interpreted the same way as the majors or the numbered minors.

The court cards' primary function is to represent people and personalities that interact with or influence us. But that's not the only thing they represent. While the face cards of tarot can represent people and personalities, their qualities can apply to aspects of ourselves, aspects of a situation or problem, or other influences. It's this flexibility that can make the court cards feel more difficult to learn.

That is why I have separated them for you in this book.

The Hierarchy of the Court Cards

In the RWS system, there is a rank and order to the court cards.

The page represents the youngest or most inexperienced of the suit. In medieval times, the page would be an apprentice or helper to a knight whose goal was to train, practice, and otherwise prove themselves worthy of knighthood. In their apprentice role, pages were also messengers. In the tarot, pages generally symbolize youth, inexperience, study, messages, and possibilities.

I like to think of them as the Magician of their suit because they contain the potential to step into any or all of the other three court roles as they evolve.

The knight represents the adolescent or young adult energy of the suit. In medieval times, the knight was a warrior and a seeker whose goal was to prove themselves through acts of bravery and adventure. In their action-oriented role, knights were called upon to protect, conquer, and explore for their kingdom. In the tarot, knights symbolize action, intensity, loyalty, bravery, and seeking. I like to think of them as the Chariot of their suit because they know what they want to accomplish and are single-minded in their determination to reach their goals.

The queens represent the mothering energy of the suit. In medieval times, the queen played a significant role in the rulership of the kingdom but also of the home. Queens needed to hold their own among the ruling class while still being present and approachable in the home. It was a demanding role, and only the strongest were suited for it. In the tarot, queens generally symbolize leadership, intuition, receptivity, and softness. I like to think of them as the Empress of their suit because they hold the space of the mother and nurturer of their suit, even if the way they nurture is wildly different for each queen.

The kings represent the fathering energy of the suit. In medieval times, the king was the ruler of the kingdom. Kings needed to decide what was best for their kingdom's prosperity, health, and safety. Good kings could be relied upon to be honest, just, and levelheaded. I like to think of them as the Emperor of their suit because they are the dynamic leaders of their suit and look after the whole of what is within their domain.

You can also look at the court cards elementally. These associations might look different depending on which school of thought you follow.

Pages: Earth

Pages represent the earthly quality of their suits. They work with their suit's energy in a grounded way. One easy way to remember this association is that pages, being youthful, are the closest to the earth in height—presumably. Visually, when you observe the pages in the RWS tarot, you'll note that they all have both feet firmly on the ground.

Knights: Fire

Knights represent the fiery qualities of their suits. They are in motion, pursuing something, and associated with seeking or questing. Knights pursue a goal with single-minded determination, so thinking of a moth to a flame helps me remember their association with fire. When you observe the knights visually in the RWS tarot, you'll notice that each knight wears a hint of red to remind you of their association with fire.

Queens: Water

Queens represent the watery qualities of their suits. They are receptive and powerful, much like water. I find it easy to remember queens as water, but if you want an easy way to remember, think of how waves can rock you gently or shove you around—very much like the queens of the tarot. When you observe the queens visually in the RWS tarot, you'll notice that each queen wears a gown that flows around them like water.

Kings: Air

Kings represent the airy qualities of their suits. They tend to look at the big picture, make big decisions, and look after the kingdom. When I think of looking at the big picture, I think about being able to zoom out or look at something from a high vantage point. The higher you go, the closer you are to the clouds. When you visually observe the kings in the RWS tarot, you'll notice that they sit on disproportionately large thrones, all seeming bigger or higher than others. To make it even easier, the King of Swords and the King of Cups look disproportionately large compared to the landscape around them.

Once you associate each court rank with an element, it's easier to remember their essential qualities.

Try This

Here's a little exercise to prove you know more about the court cards than you think you do already:

1. Take a blank piece of paper and your favorite writing implement. Down the left side of the page, write the four court card rank titles and their associated element:

   Page/Earth:
   Knight/Fire:
   Queen/Water:
   King/Air:

2. Briefly revisit the beginning of chapter 4 and refresh your recollection about the energy and keyword for each of the elements.
3. Return to your paper and, next to each court card rank, jot down some traits each of these four ranks might bring to the tarot based on their associated element.

Hold on to that piece of paper as you read the sections ahead on the court cards. You might be surprised how much you already figured out about each of the four court card ranks!

A Quick Note about Gender

Before we get started, let's have a conversation about gender and why, when it comes to the court cards, it doesn't matter.

The court cards encompass sixteen unique personalities. Those personalities could apply to someone of any gender. In the RWS tarot, the queens are the only feminine-presenting people, while the pages, knights, and kings are all masculine. However, in modern decks, you'll often find that pages and queens are depicted as feminine in appearance, while knights and kings remain masculine. There are many variations of gender representation in different tarot decks.

Originally, these visible differences between genders were there to help clarify the card's personality or energy. In the modern day, though, the genders of the court cards are often changed and rearranged to remind us that anyone can be a king, a queen, a knight, or a page.

The most important thing to remember is that, regardless of the actual gender of you, your querent, or significant people in your (or their) life, the court cards can apply to anyone or anything.

How the Keyword Method Is Different for the Court Cards

In the major arcana and the numbered minor arcana, the goal of the keyword you choose is to help you remember the overall energy of the card.

When it comes to the court cards, the goal is to associate each card with a person from pop culture, fiction, or fantasy who will remind you of the sliding scale of personality each court card represents.

What Do You Mean by "Sliding Scale of Personality"?

The court cards function on a sliding scale from their more positive qualities to their more negative qualities. To illustrate that, I'll share each court card's two related but opposing primary energies: one that is positive or constructive and one that is negative or destructive. Each court card tends to operate along that sliding scale, sometimes representing the more positive side of their personality and other times the more negative side. For example, the Queen of Swords slides between being perceptive and judgmental.

For each court card, I'll share the fictional character who I feel represents that card's sliding scale of personality. Then, I'll invite you to choose your own character or pop culture icon and write their name on your card.

A Word of Caution

It may be tempting to assign the name of someone you know in real life to a court card. While this can be effective, it can also confuse your readings. It's best to choose someone you don't know, such as a fictional character or someone you are familiar with from pop culture, so that you can read the cards objectively when they appear in readings for you.

Let's get into it.

The People of Fire: The Court Cards of the Wands Suit

Overall, the court cards of the wands suit are bold and ambitious. If they decide they want to do something, they're going to do it.

The Page of Wands: Enthusiastic to Fanatical

The Page of Wands operates on a sliding scale from enthusiastic to fanatical.

To be enthusiastic is to be intensely interested in or eager about something. In the case of the Page of Wands, that enthusiasm can be about anything and everything. To be fanatical is to be excessively and uncritically devoted to something.

In the RWS tarot, you see a young man holding a tall staff bursting with new green leaves. His feet are planted firmly on the earth, and he looks up at the growth on this staff with an expression of awe. I would, too. After all, how does a long piece of wood without branches or roots sprout new growth? Magical.

The Page of Wands, elementally, represents the earthly part of fire. An earthly fire could be a campfire or lava. Volcanic lava is molten earth, literally melted rock on fire. The Page of Wands is lava! A fun way to remember this association is to think of a fun game many people (including me) played as kids where they pretended the floor was lava and enthusiastically jumped from one piece of furniture to the next to avoid the floor, much to their parents' chagrin. The Page of Wands would be the kid in the room suggesting this game.

As the Magician of the fiery suit of passion, the Page of Wands is filled with wonder for the world, and they are all about the excitement of discovery.

The Page of Wands can turn anything into a magical, creative experience because they bring their enthusiasm and zest for life to everything they do. Like all the pages, the Page of Wands is ready to learn something new and prove themselves. Their creativity gives them the flexibility to learn new skills through various experiences. Like all the fiery court cards, the page is less concerned with rules and more concerned with experiences, which will always hold the most value for them over anything they can hold in their hands.

Strengths: The Page of Wands excels in being creative and bringing excitement and enthusiasm to anything they get involved in. They think outside the box and love to explore new ways of doing things. They are outgoing and love to try new things.

Struggles: The Page of Wands struggles when their enthusiasm becomes fanatical, and they become undiscerning about where they direct their passions. They are not always great at getting down to the nitty-gritty work of seeing things through to the end. They can be easily distracted, struggle with patience, and crave a lot of attention.

My favorite fictional character for the Page of Wands is Anne Shirley from the Anne of Green Gables book series. I love Anne's character; she is the quintessential Page of Wands. Anne has an extraordinary enthusiasm for everything and can't hide it. She sees magic and adventure everywhere but can quickly become fanatical about her interests.

Whether or not you're familiar with Anne, try to think of a fictional character or someone from pop culture who embodies the Page of Wands personality and write their name on your Page of Wands card.

I like to write only the first name on the card to keep it simple, but you can write the full name of the person or character you choose to associate with the card if you prefer.

The Knight of Wands: Adventurous to Reckless

The Knight of Wands operates on a sliding scale from adventurous to reckless.

To be adventurous is to be constantly seeking new experiences and daring methods of accomplishing your goals. To be reckless is to act without caution or concern for the consequences.

In the RWS tarot, you see a man riding a horse, brandishing a long wooden staff, and dressed in full metal armor, over which he wears a bold yellow shirt adorned with salamanders. Bright red plumage decorates his helmet and armor, and his entire outfit is flame-like. The horse is rearing up, chin tucked as if to either trample a foe or rush ahead at a full gallop. The horse's mane also has a flame-like quality to it.

The Knight of Wands, elementally, represents the fiery part of the fire. From a fire perspective, this is as hot as it gets in the suit of wands, and the Knight of Wands has the personality you would expect of someone so strongly associated with this active element. One way to remember what fire of fire can be like is to imagine a spark traveling at top speed along a fuse toward a barrel of explosives. The moment the spark meets the explosives is when fire meets fire. The adventurous Knight of Wands is always headed straight into an explosive situation!

As the Chariot of the fiery suit of passion, the Knight of Wands is always on the move, bravely facing any danger in their quest to charge into any excitement life has to offer them. Their fearlessness allows them to boldly go wherever their passion leads them, but they can also rush into situations carelessly.

The Knight of Wands is unpredictable and driven by a need for freedom and a desire for conquest. Like all the knights, the Knight of Wands is a seeker, questing for passion and whatever will light their fire. Their desire for the next big adventure opens their eyes to new opportunities. Like all the fiery court cards, the knight craves the adventure of the moment, which is often their primary focus.

Strengths: The action-oriented Knight of Wands is dynamic, self-confident, and intensely passionate. They have an intoxicating magnetism about them. They love to achieve, so while they love the thrill of the chase, they love the win even more, which makes them good at follow-through—at least on the projects they are most passionate about. Their thirst for freedom allows them to be spontaneous, making them exciting to be around.

Struggles: The Knight of Wands struggles with recklessness, which can make them unreliable. They love to charge into adventure but don't always think about whether they (or someone close to them) might get hurt in the process. They can be known to take unnecessary risks for the thrill of it. They don't mind gambling as long as the process is exciting for them, which is something they need to be wary of. The volatile Knight of Wands' moods can change rapidly, and they can be quick to anger.

My favorite fictional character for the Knight of Wands is Indiana Jones. As a character, Indiana Jones is an adventurous, fearless character who is always on a quest of some kind. Indiana's whole persona fits the Knight of Wands so well.

Whether or not you're familiar with Indiana Jones, try to think of a fictional character or someone from pop culture who embodies the Knight of Wands personality and write their name on your Knight of Wands card.

The Queen of Wands: Confident to Arrogant

The Queen of Wands operates on a sliding scale from confident to arrogant.

To be confident is to be self-assured and to fully trust yourself and your right to take up space in the world. To be arrogant is to believe excessively in your own significance and to have a condescending or overbearing attitude toward others.

In the RWS tarot, you see a woman seated at a throne decorated with lions and sunflowers wearing a long sunshine-yellow gown and golden crown. She holds a long wooden staff in one hand and a sunflower in the other. The queen faces forward, sitting upright in her seat with her knees separated confidently.

The Queen of Wands, elementally, represents the watery part of fire. When water meets fire, you get steam, and the Queen of Wands is steamy indeed. One way to remember what water of fire can be like is to think of how a boiling kettle whistles as steam comes out the top or how a steam engine sounds as it's barreling down the tracks. There's no ignoring the Queen of Wands.

As the Empress of the fiery suit of passion, the Queen of Wands is a force to be reckoned with. This queen knows their worth and oozes confidence and sensuality. They know what they can do and aren't afraid to show off their skills or tell you about them. You should never underestimate a Queen of Wands, but if you do, you can be sure they'll make sure you know you did.

The Queen of Wands is independent, determined, and confident but can also be incredibly warm, generous, and supportive. Like all the queens, the Queen of Wands will take care of you, but the Queen of Wands will do that by demanding you be all you can be. The Queen of Wands is fiercely protective of those they care about and will go toe to toe with anyone who challenges their right to be exactly who they are. Like all the fiery court cards, the queen doesn't mind being seen and appreciates being noticed.

Strengths: The self-assured Queen of Wands makes an excellent leader and never hesitates to volunteer to lead when no one else raises their hand. In addition to being fiercely protective of others, the queen is also the master of creating and defending their boundaries. They love to be in the spotlight and can be excellent at public speaking and advocating for those who struggle to advocate for themselves.

Struggles: The Queen of Wands loves to be in charge and struggles with giving up control or delegating responsibilities to others, even when that would make life easier for them. This queen has difficulty admitting they could be wrong, and their arrogance can make it difficult for them to accept criticism, even constructive, from others. Because the queen enjoys being the center of attention, they sometimes struggle with sharing the spotlight and don't have much patience for being ignored.

My favorite fictional character for the Queen of Wands is Daenerys Targaryen from *Game of Thrones*. Daenerys doesn't start out confident as a character, but once she steps into her power, there's no stopping her. As the mother of dragons, Daenerys will stand up for herself and anyone needing protection. Once she establishes a boundary, she holds it no matter what and can be unyielding. And you must admit, she does have a flair for putting on a dramatic show when she feels the situation calls for it.

Whether or not you're familiar with Daenerys Targaryen, try to think of a fictional character or someone from pop culture who embodies the Queen of Wands personality and write their name on your Queen of Wands card.

The King of Wands: Charismatic to Manipulative

The King of Wands operates on a sliding scale from charismatic to manipulative. To be charismatic is to have the ability to inspire others to follow you with loyalty, devotion, and enthusiasm. To be manipulative is to exert calculated control or influence over others for personal gain.

In the RWS tarot, you see a man in a golden flame-shaped crown sitting on a throne decorated with lions and salamanders and wearing a long red gown and a yellow cloak covered with more salamanders. A tiny salamander sits on the base of his throne, and he holds a large wooden staff loosely in one hand while the other rests on his lap. The king faces left, seeming to look out over the horizon.

The King of Wands, elementally, represents the airy part of fire. When you combine air and fire, you get smoke. Smoke rises and expands and can also be used to signal to others to mobilize their forces or spot a faraway enemy. One easy way to remember the King of Wands' association with smoke is to consider how smoke can expand to fill a space. In the same way, the King of Wands' presence commands the attention of any room they walk into.

As the Emperor of the fiery suit of passion, the King of Wands is a dynamic, powerful, and charismatic leader who can inspire others to join them in any cause they are passionate about. They are comfortable with the power they wield, holding on to it lightly, confident that it will remain theirs. They don't have to strong-arm anyone into siding with them because they believe in their cause and trust in their ability to inspire others to believe in it, too.

The King of Wands is convicted, inspiring, protective, and courageous. Like all the kings, they look at the big picture of every situation. The King of Wands, however, is uniquely equipped to devise creative solutions to overcome (or power through) those obstacles. The King of Wands won't sit on the sidelines and rule from a distance but will get right into the thick of the action themselves. Like all the fiery court cards, the king is a force to be reckoned with.

Strengths: The creative King of Wands is a visionary, able to problem solve with innovative thinking and bold action. The king loves to lead but loves to inspire others to lead as well and isn't threatened when others succeed. The King of Wands is a charismatic speaker and can often bring people around to see things their way, which makes them a powerful force in any debate. The King of Wands is like that person at the party who seems to draw others to them like a magnet and often gets exactly what they want out of life.

Struggles: The King of Wands can tend to be manipulative since they are used to getting their way. They can sometimes push themselves (or others) too far in their desire to win. They can also occasionally be a poor sport about losing. Left unchecked, this king can become domineering and overly demanding instead of inspiring.

When it comes to fictional characters, I think of the King of Wands as Xena, the warrior princess. As a character, Xena is fierce, powerful, and incredibly charismatic. She is not afraid of leadership and inspires loyalty and dedication from those closest to her. No matter what obstacles get in her way, she powers through them. Xena doesn't boss people around from outside the thick of things but fearlessly leads the battle from the front lines. It's safe to say that Xena commands all the attention in any room she enters—speaking, ahem, metaphorically.

Whether or not you're familiar with Xena, try to think of a fictional character or someone from pop culture that you feel embodies the King of Wands personality and write their name on your King of Wands card.

The People of Water: The Court Cards of the Cups Suit

The court cards of the cups suit are sensitive and caring. Ruled by their hearts, they bring a gentleness to the tarot.

The Page of Cups: Sensitive to Fragile

The Page of Cups operates on a sliding scale between sensitive and fragile.

To be sensitive is to be responsive to internal and external emotional and intuitive influences. To be fragile is to be especially susceptible to emotional stress.

In the RWS tarot, you see a young man standing in front of the ocean, dressed in light blue with pink lotus flowers and other pink accents. His head-piece looks like water flowing over his head and around his shoulders. His feet are planted shoulder-width apart. One hand rests on his hip, and the other holds a golden cup. A fish pokes its head out of the cup as if to give the page a big wet kiss, and the page looks into the cup at the fish with a slight smile on his face.

It's the fish in the cup for me. There's something about how the page looks at the little fish poking its head out that makes it seem like the whole thing is a bit of imaginative play. Of all the pages, the Page of Cups seems the youngest. It's partly in his seemingly playful approach to life and partly because he seems so full of hope and ready to see the best in everything—usually.

The Page of Cups, elementally, represents the earthly part of water. When water and earth mix, you get mud or clay; both have meaning for this page.

One way to remember the Page of Cups' association with mud is to consider the lotus flowers that adorn the page's clothing. Mud is where lotus flowers take root, deep in the most stagnant and dark waters; the lotus digs its roots deep into the mud and sends green leafy stems up through the water, reaching and reaching for the light until a bud breaks the surface and blossoms in the light of the sun. That is the journey of the lotus. "No mud, no lotus" is how the saying goes. The Page of Cups is that way—born of the mud, believing in the light, and going through it along the way because they keep trusting and believing despite it all. It's a beautiful analogy. Clay is also an excellent analogy for the moldable Page of Cups.

As the Magician of the watery suit of feeling, the Page of Cups is the believer of the tarot, believing in possibility, magic, and goodness in others and the world. They are sensitive, empathetic, and intuitive.

The Page of Cups' ability to believe is unmatched by any other court card in the tarot. They are gentle, kind, compassionate, and imaginative. Like all the pages, the Page of Cups brings a youthful spirit to their suit. This gives them a playful, childlike view of the world that can inspire others to take life a little less seriously. Their compassionate approach to others allows them to build relationships quickly and easily. Their imagination allows them to live life more joyfully. Like all the watery court cards, the page wears their heart on their sleeve.

Strengths: Because the introverted Page of Cups is sensitive to the moods and needs of those around them, they are incredibly caring, supportive, and attentive. They notice the slightest nuance and will be the first to recognize that something's bothering you. Because the Page of Cups is introspective and emotionally self-aware, they have a knack for growing and evolving within their relationships.

Struggles: The Page of Cups can be emotionally fragile, making them hypersensitive to even the hint of unkindness from others. They get their feelings hurt easily and don't always know how to advocate for themselves. They spend so much time being in tune with others that they can also find it challenging to prioritize themselves or establish and hold boundaries in relationships. This page can tend to be shy and might find themselves easily overwhelmed or overpowered by the louder or more insistent voices in a room.

My favorite fictional character for the Page of Cups is Fluttershy from *My Little Pony: Friendship is Magic*. I love Fluttershy's character. She is shy but incredibly caring. She gets her feelings hurt easily and is also easily overpowered or intimidated by others. She tends to have an idealistic view of the world and truly believes in the best in everyone. Sometimes, her naivete can get her in trouble, but she holds on to her tender heart.

Whether or not you're familiar with Fluttershy, try to think of a fictional character or someone from pop culture who embodies the Page of Cups personality and write their name on your Page of Cups card.

The Knight of Cups: Romantic to Unreliable

The Knight of Cups operates on a sliding scale between romantic and unreliable.

To be romantic is to be led by your emotions and imagination. To be unreliable is to be inconsistent in actions, commitments, or behavior.

In the RWS tarot, you see a man riding a horse that prances prettily across a river. The knight holds a cup in front of himself at heart level. He wears a watery tunic over a full suit of armor, and his boots and helmet feature wings.

I can't get over how stereotypically charming this image is. Both horse and rider are the picture of romance—a real Prince Charming vibe—which makes perfect sense for the romantic Knight of Cups.

The Knight of Cups, elementally, represents the fiery part of water. I think of the fiery part of water as boiling water. Water at a boil is quieter and more contained than steam (the watery part of fire) unless you allow it to boil over. The Knight of Cups' emotions are as visible as the bubbles in a pot of boiling water. Left without an outlet or something to spend that emotional energy on, the Knight of Cups can boil over with their desires, dreams, and feelings.

As the Chariot of the watery suit of feeling, the Knight of Cups seeks emotional experiences and connection. Led by their dreams and desires, the Knight of Cups always seeks what will fill their cup. Their desire for love, connection, and an outlet for their imagination keeps them moving forward.

The dreamy Knight of Cups is imaginative, charming, and loving. Like all the knights, the Knight of Cups is a seeker, questing for love and following their dreams. Their thirst for love and their idealism often keep their eyes roaming for the next good thing. Like all the watery court cards, the knight always leads with their heart.

Strengths: The charming Knight of Cups is loving, romantic, and emotionally available. They can sweep anyone off their feet with big gestures and pretty words. They can be surprisingly diplomatic when dealing with conflict and can be great at prioritizing those they care about. They love to love and are at their best in the early stage of relationships, when they can get to know others. The Knight of Cups is imaginative and can think creatively around problems, determined to continue moving forward.

Struggles: The Knight of Cups is at risk of getting lost in their fantasies, which is one of the shadowy qualities that sometimes makes them unreliable. They tend to avoid or escape instead of facing things when life gets tough. They like to remain in the state of love and fantasy, so when relationships get real or challenging, they are tempted to run away or at least look in a different direction, making them sometimes fickle as partners.

My favorite fictional character for the Knight of Cups is Edward Cullen from *Twilight*. Edward is the quintessential romantic. He falls head over heels for Bella Swan, and that love consumes him and drives every decision he makes. He is led by his heart and will do anything for love. Painfully loyal, Edward is charming and dreamy, able to imagine a future with someone who seems ill-suited for him from the start. He's also hot and cold sometimes; letting his heart determine his behavior sometimes has him acting a fool and causing more problems than he solves. He makes a fantastic and appropriate Knight of Cups.

Whether or not you're familiar with Edward Cullen, try to think of a fictional character or someone from pop culture who embodies the Knight of Cups personality and write their name on your Knight of Cups card.

The Queen of Cups: Nurturing to Smothering

The Queen of Cups operates on a sliding scale between nurturing and smothering.

To be nurturing is to be caring and supportive of someone or something. To be smothering is to be excessively protective or stifling of others.

In the RWS tarot, you see a crowned woman seated on a stone throne decorated with cherubic mermaids at the water's edge, staring intently at a fancy but fully covered cup. She's wearing a long blue gown that seems to merge with the water where the water meets her feet, and her cloak has a wavelike pattern.

I see the Queen of Cups as someone emotionally available and tender. Yet, the covered cup makes it seem like the queen is emotionally closed off. Then I realized that the cup is what the queen is looking at, what she is attending to. Much like the queen knows the qualities of the water contained within the covered cup, she also see past the facade that others present—their walls or their masks—to their heart.

The Queen of Cups, elementally, represents the watery part of water. It doesn't get more watery than this. Water, as a representation of emotion but also the subconscious, is powerfully represented by the queen, who is profoundly feeling, deeply intuitive, and aware of what lies beneath the surface. When the Queen of Cups gives you their full attention, you may find yourself revealing your secrets, but—so long as the queen is at their best—those secrets will be kept and held with the utmost care and gentleness.

As the Empress of the watery suit of feeling, the Queen of Cups represents the tender, loving care that only they can provide. Empathetic, gentle, and kind but firm, the queen will be fully present with you in good times and bad. Their ability to see beneath the surface makes them uniquely equipped to support those who might otherwise hide their true feelings or thoughts.

The loving Queen of Cups is compassionate, empathetic, and supportive. Like all the queens, the Queen of Cups will take care of you, but the watery queen will demand that you open up and show them your vulnerabilities. Their desire to be fully present with you can sometimes tip over into being a bit pushy or overbearing. Still, ultimately, they want to give you what you need. Like all the watery court cards, the queen's emotions are always visible in their actions and words.

Strengths: The supportive Queen of Cups is attentive, intuitive, and eager to be of service. They feel deeply and empathize authentically with others. This tender queen seems to know what is going on with others and how to best show up for them in that moment. The Queen of Cups can be your biggest cheerleader and most tender confidante. They love deep, personal conversations and will drop anything for someone in need.

Struggles: The Queen of Cups cares deeply but can sometimes care so much that they become smothering in their attempts to help. The queen can also overidentify with others, becoming codependent or overly attached, setting them up for hurt. The watery queen loves to say yes to others and can tend to do that to their detriment, neglecting their own needs in the process. Establishing and holding boundaries is often tricky for this queen as well.

The gentle and loving Belle from *Beauty and the Beast* is the perfect example of the Queen of Cups. Belle is gentle, kind, and loving but sometimes puts others' needs before hers. Her favorite pastime is curling up with a good book somewhere cozy. Belle sees past the Beast's tough exterior to the gentle heart within. That intuitive quality of seeing beneath someone's exterior is a classic Queen of Cups quality!

Whether or not you're familiar with Belle, try to think of a fictional character or someone from pop culture who embodies the Queen of Cups personality and write their name on your Queen of Cups card.

The King of Cups: Approachable to Complacent

The King of Cups operates on a sliding scale between approachable and complacent.

To be approachable is to be open, gentle, and receptive to others and to have the emotional maturity to handle complex topics, conversations, or situations in life without letting them overwhelm you. To be complacent is to lack motivation or awareness of potential shortcomings and issues and an unwillingness to strive for improvement.

In the RWS tarot, you see a man wearing a long blue gown and a chartreuse cloak sitting on a wavelike stone throne in the middle of the sea. The water all around him is active. On the left side, a fish leaps, and on the right, a faraway ship navigates the wild waves, but the king sits stoically on his throne, holding an open cup and a short golden staff, perfectly dry and untouched by the water.

The King of Cups, elementally, represents the airy part of water. With the card's imagery in mind, I think of waves crashing against the rocks, sending sea spray into the air. The King of Cups acts like the rock that shelters the town from the crashing waves and spray—solid and unyielding but fully aware and watchful of what is happening at sea.

As the Emperor of the watery suit of feeling, the King of Cups is confident and calm despite the waves of emotion thrown his way. This particular king seems to perfectly inhabit the space between sea and sky—between emotion and logic—which allows him to be diplomatic and compassionate when dealing with others. The King of Cups is a gentle leader who prefers to earn respect, not demand it.

The King of Cups is kind and generally mild mannered, making them excellent at navigating complicated interpersonal situations. Like all the kings, the King of Cups is comfortable in a leadership role, but the King of Cups is especially good at leading others in a supportive, nurturing way. This king won't merely point you in a direction and send you on your way but will walk with you, ensuring you arrive safely. Like all the watery court cards, the King of Cups feels everything deeply, and it shows.

Strengths: The gentle King of Cups navigates the tumultuous realm of emotions with steadiness, confidence, and self-awareness. This king knows how to connect with others on their level, meeting them with empathy and compassion, and can draw on their own life experiences to offer guidance and support to others. With their ability to remain composed no matter how much they feel internally, they can be depended upon to come through for you, even when the situation is challenging.

Struggles: The King of Cups can be incredibly complacent. Because this king has a softer, more sensitive side, they can be touchy, irritable, or volatile when not at their best. They can sometimes be indirect communicators, beating around the bush instead of addressing things head-on in their desire to be accommodating. Like the Queen of Cups, they can sometimes focus on others while ignoring their own needs and aren't always good at proactive self-care or asking for what they want or need.

My favorite fictional character for the King of Cups is Mr. Rogers from the show *Mr. Rogers' Neighborhood.* Mr. Rogers could make whoever watched his program feel special. His program was aimed at children, but he never seemed condescending. Instead, he talked to kids on their level. He had this ability to make others feel seen and safe with him. His show wasn't shallow but full of depth, which was only possible because of his insight and emotional maturity.

Whether or not you're familiar with Mr. Rogers, try to think of a fictional character or someone from pop culture who embodies the King of Cups personality, and then write their name on your King of Cups card.

The People of Air: The Court Cards of the Swords Suit

The court cards of the swords suit are intellectual and communicative. Ruled by their minds, they bring honesty to the tarot.

The Page of Swords: Inquisitive to Intrusive

The Page of Swords operates on a sliding scale between inquisitive and intrusive.

To be inquisitive is to have a strong desire to learn and explore new information. To be intrusive is to insert oneself into situations or conversations without being invited, causing discomfort to others.

In the RWS tarot, you see a young man with both feet firmly planted on the ground. He gazes to the left while he holds a sword in two hands over his opposite shoulder. He wears a taupe-colored outfit with yellow tights. The wind ruffles his hair and some trees in the background. Fluffy white clouds decorate the otherwise blue sky.

I've always felt the RWS version of this card was lacking.

There are few hints as to the personality of the Page of Swords in this image—with one exception: the way he looks eagerly to one side at something outside of the view of the card. The positioning of his feet indicates that he was walking one way and suddenly swung around when something caught his attention—something he wants to investigate.

The Page of Swords, elementally, represents the earthly part of air. When I think of earth meeting air, I think of the horizon. The space between the land and the sky is full of possibilities. One way to remember this association is to think of how the page gazes off into the distance at some new horizon they want to head toward. The Page of Swords is constantly taunted by the next thing they want to learn about or understand.

As the Magician of the airy suit of thought, the Page of Swords is constantly questioning and curious. They will ask a million questions or want to take something apart to see how it works. They are perpetual students and can be easily pulled off course by the temptation to learn anything new.

The Page of Swords is intensely curious, even nosy, and when they ask "Why?" they won't settle for a "because I said so" as the only answer. Like all the pages, the Page of Swords brings a youthful energy to their suit, which invites exploration. Their enthusiasm for learning allows them to approach any situation or problem with a more open mind than most of us, which can lead to innovation and out-of-the-box thinking. Like all the airy court cards, the page loves to talk and can be quite a chatterbox!

Strengths: It's always handy to have someone in the room who won't simply accept the status quo but will ask how things work or why they're being done the way they are. The Page of Swords brings this fresh insight and curiosity to anything they participate in and invites others to meet them in that space. Their curiosity makes them attentive, at least when the subject or person interests them, and they can learn to be incredible communicators. They are also very adaptable. Instead of becoming attached to a habit or behavior, they learn to roll with the punches and make changes on the fly in the interest of a better outcome for themselves, their team, or those close to them.

Struggles: With all their curiosity, the Page of Swords can become quite intrusive. In addition, the Page of Swords spends a lot of time exploring things that are stimulating to them mentally but can tend to neglect matters of the heart. This neglect can lead to a lack of emotional maturity or availability. Their curiosity and vigilance can also make them overly defensive. They're better at asking questions than answering them and prefer to be prepared than put on the spot—they hate to be wrong.

My favorite fictional character for the Page of Swords is Alice from *Alice in Wonderland*. She is the perfect character to represent the Page of Swords. After all, her curiosity not only leads her down the rabbit hole but also drives her desire to seek the garden she spots through the tiny door she encounters early in her adventure. She always asks why things are the way they are and is frustrated when dealing with the enigmatic Cheshire cat. It's easy to remember her as the Page of Swords when you think of her famous line: "Curiouser and curiouser…"

Whether or not you're familiar with Alice, try to come up with a fictional character or someone from pop culture who embodies the Page of Swords personality and write their name on your Page of Swords card.

The Knight of Swords: Ambitious to Ruthless

The Knight of Swords operates on a sliding scale between ambitious and ruthless.

To be ambitious is to have an unwavering determination to reach your goals. To be ruthless is to be willing to pursue one's goals without regard for the harm inflicted on others.

In the RWS tarot, you see a man riding a horse at what appears to be top speed, brandishing his sword in front of him with a look of pure determination. He wears a full suit of armor, and his red cloak streams behind him as he gallops ahead. Atop his helmet are what look to be two red wings also blown back as he runs. Fast-moving clouds streak the sky around him.

One thing is evident in this image: the Knight of Swords is moving incredibly fast. Whatever path they are on, there's no way you will stop them, and if you get in their way, you're likely to get trampled!

The Knight of Swords, elementally, represents the fiery part of air. I think of the fiery part of air as the lightning that streaks across the sky (or hits the ground). It's fast-moving and impossible to predict, and you'd best get out of its way.

As the Chariot of the airy suit of thought, the Knight of Swords seeks knowledge and glory. They want to stack up achievements and leave their mark on the world. They aren't galloping for the adventure; they have a mission and will accomplish it as quickly as possible.

The focused Knight of Swords is intelligent, assertive, and bold. Like all the knights, the Knight of Swords is on a mission—but their mission is to make an impact. They tend to be more spontaneous and adventurous than the other court cards of this suit. While they can be focused, they can also be flighty if a tempting enough distraction promises glory or accolades. Like all the airy court cards, they are quick thinkers and can be quickly bored with people who cannot hold their own in intelligent conversation.

Strengths: The Knight of Swords can accomplish almost anything they set their mind to and is an outstanding problem solver. They are assertive and will always go after what they want, even if the odds seem stacked against them. The Knight of Swords is brave and will fiercely defend those close to them no matter what. They will stand up for what they believe in—no matter what anyone else thinks of them.

Struggles: The Knight of Swords can have a ruthless side. Because the Knight of Swords likes to move (and think) quickly, they tend to avoid planning or thinking things through before they do them (or say them). Their impulsivity can get them in trouble in life and their relationships, which can suffer from their biting or thoughtless communication style. They can be impatient because they like to be always on the move, mentally or physically. The Knight of Swords also tends to take on too much and push themselves to burnout or get so tunnel-visioned with their ability to focus that they neglect other things or people.

My favorite fictional character for the Knight of Swords is Tony Stark from Marvel's *Iron Man* movie. Tony is a brilliant thinker who strives to achieve the next big thing. He's always thinking, innovating, and chasing his latest ideas. As a result, he sometimes neglects the people in his life who are important to him. He can be rash and impulsive, and when he has a goal or idea, there's no talking him out of it.

Whether or not you're familiar with Tony Stark, try to think of a fictional character or someone from pop culture who embodies the Knight of Swords personality and write their name on your Knight of Swords card.

The Queen of Swords: Perceptive to Judgmental

The Queen of Swords operates on a sliding scale between perceptive and judgmental.

To be perceptive is to have a keen ability to notice and understand things. To be judgmental is to form overly critical opinions about others and quickly express disapproval or criticism.

In the RWS tarot, you see a stern-faced woman wearing a butterfly crown, gray robes, and a cloak resembling a cloudy sky seated on a stone throne engraved with an angel and butterfly. The queen faces the right and holds a sword perfectly upright as she holds her other hand up dismissively. In the background behind her, a tiny river can be seen.

Judging solely by appearance, this queen means business. From the stern expression on her face to how her throne is turned entirely to the side (unlike the other queens who face at least partly forward), it's clear that this queen is not as accessible as the others.

The Queen of Swords, elementally, represents the watery part of air. When I think of the watery part of air, I think of clouds. The clouds represented on the RWS image of the Queen of Swords are situated near the horizon, but the queen's head is above them in the clarity of the clear blue sky. We know, from exploring the cups suit, that water is associated with emotion. The queen recognizes the influence of emotion but doesn't allow emotions to obscure the truth.

As the Empress of the airy suit of thought, the Queen of Swords represents the ability to navigate the realm of the mind without neglecting the emotional side of situations or people. Like all the queens, the Queen of Swords wants to support you but will do so with honesty. This queen will cut through the crap to get to the heart of a situation or problem. Honest, communicative, emotionally intelligent, and perceptive, the Queen of Swords is a powerful ally. Keep in mind that, like all the airy court cards, the Queen of Swords will not put up with dishonesty.

Strengths: Don't let this queen's stern expression fool you. While this fair-minded, intelligent queen can analyze situations (and people) like no other, they can also be gentle and compassionate when the situation calls for it. Thanks to their emotional intelligence, the Queen of Swords can navigate complex emotions without succumbing to them. Their ability to keep a cool head makes them effective communicators, and they almost always have good advice to give.

Struggles: The Queen of Swords can be incredibly judgmental and quick to speak their mind, even if their words will cut right to the bone. They can also be closed off emotionally. The Queen of Swords can have difficulty accepting help or advice, preferring to be on the other end of that interaction. They can struggle to open up to or be vulnerable with others. This fiercely independent queen wants to do it alone, which can result in burnout if left unchecked.

My favorite fictional character for the Queen of Swords is Elsa from Disney's *Frozen*. Like the Queen of Swords, Elsa tends to protect her heart and avoid too much vulnerability, but she is also fiercely independent and intelligent. Her journey in the movie *Frozen* is about learning to accept and embrace her power rather than hide it. Elsa is also the first Disney princess to call it exactly as she sees it when she points out to her sister, Anna, that she can't marry a man she just met—an iconic moment, if a bit judgmental. Ultimately, her journey to understand how to navigate complex emotions shows us what the Queen of Swords is capable of.

Whether or not you're familiar with Elsa, try to think of a fictional character or someone from pop culture who embodies the Queen of Swords personality and write their name on your Queen of Swords card.

The King of Swords: Strategic to Indifferent

The King of Swords operates on a sliding scale between strategic and indifferent.

To be strategic is to have the ability to achieve a plan by looking at the big picture and implementing appropriate action. To be indifferent is to lack interest, concern, or emotional investment in people or situations.

In the RWS tarot, you see a crowned man wearing long blue robes and a gray cloak sitting on a large stone throne, holding a large sword at a slight angle. His throne is so tall that it presumably continues beyond the card's border. Fluffy clouds decorate the sky behind him, though the sky is clear from the king's shoulder level and above.

Like the respective queen, this king's head is also above the cloud level, signifying clear-headed thinking. However, unlike the queen, no water is visible on the card, so we can safely assume that emotions are not as present with this card. The tilt of the king's sword indicates that he is willing to make difficult decisions to maintain his authority.

The King of Swords, elementally, represents the airy part of air. A suitable analogy for this is a clear blue sky. The King of Swords exists entirely in the mind realm, where they feel completely comfortable and in charge, and is at their best when there are no distractions from within or without to clutter their mind.

As the Emperor of the airy suit of thought, the King of Swords is assured of their mental abilities and has no problem taking decisive action once they have considered all factors.

The King of Swords is confident, assertive, and action oriented, but every action they take is carefully planned and calculated. Like all the kings, the King of Swords prefers to take the lead in life and is especially good at untangling complex situations to find the best possible solution. When the Knight of Swords rushes into action, the king will hold back, taking in as much information as possible and planning their moves carefully. Like all the airy court cards, the King of Swords is most at ease with situations that can be explored logically.

Strengths: The King of Swords is a rational thinker who will make decisions objectively and levelheadedly. The ultimate chess player, this king is a big-picture thinker who always tries to zoom out and look at every situation from multiple angles before determining the appropriate action. This king values respect and the ability to take accountability and models these behaviors in their interactions with others.

Struggles: The King of Swords can sometimes overidentify with logic and strategy to the point where they become indifferent to others' feelings, isolating them from others. They also tend to overthink situations, introducing complications that would otherwise not have been present. This king is less comfortable when it comes to matters more affected by emotions or requiring a degree of vulnerability. The King of Swords prefers to stay somewhat reserved in this area, making it difficult for them to get close to people. This king can also be rigid and controlling.

My favorite fictional character for the King of Swords is Spock from *Star Trek*. Always logical, strategic, and rational, sometimes Spock can miss the finer nuances of interpersonal relationships and can struggle to relate to others on an emotional level. Spock brings incredible value to his team by always thinking ahead and planning for all scenarios. After all, he said, "Insufficient facts always invite danger."

Whether or not you're familiar with Spock, try to think of a fictional character or someone from pop culture who embodies the King of Swords personality, and then write their name on your King of Swords card.

The People of Earth: The Court Cards of the Pentacles Suit

The court cards of the pentacles suit are grounded and responsible. Ruled by their hearts, they bring stability to the tarot.

The Page of Pentacles: Diligent to Perfectionistic

The Page of Pentacles operates on a sliding scale between diligent and perfectionistic.

To be diligent is to be consistent, conscientious, detail-oriented, and committed to your responsibilities. To be perfectionistic is to set extremely high standards while striving for flawlessness.

In the RWS tarot, you see a young man standing among wildflowers in a green field carefully holding and peering at a coin-like pentacle. He is dressed in earthy tones of brown and green (other than his red headpiece). The landscape behind him is green with a visible mountain and some trees on the horizon. The sky behind him glows yellow.

The way the Page of Pentacles examines the pentacle in this card always makes me think of this simple phrase: "The page doesn't wait for someone to offer him an opportunity. He creates his own."

The Page of Pentacles, elementally, represents the earthly part of the earth. You don't get much more grounded than that. The Page of Pentacles represents being in touch with all the earth's resources and life's material and mundane realities. They love to learn, but they want practical knowledge more than they want book knowledge. They want to put what they learn into practice.

As the Magician of the earthly suit of resources, the Page of Pentacles is determined to create the life they imagine with hard work and their own two hands. They would feel frustrated at being handed everything in life and get deep personal satisfaction from accomplishing even small goals that take them in the direction they want to go.

The Page of Pentacles takes a practical approach to life and prefers that anything they undertake has a measurable, observable outcome. Like all the pages, the Page of Pentacles is eager to prove themselves and loves to do so by making the most of everything they have acquired. Their grounded approach to life means that they rarely squander opportunities. Like all the earthly court cards, the page wants others to value them as a resource.

Strengths: The Page of Pentacles is almost always diligently working away at something. Their pragmatic approach to life makes them especially good at detail-oriented work, as they tend to be incredibly thorough with everything they do. This page is also risk averse and tends to be responsible with their financial resources, erring on the side of saving instead of spending.

Struggles: The Page of Pentacles cares so much about proving themselves that sometimes they can overfocus on perfection. They can be intensely perfectionistic, which can keep them from making forward momentum at all. It's hard to get anything done when you're too focused on the details, even to consider the bigger picture or end goal. The Page of Pentacles can sometimes get stuck in this detail-oriented view, which keeps them from moving forward.

My favorite fictional character for the Page of Pentacles is Hermione Granger from *Harry Potter*. Hermione is incredibly hardworking and diligent in her studies. Still, she tends to push herself (and others) too hard in her quest for perfection. She's grounded and knows how to apply herself but is steadfast in pursuing her goals.

Whether or not you're familiar with Hermione, try to think of a fictional character or someone from pop culture who embodies the Page of Pentacles personality and write their name on your Page of Pentacles card.

The Knight of Pentacles: Dependable to Inflexible

The Knight of Pentacles operates on a sliding scale between dependable and inflexible.

To be dependable is to be trusted or relied upon to do what you say you will do to fulfill your commitments. To be inflexible is to be resistant to change and compromise or to be rigid and unyielding.

In the RWS tarot, you see a man sitting atop a large dark horse standing still on a hillside, overlooking the valley below. He sits upright and carefully holds a pentacle in front of him, gazing at it intensely. He is dressed in full armor with some red accents, and his horse also wears red accents. The sky is bright yellow.

Unlike the other knights, the Knight of Pentacles and his horse appear to be standing still. It's clear that he is on a journey, so perhaps he pauses before continuing, but he is focused on his goal.

The Knight of Pentacles, elementally, represents the fiery part of the earth. When I think of fiery earth, I think of quartz. Quartz crystals are dynamic in that they grow and change, transforming over a long period of time. They also generate a form of energy naturally, which gives them the dynamic force I associate with the element of fire. Like quartz, the Knight of Pentacles moves and changes over time, but slowly.

As the Chariot of the earthly suit of resources, the Knight of Pentacles seeks financial security and long-term comfort. Short-term benefits or accolades don't drive them. Instead, they want to serve a purpose, perform a duty, and be relied upon.

This slow-moving knight is steady, reliable, and honest. Like all the knights, the Knight of Pentacles wants to continue moving forward, but unlike the other knights, this one will take their time to get where they're going. They take the safe path whenever possible. Like all the earthly court cards, the knight is stable. Unlike the other knights, whose horses are depicted in positions of active movement, this knight's steed stands steady and still.

Strengths: The Knight of Pentacles is the most reliable character of all the court cards. If you ask them to do something, they will do it to the best of their ability and will not stray from the task. They are loyal and eager to commit to long-term projects and relationships, preferring stability. They are practical and risk averse and will not squander their resources.

Struggles: The Knight of Pentacles can be so fixated on their task that they become intensely inflexible and stubborn. They lack spontaneity and have difficulty shaking things up, making them predictable and boring to some. They can overly focus on the need to protect their resources, preferring frugality to extravagance, which can make them rigid when it comes to spending. They're slow-moving but can sometimes stop moving altogether and hesitate to move forward.

My favorite fictional character for the Knight of Pentacles is Frodo Baggins from *The Lord of the Rings*. Frodo may have been hesitant to leave the comfort and stability of his home, but when given an important quest, he will not be swayed from his task and sees it through despite all the difficulties he faces. He proves himself trustworthy, reliable, and dependable through it all.

Whether or not you're familiar with Frodo, try to think of a fictional character or someone from pop culture who embodies the Knight of Pentacles personality and write their name on your Knight of Pentacles card.

The Queen of Pentacles: Comforting to Enabling

The Queen of Pentacles operates on a sliding scale between comforting and enabling.

To be comforting is to be reassuring and to ensure the comfort of those around you. To be enabling is to provide support, resources, or opportunities that inadvertently facilitate harmful or undesirable behaviors.

In the RWS tarot, you see a woman in a golden crown seated on a stone throne in the middle of a lush garden. She is wearing a long red gown with a flowing green cape. She looks down at a pentacle that she cradles in her lap while, in the foreground, a brown rabbit hops into view and roses drape overhead.

This scene seems so cozy to me. The flowers are in full bloom around the queen, and the way that the pentacle rests in the queen's lap always feels as though it could be a small child instead. The queen's posture and facial expression are lovingly attentive.

The Queen of Pentacles, elementally, represents the watery part of the earth. When I think of the watery part of the earth, I think of a rainforest, lush and fertile with ripe fruit and blooming flowers everywhere. No one lacks anything in this space where there are ample places for the forest's creatures to live and thrive. It's an appropriate allegory for the Queen of Pentacles, who likes to make sure that no one near them is left wanting.

As the Empress of the earthly suit of resources, the Queen of Pentacles represents a careful but thoughtful use of resources. Unlike the page, who is trying to build up resources, or the knight, who is trying to protect them, the queen knows how to spend wisely and does so to take care of those close to them. Like all the queens, the Queen of Pentacles wants to nurture you, and this queen does so by providing for your material comforts. If you are cold, the Queen of Pentacles will offer you a blanket or knit you some cozy socks. If you're hungry, this queen will make you a nice meal. Attentive and steadfast, the Queen of Pentacles naturally provides for all around them and loves to be of service by providing tangible support to those in their charge. Like all the earthly court cards, the Queen of Pentacles shows up and isn't afraid to roll up their sleeves and get dirty if it means getting things done or helping others out.

Strengths: The Queen of Pentacles is nurturing in a way that is instantly recognizable because they nurture in tangible ways, providing others with practical support. This queen is known for being generous and quick to offer a helping hand, but the Queen of Pentacles is also a great person to turn to for life advice or emotional comfort. This earthly queen is incredibly loyal and makes a reliable friend and ally.

Struggles: The Queen of Pentacles means well but can often take their help too far, enabling people to engage in unhealthy or harmful behaviors. While the Queen of Pentacles can be incredibly generous with their time and energy, they sometimes don't treat themselves with the same care and attention. Like all the nurturing court cards of the tarot, the Queen of Pentacles can tend to neglect their own needs while focusing on helping others. This queen also struggles with being overbearing or helicoptering around those they care for, creating tension with their loved ones. If the Queen of Pentacles focuses too much on material resources, they can become materialistic or overly focused on wealth, which can tip their priorities out of balance.

My favorite fictional character for the Queen of Pentacles is Molly Grue from the book and movie *The Last Unicorn*. Molly will forever be the perfect representation of the Queen of Pentacles to me. She is grounded and steady, loyal and loving, but she will always be there to give some life advice (while ensuring you have a hot bowl of soup or a cuddle). Molly is earthly and practical but kind and loving. She's gentle but a little rough around the edges.

Whether or not you're familiar with Molly, try to think of a fictional character or someone from pop culture who embodies the Queen of Pentacles personality and write their name on your Queen of Pentacles card.

The King of Pentacles: Wise to Cynical

The King of Pentacles operates on a sliding scale between wise and cynical.

To be wise is to know how to apply your knowledge and skills effectively and to understand how to use good judgment. To be cynical is to have a skeptical, distrustful mindset and a general belief that people are motivated by selfishness or dishonesty.

In the RWS tarot, you see a man wearing a flowing gown decorated with grapes over a suit of armor. His crown is adorned with red flowers, and he is surrounded by thriving grapevines. His gaze makes it clear that he has his eyes on the pentacle he holds. Behind him, a castle sits close enough that it's safe to assume that it represents this person's home.

The King of Pentacles is surrounded by signs of wealth and luxury in this image. There are so many grapes in this image, both on the king's gown and growing all around them, that you can't help but notice their abundance.

The King of Pentacles, elementally, represents the airy part of the earth. With the lush grapes all over the RWS image of this court card, I can't help but think of the way tree branches reach for the sky, slowly growing over time, drawing up resources from the earth until they bear their fruit—which eventually falls, when the time is right, further seeding the ground for new growth. It makes me think of how the King of Pentacles has built up their wealth and resources throughout their life and now has enough to invest in future growth—wealth that will continue to grow throughout their lifetime.

As the Emperor of the earthly suit of resources, the King of Pentacles has gained wisdom through life experience, both in work and in personal relationships, and knows how to navigate the twists and turns and ups and downs of life with more ease than others.

The King of Pentacles is self-assured, confident in their skills, secure materially and personally, and pragmatic. Like all the kings, the King of Pentacles can remove themselves from the nitty-gritty of a situation and look at the big picture. This king will often spot the risks or dangers in a situation before anyone else. Like all the earthly court cards, the King of Pentacles values security and stability over fun and adventure.

Strengths: When it comes to managing finances or other resources, there is no one with better advice than the King of Pentacles. This wise and earthly king is a business expert who does well as an entrepreneur or as part of a larger corporate entity. The King of Pentacles is a wise and pragmatic leader who values structure, routine, and steady progress but will take some carefully considered risks if they can manage the outcome if it doesn't go as well as they hope. They always account for what could happen in a worst-case scenario and ensure they have a fallback plan in place if needed. This king is reliable and resilient and can be depended upon to provide for those around them.

Struggles: The King of Pentacles has worked hard to get where they are, and their pragmatism can predispose them to think negatively about others, becoming cynical in the process. The King of Pentacles also doesn't cope well with change. They prefer their life to be routine and orderly and can flounder when something throws a wrench in the steadiness of their day-to-day life. While they adapt eventually, they can be inflexible and stubborn. They've learned the hard way how to succeed in business and life. Their pride can get in the way of them reaching out for help or advice—especially from those who do not have the same proven track record they do. They tend not to trust others easily and generally expect the people in their lives to earn their trust and respect.

My favorite fictional character for the King of Pentacles is Richard Gilmore from *The Gilmore Girls*. He is the perfect example of a wise and earthly king. Richard is a businessman who has spent his life building his knowledge, skills, and material wealth and has reached a point where he can provide for his comfort and those around him. However, he could be extremely stubborn and rigid about some things, and his pride could be wounded easily. He couldn't always roll with the punches, but he cared for those around him and wanted to ensure they felt safe and secure in his presence.

Whether or not you're familiar with Richard Gilmore, try to think of a fictional character or someone from pop culture who embodies the King of Pentacles personality, and then write their name on your King of Pentacles card.

Getting to Know Your Court Card Keywords and Personalities

Now that you have a complete set of court cards, each labeled with your personal keyword and the name of a person or character they remind you of, it's time to put them to work so you can get to know them better.

One of the most common questions I get about the court cards is: "How do I know if the court card is an aspect of myself, someone else, a situation, or energy?"

There's an easy answer to this question, and there's a difficult answer.

The easy answer is: you learn to trust yourself.

The difficult answer is: you learn to trust yourself.

I'm not being flippant, honestly. Learning to trust the way you read a card is the easiest and the most challenging way to determine what a court card (or any card) means in a reading. I assure you, though, that learning to trust yourself gets easier the more that you practice it, and so the sooner you start, the better. If you practice trusting your initial gut feeling about a card when it first comes up from the beginning, you'll build that self-trust early in your practice, and I highly recommend it.

With that said, some readers have systems to help them narrow the focus of a court card in a reading if they shuffle reversed cards into their decks. One method is to predetermine that a court card that appears upright means the card is about you and one that appears reversed refers to someone else—but this doesn't account for situations or energy interpretations. Another method is to assign upright cards to people and reversed to energy or situations—but this doesn't help you determine when the card is about you or someone else.

If you want to create a system to know what a court card is referring to, please do! My only advice, in that regard, would be that you be consistent in how you apply it. For myself, after experimenting with systems like these, I found that they either felt too specific or not specific enough and left me feeling frustrated with the court cards. The day I decided I would simply trust myself was the day it got easier for me to interpret these cards.

With that said, it's time to test-drive your new set of court card keywords by practicing doing some readings for yourself (or willing friends and family) with them.

Below are a few spreads to try out with your marked-up court cards. Try each spread a couple of times to see how working with your personal set of keywords feels. If you find your keyword or the person you assigned to the card doesn't hold up throughout these exercises, feel free to revisit that card and make some changes. Once you're satisfied with the keywords and characters you've chosen for these, you're ready to move on to the next chapter!

One-Card Embodiment Spread

For the one-card embodiment spread, pull one court card to represent qualities you should embody. Lean into this court card's strengths in the day (or week) ahead. Let this personality be your ally; lean into their strengths and consciously work to surpass their struggles. At the end of the day or week, reflect on your experience and note what you learned.

CARD 1: Qualities to embody in the day/week ahead.

Two-Card Situation/Advice Spread

This is a simple two-card spread that can help you explore a current predicament or situation. The first card focuses on providing more information or context about what you're dealing with. The second card focuses on empowering you with helpful advice or an action you can take to move the situation forward.

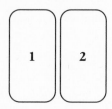

CARD 1: What do I need to know about this situation? Use the court card drawn to understand the energy or personality of the situation.

CARD 2: What action should I take? Use the court card drawn to understand the best approach to navigate the situation.

Three-Card Me, Them, Us Spread

The three-card me, them, us spread is a powerful relationship spread that can provide a lot of information about a relationship in just a few cards. This spread works well no matter what type of relationship you are reading about: romantic, platonic, professional, or familial.

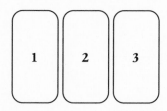

CARD 1: What personality traits are coming forward prominently for you in this relationship?

CARD 2: What personality traits are coming forward prominently for the other person in this relationship?

CARD 3: What traits should both lean into to create more harmony in the relationship?

Four-Card Personal Development Spread

The four-card personal development spread is an effective one to use when you want to explore your own personal growth and development, but you can also use this spread for querents.

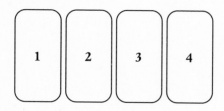

CARD 1: Strengths to lean into.

CARD 2: Struggles you are currently dealing with.

CARD 3: Advice from a court card. (What advice would this character give you to navigate your struggles from card 2?)

CARD 4: Action step to take. (What would this court card do next?)

Chapter 6
Don't Let These
Mix-Ups Trip You Up

One of the most common issues that new tarot readers face is the way that some cards seem to have similar meanings. I get asked, frequently, what the difference is between this card and that card. In fact, I created an entire YouTube content series based on differentiating seemingly similar cards.

I'm confident in my assertion that each tarot card is completely unique in its meaning; however, there are certainly cards that—at first glance—appear to have the same message. This can certainly trip you up in a reading, especially if you can't remember which is which.

So, let's discuss some of the most common mix-ups that tarot readers might struggle with.

Justice vs. Judgement

Accountability vs. Evolution

These two cards get mixed up with one another the most often by both new and more experienced tarot readers. Why?

The fact that both card titles begin with *Ju* doesn't help. Even the names alone could be easy to misread. The biggest issue is that the concepts of justice and judgment feel closely related, particularly when you look at these cards through the lens of the legal system. After all, a judge passes judgment and works to uphold justice.

As we explored earlier, the Justice card is not only about being in a courtroom but about facing the consequences of your actions and behavior and taking accountability—for good or bad. Remember, my keyword for this card is *accountability*.

Judgement is not about being judged in a literal sense. It's about being called to evolve into a new version of yourself. My keyword for this card is *evolution*.

It's not nearly as easy to mix up *accountability* and *evolution* as it is to mix up Justice and Judgement—another point in favor of this single-keyword method to learning the tarot!

The Hermit vs. the Hanged Man

Introspection vs. Suspension

These two cards seem similar when you think about how both cards represent a sense of solitariness. The Hermit intentionally retreats from society, moving within and isolating themselves to learn and grow. On the other hand, the Hanged Man's state of suspension could be either voluntary or involuntary. Both are removed, in a way, from the everydayness of the world.

Both cards present an opportunity to learn and gain insights about oneself, but energetically, these cards represent different archetypes.

The Hermit actively and intentionally looks within to gain a deeper understanding of the self so that they can light the way for others. In the Hermit, we see an active search for insight and wisdom that necessitates pulling away from others and finding truth in a solitary way. The Hermit represents the active practice of introspection.

The Hanged Man, however, is held in a state of waiting that is inherently uncomfortable. They may have arrived there voluntarily or involuntarily. The Hanged Man may represent what it feels like to be cast out or forced to wait for something. In that period of isolation or waiting, one has an opportunity to learn from the experience, but it's deeply uncomfortable. The Hanged Man is primarily about the experience of being in a state of *suspension*—my keyword for this card.

Death vs. the Tower

Ending vs. Destruction

Both the Death card and the Tower card are about transformation and the end of something as you know it, which can make them seem similar. Both cards can involve learning to come to terms with a new reality, and both cards invite you to grow from the experience. In both cases, you'll need to learn to let go of what is no longer and invite a new way of experiencing the world.

While it's true that both cards involve an element of transformation, the experience of these cards and what they mean in the practice of reading the tarot is different. The Death card speaks to the natural cycle of life and death—things and situations that reach a natural, inevitable conclusion or end. The Tower, on the other hand, involves an often sudden, destructive ending to a situation, relationship, or way of thinking.

Thinking about these cards from the perspective of the keywords you've assigned can shed additional light on their differences. For me, Death is *ending*, and the Tower is *destruction*. The Tower tumbles down as a result of knowledge or insight. It's a sudden shift, the thing you have seen—and now can't unsee—that rocks your world. Sometimes, it's you who destroys the tower. It doesn't always come from outside of yourself. Death, however, is entirely outside of your control.

I want to say it's as simple as Death being gentler than the Tower, but that's not always the case. Any ending can be brutal. Instead, I will say that Death is something that you can't prevent, even when you try to resist it. Tower experiences, when foretold, can sometimes be prevented, but once that Tower starts to fall, it's coming down.

The Sun vs. the World

Radiance vs. Completion

One of the reasons the Sun and the World can have a similar vibe is that both cards are inherently joyful. Both cards are strongly associated with positive outcomes and success. Both cards indicate a certain amount of safety or containment. In the Sun card, the garden walls symbolize safety. In the World card, the laurel wreath that circles the central figure can represent boundaries or containment.

The Sun represents the radiant joy that comes from successfully being in the world as your authentic self—allowing the trappings of society and others' expectations to disappear. The Sun card is a happy, carefree card. When this card speaks about success, it's a stress-free, joyful success.

The World, on the other hand, is about the completion of a journey or cycle. It's the moment when everything falls into place. It's wholeness, fulfillment, and success. However, not all fulfillment is joyful. Completing something can be a bittersweet experience. There have been ups and downs. Remember, this card contains the entirety of the Fool's journey and is both the fulfillment of one cycle and the beginning of another.

For me, the Sun conveys radiance, joy, and authenticity, while the World speaks about completion, fulfillment, and cycles.

Two of Wands vs. Three of Wands

Possibility vs. Commencement

The Two of Wands and Three of Wands are easily mixed up. These cards have more in common than different.

They both feature people standing on a high vantage point looking out over the horizon. In both scenes, a person holds one staff while the other is planted nearby. To make matters worse, both seem to be looking out at the water. Confusing much?

With all their similarities, some unique qualities of each scene make it clear they mean different things. The first detail to notice about these cards is the location. At first, it seems similar: a high-up place.

In the Two of Wands, that high-up place is incredibly safe. The person looking out over the horizon in this card is secure within their castle walls. From this place, the person in the card feels comfortable exploring what is possible. They are still weighing their options here.

In the Three of Wands, the main character is fully exposed, high up on the cliff's edge. They've made decisions, stepped away from the safety and security of their comfort zone, and begun taking real action toward their goals. There's risk in this exposure as they look out at the ships in the sea. Whether you imagine those are ships they've sent out or ships they're welcoming home, it's clear that this person has already commenced their journey or venture.

Nine of Cups vs. Ten of Cups

Contentment vs. Bliss

Much like the Two and Three of Wands, the Nine and Ten of Cups are compositionally similar. Both cards feature an arc of cups, and both feature happy people. From an interpretation point of view, I'd be glad to get either card in a spread—although, if I had my choice, I'd pick the Nine of Cups every time.

The Nine of Cups shows a happy person seated in front of nine neatly displayed cups on a curved table behind them. It's the satisfied smile this person wears that gets me every time.

The Ten of Cups shows a rainbow of cups over what looks to be a happy family. All is beautiful and blissful.

What is the difference?

This one is easy: the difference is how many people you see on the card.

The Nine of Cups features one person who is satisfied and content with their life. They know that they, alone, are enough.

In the Ten of Cups, everything goes further. One person's contentment becomes a family's bliss. Still, that bliss is dependent on everyone in that picture being similarly content at the same time.

The Nine of Cups is about individual contentment and happiness, while the Ten of Cups is about what happens when multiple people who have reached a Nine of Cups level of contentment come together to share their bliss.

Five of Wands vs. Five of Swords

Competition vs. Tyranny

The Five of Wands and Five of Swords don't look anything alike visually. Yet, quite a few tarot readers struggle to differentiate them when interpreting the cards in a reading.

That's because, fundamentally, both cards are about the type of conflict that occurs when people clash. Essentially, both are fighting cards. Sort of.

The Five of Wands shows five people in a chaotic battle, each with their own wooden staff.

The Five of Swords, on the other hand, shows one prominent person holding three swords and standing triumphantly over two other swords at their feet. Two people slink away dejectedly in the background.

Other than the fact that the Five of Swords depicts a clear winner, the ideas here are similar.

The key difference here is how the people pictured on the card participate or not in the battle.

In the Five of Wands, everyone is equipped with a single staff. No one seems overpowered by the other, and everyone willingly engages in the activity. This looks like a healthy and consensual competition.

By contrast, the Five of Swords shows one person who has overpowered the others. This individual holds three swords already, indicating that they came to the battle more equipped than the other two individuals who surrendered their swords, and they don't seem to have done so willingly at all. The tyrant with all the swords doesn't seem interested in fair play; they'd prefer to win—at any cost.

Eight of Swords vs. the Devil

Overwhelm vs. Bondage

The Eight of Swords and the Devil card are both about being trapped or restricted. To make matters worse, there is usually some evidence in both cards that the person (or people) who are trapped could free themselves if they choose.

In the RWS version of the Devil card, a primary character represents a devil with two people chained at its feet. The chained people wear collars that they could, if they chose, slip over their heads to free themselves, but they don't.

In the Eight of Swords, you see a person loosely bound and blindfolded, surrounded by eight swords stuck in the ground around them. Notably, no blades are directly in front of or behind the figure. The ties that bind them are draped so that if they wiggled even a little, they would fall to their feet, and then they could remove the blindfold and walk away.

What gives? What makes these cards different?

Arguably, the fact that one is a major arcana and one a minor arcana sets them apart. Major arcana cards have a bigger energy and are connected to more significant experiences. That isn't the only difference between these cards that are themed around restriction and bondage.

Visually, the most significant difference is whom you see—or don't see—on the card.

In the Devil card, there is an external force, represented by the devil, that the people in the card are bound to. That is because the Devil card is all about being bound to a habit, a way of being or thinking, or some other form of addiction.

In the Eight of Swords, there is simply the main character of the card, all by themselves, surrounded by all those swords. In the suit of the mind, the swords represent thoughts, ideas, decisions, worries, and other thought-based forms. The person in the card isn't bound to something or someone; their internal thoughts bog them down. It's their thoughts that keep them stuck, not an attachment to someone or something else.

In both cards, the trapped person(s) can free themselves if they choose. The difference is in what they need to free themselves from.

Two of Cups vs. the Lovers

Connection vs. Commitment

The Two of Cups and the Lovers are easily confused. Both cards can be about romantic love or, at least, about a deep connection between two people, but that is where their similarities end.

Like examining the differences between the Eight of Swords and the Devil, you can begin the exploration of the Lovers and Two of Cups by remembering that the Lovers is a major arcana card, so it references an impactful life experience. Conversely, as a minor arcana card, the Two of Cups is more likely to describe an everyday occurrence that may not have such a lasting impact.

The scenes in the two cards do look a little alike, but there are a couple of differences that can help you remember each card's unique interpretation.

First, we can see that both people are clothed in the Two of Cups, whereas in the Lovers card, both people are nude. The type of connection we feel with someone when we're beginning to get to know them (as represented in the Two of Cups) is very different from the type of connection we feel with someone we can be fully vulnerable enough to commit to (as represented in the Lovers).

Second, notice how the two primary characters on the cards interact with each other. In the Two of Cups, the couple are close, with eyes only for each other. In the Lovers card, the couple stand further apart and, while the man looks at the woman, the woman looks up at the angel, as if she is seeking some sort of divine guidance to help her make a wise decision.

The Lovers card, ultimately, is more about committing to a path—making a choice—than it is about love specifically. The Two of Cups is about a connection that involves an equal exchange of energy and interest. When you look at these cards as stages in a relationship, the Two of Cups represents the budding beginning of a romantic connection, while the Lovers represents the long-term commitment of a marriage or partnership.

Two of Pentacles vs. Temperance

Priorities vs. Moderate

The Two of Pentacles and Temperance are about weighing and balancing two opposing forces.

In the RWS version of the Two of Cups, a person juggles two pentacles that show an infinity symbol around them. Behind them is an image of an active sea with big waves tossing ships around.

In the Temperance card, you see an angel with one foot on land and the other on water, pouring one cup into the other in a motion that indicates the cups' contents flow back and forth between them.

Again, we find ourselves comparing a minor arcana card with a major arcana card, so I won't belabor that particular point.

Instead, I will point out how the two objects are handled in both cards. In the Two of Pentacles, the pentacles are being juggled but are individual. On the other hand, in Temperance, the two cups' contents are mixed or combined. One cup's contents tempers or moderates the other's.

The Two of Pentacles is about juggling parts of your life or resources to determine which needs to take priority at any given time. It can represent the stress of figuring out what to prioritize without letting any balls drop.

Temperance is about alchemizing two extremes to find the point of moderation between them. The two cups represent two extremes or two sides of the same coin, and this card is about finding a compromise or middle point between them. It's about moving away from extreme opposing things or points of view and finding the moderate middle ground.

Six of Swords vs. Eight of Cups

Escape vs. Departure

The Six of Swords and the Eight of Cups are both cards about leaving, a quality that can make them feel similar. Yet, they couldn't be more different.

In the RWS version of both cards, you view the central person (or people) from behind as they head into their future. What difference is there besides that one departs on land and the other over water?

The Six of Swords is all about escape, getting away from a bad situation. In the RWS version of the card, we see a cloaked adult and a child from behind being ferried from rough water to smooth by a ferryman. These people need to get away from something and need a little assistance.

In the Eight of Cups, however, we see someone walking up a hill, leaving a neat stack of eight cups behind them. They're leaving, alone, with only what they can carry and a walking stick to assist them as they begin a new chapter of their life.

One of the key differences between these cards is the reason for leaving and the level of empowerment the main characters in the scene are experiencing. In the Six of Cups, there's a sense of disempowerment, of running away. In the Eight of Cups, the central person chooses to walk away.

Another key difference is the trajectory of their paths. Whereas the Six of Swords shows movement from rough water to smooth, implying that life is on the way to becoming a little easier, the Eight of Cups shows someone turning their back on a stack of cups—a life they've emotionally invested in—to walk uphill, where the path may not be so smooth.

One of the best tips for unpacking the differences between cards that might be easy to mix up is exploring what they mean in the context of their suit. The escape depicted in the Six of Swords follows the tyranny of the Five of Swords. The divergence of the Eight of Cups, on the other hand, is what follows the fantasizing of the Seven of Cups. Thinking about where each card falls within the context of the suit can help you unlock so much more depth of meaning!

Pages vs. Aces

Another common trip-up for tarot readers is understanding the differences between the ace and the page. Both indicate beginnings, newness, and opportunity—no matter their suit.

Remember, the ace is the seed of its suit. It contains all the potential of its suit.

The page is like the Magician of their suit. They are bright-eyed and full of possibility, ready to take the world by storm—within the context of their suit.

The simplest way to differentiate these two types of cards in the tarot is to remember this simple analogy:

The ace is the seed of the suit. The page represents someone who will plant that seed.

Other Combinations

We could combine many other cards to analyze their similarities and differences. Now that we've gone through some of the most common ones together, I will leave you with a few tricks you can use to differentiate any combinations that trip you up in the future:

1. Compare the cards visually. First, notice what is similar. Then, see what's different. What could those differences mean?
2. Compare your keywords. Explore the keyword you chose for each card. Think about how those two keywords are different.
3. Practice answering the same question with each card and see how, in practice, you interpret them differently.

Going through these steps will not only help you get clarity on how the cards are different, but you'll find that you deepen your understanding of and relationship with each card in the process!

Chapter 7
Making Connections

The system of the tarot is unendingly fascinating to me. Not only does every card open the door to a wide variety of interpretations, but you can find countless connections between cards within it. A wealth of secrets awaits your exploration as you delve into the intricacies of the tarot.

One of my favorite things to do is to look for cards that have a connection to one another. The major arcana contains several fabulous examples of these types of connections.

Fool and the World

Risk and Completion

Both the Fool and the World contain the entirety of the major arcana within them.

The Fool contains all the potential of the Fool's journey: every card or experience contained within the majors. This fresh and untested character goes through the experience of the major arcana, completing their journey in the World, only to begin again.

The World, also like the aces of the minor arcana, has within it the entirety of the Fool's journey: every up and down, every test and every epiphany. This card represents wholeness, completion, and the doorway between the end and a new beginning.

The Fool becomes the World only to become the Fool once again. These two cards are inexorably linked. Both are the beginning and the end, always in motion as representatives of the cycle of life.

Cool, right?

The Magician and Strength

Potential and Fortitude

It always struck me as fascinating that both of these cards show a figure with a lemniscate or infinity symbol above their heads. Eventually, I realized that the roses that grow above the Magician's head are now worn around the waist of the person in the Strength card.

The Magician represents potential and manifestation: the ability to transform spiritual energy into physical energy—as above, so below. This card represents a point of balance between spirit and matter.

Strength represents the ability to harmonize with ferocity and wildness to tame the beast within (or without). This card represents a point of balance between the conscious and unconscious—between what is known and unknown.

Looking at these cards side by side, I noticed something interesting. The Magician creates in an active, dynamic way. On the other hand, the Strength card shows a softer, more receptive quality. Strength shows how receptivity, acceptance, and gentleness also create progress. On the one hand, we have this dynamic, active force, and on the other, a gentle, supportive force. Both are strong. Both are necessary. Neither is stronger or better than the other. Both powerfully master their environment, but they use their power in different ways.

Like the Fool and the World, these cards are two sides of the same energy.

The High Priestess and the Moon

Intuition and Illusion

The High Priestess, the keeper of secrets, seems to guard a body of water that we can barely make out in the background. We know that the High Priestess is deeply associated with intuition, the inner voice, and, therefore, the subconscious.

The Moon card is deeply connected to the idea of the subconscious. The crayfish coming out of the water is a symbol of the fears and perceptions that rise out of the waters of the subconscious and our opportunity to walk through those illusions to seek the truth and clarity we will later find in the Sun card.

Is it such a stretch, then, to think about the water pictured in the Moon card being the water we spy in the background of the High Priestess card?

I believe it's entirely possible that the veil behind the enigmatic priestess blocks the direct view of our subconscious and instead directs us to start slow by connecting, first, with our inner voice before we do the deeper, more difficult work of confronting our subconscious directly.

Death and the Moon

Ending and Illusion

What's not a stretch is the matching pillars that link the Death and Moon cards to one another.

If you look closely at the RWS images of both cards, you will see that the pillars in the background of the Death card ARE an exact duplicate of the pillars shown in the Moon card.

Death and the Moon may not seem to have anything in common, but I think they are linked energetically by the transformation both cards represent. The path between the towers that appears to lead to the light feels very poignant.

With the Death card, we are transformed when one thing ends so another can begin. In the Moon card, we are transformed by learning to step into the inner wilds of the subconscious to face our fears, cast aside illusions, and discover who we truly are.

Having grown up in the '80s, I must admit that both sets of pillars remind me of the twin sphinxes from the *The NeverEnding Story* that the main character, Atreyu, must pass between to prove his worthiness to complete his quest.

I think I will nickname these towers the Two Towers of Transformation!

The Empress and the Emperor

Nurture and Authority

It's plain to see that the Empress and Emperor are connected. They are the dual forces that rule the universe of the tarot.

I like to think of these two in terms of their energetic connection to each other and how they represent a dualistic view of the world that can be incredibly relatable to our real life.

Visually, several elements link them together yet also help us differentiate their individual energies. The Emperor sits on a heavy stone throne, wearing metal armor and a bold golden crown. There is an earthbound heaviness to the imagery. The Empress, however, lounges on soft pillows out in nature and wears a crown of twelve stars—one for each sign of the zodiac, linking this archetype with the heavens. They both hold symbols of power, but their symbols are different. The Emperor wears metal armor and holds tightly to a staff and sphere. On the other hand, the Empress wears flowing garments and has a shield within reach but not even held within the hand. One seems tense and ready for battle; the other is soft and relaxed but prepared to defend what is important to them.

Separately, these cards are complementary, rather than contrary, to one another. Where one pushes, the other pulls. Where one gives, the other receives. Where one charges forth, the other softens and accepts. Both contain strength, authority, and power—but they wield it in different ways, and it is through the combination of the two that we see the true nature of power and authority.

The Empress is a force of creative power and wields that power by nurturing and supporting action that creates fertile ground for growth. The

Empress is associated with beauty, love, harmony, sensuality, and the pursuit of pleasure. This card feels like a soft place to land.

By contrast, the Emperor is a force of active power and wields that power through authoritative and strategic action that draws firm boundaries and demands accountability. The Emperor is associated with independence, desire, action, initiative, and pursuing one's goals. This card feels like a call to action.

Together, these cards provide both active and supportive forces. Like the Taoist idea of yin and yang, neither can exist without a little bit of the other. If we lean too hard into softness, we risk nonaction or self-indulgence. If we rely solely on action and drive, we risk the abandonment of pleasure and joy.

These two energies are designed to work in concert with one another. We may need more than the other at any given time, but we need both throughout our lives.

The Lovers and the Devil

Commitment and Bondage

The first connection between major arcana cards that I became aware of as I studied the tarot over the years was the connection between the Lovers and the Devil. It was one of those amazing moments of seeing a connection that I can never unsee. Understanding the link between these two transformed how I interpret each of them.

One of the simplest ways to understand these two cards is to lean back into your keywords. For me, the Lovers card represents a choice to commit. The Devil card represents bondage. It's not hard to see how a choice to commit can become an unhealthy attachment and, thus, a state of bondage.

It happens in relationships of all sorts. The line between healthy and unhealthy attachment is thin. It doesn't happen only in relationships. Anything you love or commit to can become a dependence that you chain yourself to. It can be a joyful hobby or indulgence that becomes an unhealthy habit or addiction.

Both cards are linked to our values and what significantly impacts us energetically. The Lovers card, overseen by a representation of what is good in the form of an angel, speaks to choosing the path that aligns with your values in pursuing all that is good. The Devil card, depicted as a representation of what is bad, speaks to the consequences of choosing a path that contradicts the greater good and negatively impacts you and anyone affected by your attachment to that path.

In their positive aspects, both invite you to choose what is right and good for you. Sometimes, a little bit of the Devil can unbind you from enslaving yourself to virtuousness. In the same way, a little bit of the Lovers can open your heart to love and possibility so that you don't bog yourself in attachment to the material pleasures of life.

Again, these cards show two sides of the same coin—choices, desires, commitments, and what we bind ourselves to. The Lovers card asks you to mindfully decide what you will attach yourself to so you can live in harmony with your highest self. The Devil warns you that your attachments are taking you away from your highest self but reminds you that you can free yourself— if you choose.

Much like the Fool leads to the World and back to the Fool, the Lovers may sometimes lead you to the Devil and then back to the Lovers with the choice to choose a new path.

Pretty cool, right?

The Tower and the Star

Destruction and Hope

Visually, the RWS versions of these two cards look nothing alike, but I always notice that my eyes are drawn to the top third of both images.

In the Tower card, my eyes are drawn to the arrow of lightning striking the top of the tower, erupting it in flames and sending its inhabitants flying: destruction. In the Star card, my eyes are drawn to the bold yellow star and the seven bright white stars surrounding it: peace.

These cards represent both sides of a life shake-up. While the Tower destroys the constructs that have taken you away from the path that is right for you, the Star recalibrates you so you can rebuild and find your way again. Both cards invite you to soften and give yourself over to the experience you're having.

The Star is one of my favorite cards in the deck because it speaks of hope and offers a guiding light to help you get on track with what is truly meant for you. It's no accident that the Star falls immediately after the Tower in the order of the major arcana. The Star is there to help guide you after the destruction of the Tower so you can figure out what to rebuild—and how to start over.

What They All Have in Common

Each of these connected pairs is a powerful representation of duality by showing two sides of the same coin. Using my keywords, here's a simple summary of each pair:

The Fool and the World represent risk and completion.

Without some risk, what could we start? Unless we start something, we cannot complete anything.

The Magician and Strength represent potential and fortitude.

We hold the potential to do and create great things, but we must have the fortitude to navigate the obstacles that arrive in our path or that potential is wasted.

The High Priestess and the Moon represent intuition and illusion.

We use our intuition to navigate the illusions that cast shadows on our path and to find our way.

Death and the Moon represent ending and illusion.

We fool ourselves that both good and bad things will last forever. Death teaches us everything ends, and the Moon asks us to dig deeper for the truth.

The Lovers and the Devil represent commitment and bondage.

If you never commit to anything, you are never at risk of bondage, but with any commitment—truly any choice—there is the danger of bondage and an invitation to make choices and commitments that align with your values.

The Tower and the Star represent destruction and hope.

After every storm, there is a rainbow. With everything that is destroyed, there is an opportunity to rebuild. After destruction, there is hope.

There are many powerful connections between cards in the tarot. Whatever deck you are working with, taking time to get to know every card will unlock more possibilities for noticing repeating themes or symbols that may link cards together, opening up more insight for you!

Chapter 8
Card Combinations

I t's all well and good to learn what cards mean individually, but how the heck do you read them when they come up in combination?

Let's tackle this together. It's going to be a breeze. I promise!

The Five-Step Method for Reading Tarot Card Combos

I get it. Reading cards in combination seems complicated. How do you know what the Lovers and the Five of Cups mean together? What about the Seven of Wands and Ten of Cups?

Over the years, through studying other divination systems that are much less intuitive in their interpretation than tarot is, I found myself stumbling into the most straightforward method ever for reading cards in combination. This method requires only one easy step and four slightly more involved— but optional—steps.

I call it the Five-Step Method, but I promise you that you will get great results even if you stop at the first step. Maybe we should call this the One-to-Five-Step Method.

For this method, I'll assume that you want to shuffle your cards and pull a set number of them from the deck to answer your question. This method works whether you draw two or ten cards without predefined positions.

Step one is the most important. If you feel comfortable with step one, try adding step two. Once you feel satisfied with those, try adding step three and so on. Or, if you're like me and want to dive right in and do everything, try going through all five and see where you land. You might love doing all the steps right from the beginning.

As with everything else I've shared in this book, make it yours so that it works for you!

Step 1: Do the Math

I'm not fond of math, but "do the math" is the simplest way to explain this step.

Ideally, you've spent time with me throughout this book associating a single potent keyword to every card. When you see the cards in combination, it's simply a matter of adding up the words to equal an interpretation.

To get comfortable with this method, start by answering questions with only two cards in combination and then gradually add cards to build more complicated "equations."

For a two-card example, imagine you've asked your cards what you need to know about your recent meeting with your boss about a possible shift in your work responsibilities. You concentrate on the question, shuffle your cards, and draw the High Priestess and the Nine of Cups. My keyword for the High Priestess is *intuition* and for the Nine of Cups is *fulfillment*.

Here's the math:

Intuition + Fulfillment =
Trust your gut and prioritize personal fulfillment.

If the job duty change feels like a positive move, that will increase your satisfaction on the job. Make the leap!

How might you interpret the math using your keywords instead of mine? Remember that there is no one right way to interpret the answer, even based on the math. The math gets you thinking about how the two card concepts work together to answer the question!

Let's look at a three-card example, answering the same question. This time, you shuffle and draw the Devil, the Seven of Swords, and the Three of Cups.

My keyword for the Devil is *bondage*, for the Seven of Swords is *rebellion*, and for the Three of Cups is *support*.

Here's how the math might look:

Bondage + Rebellion + Support =
This role change could put you in a situation where you experience
a loss of flexibility or mobility in how you do your work, which
could feel restrictive or even make you feel trapped. You want to be
creative in your work—not just follow prescribed processes—but
also work collaboratively with a team that supports one another.

Again, you might interpret these three cards in multiple ways, particularly
when you have more information about the situation because it's close to you
or you have more details that your querent has shared with you.

How might you interpret these three cards using your keywords to answer
the question?

Step 2: Order

For this step, you'll need to decide what significance, if any, the order of the
cards you lay down will have on your interpretation. You can assign any meaning to the card order that makes sense. As with any method you use, the most
important thing is that you're consistent with your method.

For me, the order from left to right has a timing significance. For example,
if I lay three cards down in a row, the center card will have an association with
the present, the left card will have an association with the past, and the card
on the right will have an association with the future. That past, present, and
future could be close together, like yesterday, today, tomorrow or even before,
during, or after a moment in the day. It could also be far apart, such as last
year, this year, or next year. How much time is something that has more to do
with the question and the overall interpretation, but the idea is that there is a
trajectory of time in a line of cards.

You might prefer to answer present-based questions only, in which case
you may choose to have the order mean something else. Perhaps the fur-
thest card to the left is the most significant and cards to the right qualify or
add clarity to that first card. I've known readers who lay down nine cards in
a square and interpret the top three as the current message, the cards below
that as clarifiers to that message, and the cards below the clarifiers as unseen
influences. The sky is the limit for what you can associate with the order or

arrangement of the cards. Having an association can add a lot of helpful context to how you interpret groupings of cards.

Let's revisit the three-card answer to the shift in work responsibilities. Remember that the math for me was bondage + rebellion + support. Now, let's apply the trajectory of time to these three cards before coming up with the final interpretation:

Past Bondage + Present Rebellion + Future Support =
The role that you're in now may feel restrictive or as though you've reached a dead end. You have been feeling trapped. The new opportunity makes you feel conflicted because you want to protect what you've built in your current position. You may be nervous about sticking your neck out in a new role. Support is there to help you grow in the new role, should you choose to take it.

What a difference this step made in adding more context to the interpretation! That is why coming up with systems of association that work for you can help build confidence when you're reading the tarot.

I love this stuff!

Okay, it's your turn. Play around with an association for the order of the cards that might be fun to try. Then, try answering some made-up questions using three or more cards, adding up the keywords with their order association. See what interpretations you can come up with!

Step 3: Elements

Let's add a little more to our equations now. By the way, I'm sorry to all my fellow math-haters out there, but once the math analogy clicked for me, I couldn't shake it. I wish I had created an artsy analogy, but here we are.

The day I began paying attention to the elemental balance (or lack thereof) in my tarot interpretations, everything came together so quickly for me. Your mileage may vary, but you've already laid the groundwork. I know you have because I introduced you to the elements back at the beginning of chapter 4! This means we now have a keyword association for every element we can play with.

Adding this step works best with larger groups of cards—ideally six or more. All you need to do is add up how many cards for each element are on the table and consider the impact of the associated keyword. I know … more math (sorry!). To avoid complicating this, concentrate on the minor arcana. Don't worry. Before we move on to the next step, I'll address how to factor in the major arcana.

Let's try answering another sample question. This time, let's say you want to check in on the status of a relationship. For the sake of the example, we'll assume this is a romantic relationship. You shuffle and draw your cards, and here's what you have on the table. If you went with time for your order association, you might have something that looks a little like this math-wise:

PAST: Four of Cups / Stagnant + Hierophant / Tradition

PRESENT: Five of Swords / Tyranny + Ten of Pentacles / Legacy

FUTURE: Page of Cups / Sensitive to Fragile + Four of Swords / Respite

Looking at this layout, let's now factor in the elemental balance.

There are two cups cards—that's the watery suit of feeling. There are two swords cards—that's the airy suit of thought. There is one pentacles card—the earthly realm of resources—and no wands—the fiery suit of passion. Overall, passion is lacking in the relationship. There is a good amount of emotion and thought and only a little stability.

Add the impression you get from the elemental balance to the overall interpretation and you might get something like this:

This relationship has a long history of getting stuck in the rut (stagnant) of how things have always been done (tradition). It seems that in the present, at least one of you is either intentionally or unintentionally taking advantage of the other—or taking them for granted (tyranny). Perhaps this is done to hold on to the relationship as a resource—something you both have invested in for a long time (legacy). Emotions will rise to the surface in the future. One of you will feel the shift, bringing any issues to the forefront (sensitive to fragile). The result will be a stabilizing, at least for a time, of the relationship dynamics (respite). Overall, you both are mentally (air / thought) and emotionally (water / emotions) invested in the relationship. You both rely on it for a sense of stability, particularly regarding your resources (earth/resources). Still, there is a lack of passion, fire, and heat in the relationship (fire/passion).

With this example, you can see how much more context you can add to a combination of cards by considering how much (or little) of any element is on the table.

What about the Major Arcana Cards?

The elemental association of the major arcana cards is less obvious, which makes it difficult to factor them into the elemental balance of a reading. Frankly, I usually don't bother to factor them into the elemental balance at all. Instead, I pay attention to how many (or few) majors are present in the reading to determine how fixed (or changeable) the reading is.

If there are no major arcana cards in your reading, or very few, the reading may be considered more flexible or mutable. If major arcana cards make up half or more of the cards in the reading, then I will tend to see the reading as more fixed and unchanging.

In the above example, there is only one major arcana card (the Hierophant) out of all six cards in the spread. I would note this to mean that this reading is somewhat changeable.

Now, you try! Answer a question for yourself and try to incorporate steps 1, 2, and 3 in your interpretation.

Step 4: Numbers

In the numbers step, you look for any number patterns or repeating numbers on the table. You can work on this flexible step in several different ways.

First, look for any numbers that appear repeatedly on the cards on the table. For example, if among the cards on the table you have the Two of Pentacles, Two of Swords, and the High Priestess (major arcana card number two)—that's some considerable two energy. For me, twos are often about choices, which would tell me that some considerable *choice* energy is involved in this reading.

Another way you can look at numbers is to look for the order of the numbers. For example, if you lay down a line of cards and notice the numbers reflected on the cards are increasing, such as a Two of Wands, Three of Cups,

Five of Pentacles, Ten of Swords, that can tell you that something about the situation is increasing or escalating. The opposite may be true if you see a lot of descending numbers. This can add context and information to the reading.

You might have other ideas about incorporating the numbers you see on the cards into your interpretation. You should experiment with them when you're ready to see if this step adds value to your interpretations.

Step 5: Directionality

Directionality is a fun additional step to add to how you interpret cards on the table. This works much better with scenic cards than it does with pip cards since you'll want to be able to look at the imagery on the card to determine what, if any, significance there might be to which direction characters seem to be facing or what (or whom) they seem to be looking at.

First, based on the card order association I use (see step 2), I will pay attention to whether there is a heavy past or future focus.

If I see several cards with people facing the left, I could add to my interpretation that perhaps I or my querent is spending a lot of time and energy looking to the past. Similarly, if several people face to the right, that could indicate a future focus.

Second, I will make notes on any interesting things happening between cards. For example, two knights facing each other could highlight a conflict between two different people or energies. Two people facing away from each other could indicate that they aren't seeing eye to eye.

You can incorporate directionality in hundreds of creative ways to add flavor to your interpretations!

Summing It Up

Apologies, but I couldn't resist one final math reference. Let's sum up how these steps can help you build confidence in interpreting card combinations.

First, start with step 1: the simple math of combining your keywords to build an interpretation.

When you're comfortable with that, consider adding some meaning to the order of the cards on the table and incorporate that.

If you're comfortable with the math and the order, try factoring in the elemental balance or any interesting numerical patterns on the table.

If you still want even more context to what the combination of the cards on the table has to say, consider how the people on the cards are interacting (or not) with one another by which direction they're facing or whom or what they are looking at or turning their back on.

This is the point in this chapter where I remind you, again, to go at your own pace.

You don't need to be comfortable with all these steps to read tarot effectively. These steps are meant to give you tools you can use, if you choose, to build a working conversation with your cards so that you can get the answers you seek for you or your querent.

I cannot stress enough how important it is to constantly check with yourself to ensure that how you interpret the cards works for you. If something you incorporate into your reading process makes getting an interpretation more challenging, do a little pruning. Cut back on what complicates things and return to the simplest method to get your answers.

Remember that you don't have to show your work to anyone. As long as you get the answer, how you got there doesn't matter to anyone but you.

Chapter 9
Common Tarot
Spreads to Practice

N ow that you know how to read the cards without a spread, which is arguably the most challenging way to read them, let's return to tarot spreads.

Throughout this book, I've shared several smaller card spreads so that you can get comfortable with your majors, numbered minors, and court cards. I certainly encourage you to revisit those spreads with the entire deck, but I also wanted to share with you a few more of my favorites.

What Is a Tarot Spread and How to Use It

I went over the basics of tarot spreads at the end of the chapter on the major arcana, but just in case you skipped ahead—no judgment, I promise—let's revisit that in a little more detail.

A tarot spread is simply a predefined layout for the cards where every position has its own meaning.

To read the cards in a spread, you combine the card's meaning (your keyword) and the spread position's meaning to get your interpretation.

If the spread position is "unconscious influences" and the card you drew is the Nine of Swords (my keyword is *anxiety*), you would interpret that the person is being unconsciously influenced by their fears or anxieties.

Working with spreads is an accessible way to read tarot because you can incorporate the extra context of the spread position into your interpretation of each card.

Why did I place this chapter after the more difficult chapter on reading cards in combination without a spread? Because now that you've read without a spread, this will be a piece of cake for you—and also because, if you want to get wild, you can incorporate some of those steps from the last chapter into your interpretation of spreads, too!

Let's go over the three most common spreads I have encountered in my years of reading tarot.

The Single-Card Draw

Don't underestimate the power of a single-card draw to answer a question. You can answer any question with a single card, but patience is the key.

When you get a card that doesn't immediately make sense, it's tempting to decide it must not be right and redraw. I'm not judging; I have been guilty of it, too!

The truth is that working with single-card draws will rapidly improve your confidence in reading the tarot. It's easy to reach for more and more cards to clarify or add context, but the more you let yourself sit with a single card and dig deeper to uncover the message, the more you will understand the nuances of that card. I couldn't recommend it more.

To make it an actual spread, experiment with giving the single-card position a name or focus. This will provide a little context and let you dynamically engage with the card. Here are some examples of flexible single-card spreads you can try:

Daily Advice: What piece of advice can ensure a better day today?

This reading will stretch your understanding of the tarot by asking you to take whatever card you draw for this prompt as advice. Let's look at a couple of examples and one possible interpretation for each. The best way to work with this is to start with a single-sentence piece of advice and then journal or expand on it if you want to go deeper.

- The Devil (Bondage): Avoid getting caught up in negative patterns or habits today.
- The Queen of Swords (Perceptive to Judgmental): Take things and people at face value today and pay attention.

- Eight of Cups (Departure): Remember that no matter how much you have invested in a conversation, a task, a person, or anything else, you can choose to walk away if that is what's best for you.

Evening Reflection: What lesson can I learn from my experiences today?
Using the tarot to look back on your day so that you can learn from it is a lovely way to end the day and can help you look at tarot cards from a different perspective. I like to word these interpretations as questions I can think about. Here are a few examples:

- The Fool (Risk): What risks did you take today? How did those situations turn out?
- The Hierophant (Tradition): What rules did you follow or break today? What can you learn from your decision to go with the flow or buck the system?
- Ten of Pentacles (Legacy): How did your choices, today, impact your legacy? What will you leave behind when you're gone?

Preparation: What do I need to be prepared for today?
I like to think of this spread as a daily forecast, but one that empowers me to be prepared for the day ahead. You can have fun with this one by interpreting it literally or metaphorically. Let me give you a few examples.

- Five of Wands (Competition): Get your game face on because today you'll need to be ready to hold your own when faced with some opposition.
- The Moon (Illusion): You don't have all the facts today, at least not on the surface, so don't make assumptions and be ready to ask questions so you can shine a light on the truth.
- Judgement (Evolution): Be ready to heed the call when offered an opportunity to step up and step in today.

Outside of specific prompts or spreads, you can also pull a single card to answer any direct question. The sky is the limit! Remember to sit with the card you draw. Sometimes, your answer will be apparent; other times, you might need to tease it out after thinking about it for a while.

The Three-Card Spread

There are hundreds of three-card spreads that you can learn and work with. I have used many of them over the years. Three cards provide enough context, so you shouldn't have to flounder, but not so much that it becomes overwhelming.

Past, Present, Future

This spread is the most common of all the three-card spreads. It's honestly iconic, and for good reason. This spread lets you pull cards in a simple timeline to answer any question.

Let's say you'd like to know if you should say yes to a second date with that person you went out with last week. You draw the Eight of Cups, the Wheel of Fortune, and the Five of Cups. Meeting this person may feel like a stroke of good luck after your recent isolation and restriction, but grief is ahead. The answer is no.

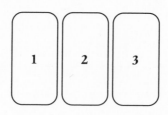

CARD 1: Past
CARD 2: Present
CARD 3: Future

Within, Without, Advice

This spread is helpful if you are trying to sort out or untangle a situation. The within position identifies any internal influences, such as your thoughts or emotions about the subject of the reading. The without position signifies external forces or things affecting the situation that are outside your control, and the advice position tells you what you should consider or how you should take action.

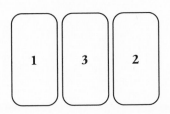

CARD 1: Within
CARD 2: Without
CARD 3: Advice

Body, Mind, Spirit

This spread is a beautiful present-based reading you can do to identify what is going on or what you need to know about the state of your body, the state of your mind, and the state of your spirit at this moment.

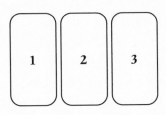

CARD 1: Body
CARD 2: Mind
CARD 3: Spirit

Energy, Obstacle, Advice

This is my favorite three-card spread because it's the one I created for myself. I often found that some of the more popular three-card spreads left me wanting something else, so I came up with this to solve that problem.

What I love about this spread is that it helps me identify what is going on energetically with the situation, what obstacle is causing trouble, and how I should move forward. It feels grounded and has not failed me yet!

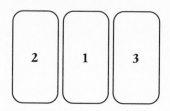

CARD 1: Energy
CARD 2: Obstacle
CARD 3: Advice

After working with predefined spreads for a while, you may want to create one that is custom fit to how you read the cards as well!

Now, let's address the elephant in the room, shall we?

The Celtic Cross

Before you slam this book closed because you're, frankly, sick of tarot books talking about the Celtic cross AGAIN and you are not about to put up with that here, please ... bear with me. I promise it will be worth it.

You will hear from some people that the Celtic cross tarot spread is complicated and outdated. However, I have never found another tarot spread that is as versatile or easy as this one. I also can't tell you how often the Celtic cross has saved my butt as a tarot reader when a querent has asked a complicated question. In my experience, the Celtic cross provides a road map that can guide you through the various layers of a nuanced question to help you get real clarity.

If you take the time to memorize one tarot spread, it should be this one.

Knowing this spread is empowering to me as a reader because I can lay one out anytime, anywhere, for any question and get right into interpreting the cards instead of worrying about what method or spread I will use.

The Celtic cross is also my favorite spread for general readings without a specific question. This spread homes in immediately on what the reading will be about from the first card. I love it!

I don't understand how or why the Celtic cross got its reputation for being complex, but I don't think it's deserved.

Perhaps the Celtic cross's reputation for being complicated is based on a more complex version of this well-known spread.

The version I use has always felt pretty accessible to me. I couldn't tell you whom I first learned this version from. I may have modified another version years ago or learned from a fellow tarot enthusiast. What I do know is that this version is a breeze to work with once you familiarize yourself with it.

Let's analyze the following Celtic cross reading in two ways:

#1: Your querent asks you to give them a general reading.

#2: Your querent lets you know they are struggling at their job and want to know if they should stay put or look for a better opportunity elsewhere.

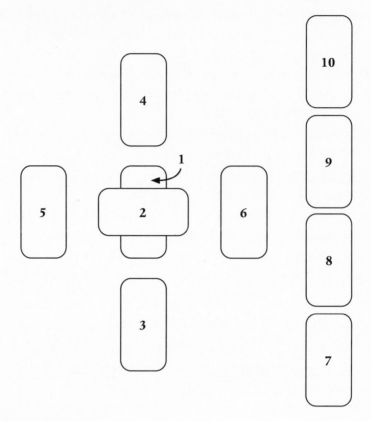

CARD 1: Heart of the issue
CARD 2: What crosses it
CARD 3: Unconscious influences / the unknown
CARD 4: Conscious influences / the known
CARD 5: Recent past
CARD 6: Near future
CARD 7: Internal influences
CARD 8: External influences
CARD 9: Greatest hope / greatest fear
CARD 10: Key to the outcome

1: The Heart of the Issue—Two of Cups (Connection)

The card in this position is the central focus of the reading.

> #1: In a general reading, this position lets you know what the reading will be focused on. In this case, the Two of Cups indicates the reading will be about an important relationship.

> #2: In response to a specific question, this position often confirms the subject of the reading or adds additional context. In this case, the Two of Cups indicates that the querent needs to make an important decision and that a relationship that is important to them is a factor in the decision.

2: What Crosses It, for Good or Bad—The Devil (Bondage)

The card in this position is traditionally laid horizontally on top of the first card and modifies it. I memorized this position to be "what crosses card one, for good or bad," meaning that this card either supports or hinders the card beneath it and can be interpreted either way.

> #1: The Devil covering the Two of Cups lets you know that your querent might feel trapped or restricted in their relationship. The Devil could also indicate unhealthy patterns or toxicity.

> #2: The Devil crossing the Two of Cups indicates that the current job feels restrictive. Your querent probably feels stuck. This could also suggest that the work culture is unhealthy or that there is an unhealthy dynamic between your querent and one or more of their coworkers.

3: Unconscious Influences, the Unknown—Eight of Wands (Momentum)

The card in this position lets you know what you may not be aware of, what is unconscious in relation to the situation. It offers additional context.

> #1: The Eight of Wands in this position indicates a lot of passion in the relationship, but it also doesn't seem like the querent feels

like they have much control—the relationship has taken on a life of its own.

#2: The Eight of Wands indicates that your querent has a lot invested in their current work situation and built a lot of career momentum there, undoubtedly making the querent hesitant to consider starting over elsewhere.

4: Conscious Influences, the Known—The Empress (Nurture)

The card in this position lets you know what you are aware of and what is conscious about the situation.

#1: The Empress indicates your querent cares deeply about the relationship and wants to nurture it. They may be doing much of the emotional labor in the relationship, perhaps more than their partner.

#2: The Empress indicates your querent cares about their job and the people they work with. It's their relationships and the way they care about the work they do that keeps them at the job despite the difficulties they've been experiencing. This card also underscores that it would be important to your querent to do work they care about and work among people they feel comfortable with.

In both cases, the Empress and the Eight of Wands work together to underscore that your querent cares deeply and has invested heavily in their current situation.

5: Recent Past, Journeys Ending—Seven of Swords (Rebellion)

The card in this position shows something from the recent past that influences the current situation.

#1: The Seven of Swords indicates that there could be a disconnect in the relationship about a significant issue. Perhaps your querent or their partner wants to do things differently and is rebelling against the status quo. It could also hint at deception within the relationship, which could tie in with the Devil in position 2.

#2: The Seven of Swords indicates that your querent or one of their coworkers has been taking shortcuts or is not being straightforward. Your querent may be dealing with a duplicitous coworker. It's also possible your querent is tempted to break the rules and rebel against whatever restriction they feel in their current job, which also ties in nicely with the Devil in position 2.

6: Near Future, Journeys Beginning—Ace of Pentacles (Opportunity)

The card in this position is about journeys just beginning or what is coming around the bend, adding clarity to the future.

#1: There is hope for your querent's relationship. The Ace of Pentacles indicates a golden opportunity soon, particularly if your querent is prepared to inject new energy into the relationship or engage with their partner in new ways.

#2: The Ace of Pentacles strongly indicates that your querent will be getting a new job offer soon or will encounter a new opportunity that will seem too good to pass up.

In both examples, the Ace of Pentacles represents an opportunity for something positive coming soon.

Because this position can be more predictive, it could be confusing if you don't read predictively. If you're struggling with this position because you prefer to keep your tarot readings grounded in the present, you could rename this position to something else that might support your reading style better.

Remember: your tarot practice, your rules!

7: Internal Influences, What's Within Your Control—Ace of Swords (Discovery)

The card in this position explores how the querent is influencing the situation. This is often an area the querent has control over. If a court card is drawn in this position, you would know that the court card indicates personality traits or energy coming from the querent.

#1: The Ace of Swords in this position indicates that your querent has control over how they think about their relationship. It can also suggest that your querent has recently come to a new understanding about their relationship.

#2: The Ace of Swords in this position indicates that your querent has control over how they think about their current position. It can also suggest that your querent has recently uncovered new insight about what is contributing to their job dissatisfaction.

8: External Influences, What's Outside Your Control—King of Wands (Charismatic to Manipulative)

The card in this position shows how forces outside the querent are impacting the situation. It also can point to what is not within your querent's control. A court card drawn in this position would typically signify someone other than the querent.

#1: The King of Wands in this position indicates that your querent's partner is engaging, charismatic, and passionate. It could be that tempers flare or that their partner sometimes behaves manipulatively.

#2: The King of Wands in this position indicates that someone at your querent's current company is either engaging, charismatic, and passionate or overly domineering or manipulative with a hot temper.

Court cards offer a unique opportunity to examine how other people or aspects of your querent impact the situation. They can also point out energies or dynamics in a broader environment. For example, in the relationship reading, you're really looking at just two people, but in the work reading, the qualities of the King of Wands could apply to the office culture in general.

Additionally, for every position, don't forget to look at all the surrounding cards to get a better feel for what each card is telling you.

Given the Devil in position 2 and the sense of restriction for the querent, I'd look at the more negative qualities of this court card as an influence on the situation for both interpretations.

9: Greatest Hope, Greatest Fear—Six of Pentacles (Reciprocity)

This is my favorite position in the Celtic cross spread because it can often get straight to the most pressing issue for the querent.

The card in this position tells you the greatest hope and greatest fear concerning this situation. The *and* is important because it identifies how your querent's greatest hope and greatest fear are usually the same thing or two sides of the same coin.

To interpret the card in these sample readings, ask yourself, "How could the Six of Pentacles (*reciprocity* is my keyword) represent both hope and fear for my querent?"

#1: The Six of Pentacles in this position indicates your querent craves equal give and take in their relationship. Your querent may be overextending themselves and needs their partner to do more (or perhaps it's the other way around). Your querent recognizes this imbalance is negatively impacting their relationship. The fear could be that if the relationship were equal, the other person may feel unneeded (or your querent might), and the relationship would be damaged.

#2: The Six of Pentacles in this position represents a more tangible reciprocity for your querent. They may not be receiving fair compensation or opportunities to advance and may hope for that to change. At the same time, they might be afraid that getting a raise or promotion won't ultimately solve the problem of their job dissatisfaction, and they'll want to leave anyway.

10: The Key to the Outcome—Four of Pentacles (Security)

Traditionally, the tenth position in a Celtic cross identifies the outcome. However, I was taught that the tenth position is the key to the outcome, not the outcome itself. Instead of a fixed prediction, the card in this position indicates what the querent needs to do to reach the outcome that is in their best interest. I find this version much more empowering!

#1: The Four of Pentacles in this position indicates that the querent should focus on their comfort and security to find their answer.

Do they feel more comfortable and secure within their relation-ship—when they are with their partner—or outside of it? It can also indicate that your querent clings too tightly to their comfort zone or the known. My advice for this querent would be not to allow their desire to maintain the status quo keep them from addressing the issues they know are present in their relationship.

#2: The Four of Pentacles in this position indicates that material stability and security are important to your querent but that this is not the only factor that matters. Your querent may need to release their attachment to their comfort zone to take the necessary steps to find a job that is a better fit for them.

Putting It All Together

This is the point where you pull together all the individual cards into a cohe-sive overall interpretation that, ultimately, answers your querent's question or gives them tangible advice to help them move forward. Since the first exam-ple is a general reading, you're summarizing what came through during the reading, how it applies, and what your querent should do next. In the second example, you're answering the querent's question about how to handle their difficult work situation.

#1: If I were giving this reading, I would advise the querent that their fear of change or of rocking the boat keeps them in an unhealthy relationship dynamic. They need to bring their concerns and fears to their partner to improve this situation together. Failing that, they might need to consider whether staying in that relation-ship is in their long-term best interest.

#2: If I were giving this reading, I would advise the querent that it's essential to be honest with themselves about their level of satisfac-tion in their job. There is more contributing to their unhappiness than just money, including some unhealthy relationship dynamics in the workplace. They should consider raising their concerns to their workplace directly, and failing that, they should consider looking for a better job.

One of the beautiful things about the Celtic cross is that several position pairs offer a dualistic look at what affects the situation: past and future, unconscious and conscious, internal and external influences.

These pairs allow you to look at the situation from multiple angles to get a comprehensive view of the situation and contributing factors. Each position offers helpful information that adds context to the situation and to things that may be obvious and things that you or your querent may not have considered, and at the end of it, you're offered tangible action steps to take to solve your problem.

Give it a try.

If you find that some of the positions don't work for you, tweak them until they do work for you. You'll find that the Celtic cross will serve you well.

Taking It to the Next Level

N ow that you've created your own personal set of tarot keywords, explored reading groups of cards organically, and learned how to work with spreads, you are ready to hit the ground running!

Before you do, though, can we talk for a minute about breaking the rules?

Breaking the "Rules" of Tarot

The best advice I can give you for upping your tarot game is to learn the rules so you can break them.

The most profound readings I've ever given or received have resulted from breaking the rules by going off book and interpreting the cards in whatever way feels right in the moment.

After all, the best intuitive readings come about as a springboard from what you already know about the cards, or at least that's been my experience.

I have an extensive tarot deck collection. If I only read the cards based on my basic understanding of the card's meaning, I would never have kept that second, third, or hundredth deck.

Each new deck I have picked up, gotten to know, and read with has offered me new insights. Every new variation on a tarot card provides a unique perspective. As a result, my understanding of the cards' meanings has evolved a number of times over the years. Never was this more evident than when I sat down to write this book and realized that the keywords that used to be my go-tos had changed long ago.

I hope that what you've gotten from this book is enough of an understanding of the basics of tarot to empower you to go deeper with your studies and to play more so you can expand your tarot vocabulary and have fun breaking the rules!

There are a variety of places you can take your exploration of tarot. When you've gotten comfortable with all this book contains, I encourage you to pick an area of study to add a new layer to your tarot knowledge.

Are you interested in astrology? Take some time to study the astrological correspondences of the major arcana. Want to go even further? Study the astrological associations of the minors.

Are you drawn to mysticism and the deep esoteric associations of the tarot? Consider learning about the Order of the Golden Dawn and how the group influenced tarot.

The sky is the limit.

Most importantly: practice.

Practice reading tarot for yourself. If you want to be comfortable reading for others, practice reading tarot for others.

You don't need to know every single correspondence for every single card. You don't need to know the astrological associations, understand the influence of color, or what all the most well-respected tarot experts have to say about every card.

All you need to do is learn to trust yourself and your interpretations each and every time you read cards. And that is something that will only come with time and lots … and lots … of practice.

A Few Parting Words

Most people believe that tarot is difficult to learn because there are seventy-eight different cards with meanings to memorize.

The truth is that I've never felt like I had to memorize a thing. I never tested myself with tarot flashcards or asked my friends to quiz me on what a card meant. I didn't approach learning tarot as if I had a test to pass, nor should you.

Instead of thinking of the tarot as a set of seventy-eight cards with meanings you need to memorize, think of the tarot as a house with seventy-eight rooms that you get to explore. You might not understand everything you see in those rooms. There might be symbols you don't understand or secrets tucked away in drawers. You don't need to unpack every detail; you simply need to experience each room to begin to understand who lives there.

My goal in writing this book and teaching you the single-keyword method of learning the tarot is to provide you with a set of keys that you can use to unlock each of the seventy-eight doors of the tarot.

How far you choose to venture into each room, how much exploring you want to do, and how many drawers you want to peer into is all up to you.

Enjoy the adventure.

Acknowledgments

Writing this book has been a grand adventure and one that I never could have undertaken without the help and support of so many.

First, and foremost, I want to thank the people who have watched and supported me on YouTube. You have helped my dreams come true. Thank you.

To Peggy, who willingly became a tarot-widow while I worked diligently on this book, thank you. Your sacrifice didn't go unnoticed, and your steadfast support means the world to me. When I hit moments of frustration or writer's block, you helped me roll the boulder from the top of the hill down instead of sitting back and watching me try to roll it uphill. You are an incredible wife and partner, the balm to my wounds, and my greatest love. I am so grateful for everything you are to me and everything you do to help my dreams come true. I love you.

To Jon, your enthusiasm and support for my creative pursuits means more to me than you could ever know. Thank you for allowing me to be a part of your life and for always being a safe person in mine. I love you.

To my friends, all of whom have put up with a barrage of video and text messages as deadlines creeped ever closer or I faced periods of impostor syndrome, thank you. To Dani, Dawn, and Tori, what would I do without you? Thank you for your belief in me, for helping me unpack tough stuff that this project brought up for me, and for your perspectives as fellow tarot readers that helped me make this a better book. To Duane, thank you for the laughs, the gainful employment, and for putting up with my never-ending tarot deck deliveries. I appreciate you.

To Benny, thank you for sharing your thoughts and experiences with my Tarot with Training Wheels course. Your input made this a better book than it would have been without it. Thank you.

I'm not sure I have the right words to express my gratitude to my brilliant acquisitions editor at Llewellyn, Barbara Moore. Barbara, you have been an inspiration for me for a great number of years. I knew your name before I knew the name of any other tarot author. Your contributions to the tarot world are an incredible legacy, and working with you on this book has been an unimaginable joy. Never, in a million years, would I have thought it possible that one day I would be sitting down over sandwiches and discussing a book idea with you. Working with you has been a dream come true. I'm immensely grateful for your belief in me and my work and am astonishingly humbled by your beautiful foreword. Thank you for everything you have and continue to do for the love of tarot.

To Brittany Keller, thank you for your gorgeous cover art! I love it!! To Marysa Storm, for your keen eyes for detail, thank you. It's easy to get lost in the big picture of a project. Thank you for catching what I missed and more so this book could be the best version of itself. To Verlynda Pinckney and Christine Ha, thank you for your beautiful design work. To Markus Ironwood and the rest of the team at Llewellyn who helped make this book a reality, thank you.

I owe a debt of gratitude to the other tarot authors who have inspired me throughout the years, including (though certainly not limited to) Rachel Pollack, Mary K. Greer, Robert M. Place, Marcus Katz, T. Susan Chang, Sasha Graham, M. M. Meleen, Benebell Wen, and Melissa Cynova.